The Archaeology of European Expansion in India

Gujarat, *c.* 16th-18th Centuries

The Archaeology of European Expansion in India

Gujarat, *c.* 16th-18th Centuries

Dilip K. Chakrabarti

Aryan Books International
New Delhi

THE ARCHAEOLOGY OF EUROPEAN EXPANSION IN INDIA

ISBN-81-7305-250-6

Published in **2003** by
ARYAN BOOKS INTERNATIONAL
Pooja Apartments, 4B, Ansari Road, Darya Ganj, New Delhi-110 002 (India)
Tel. : 23287589, 23255799; Fax : 91-11-23270385
E-mail : aryanbooks@vsnl.com

Computer Typeset at ABI Prints & Publishing Co., New Delhi
Printed in India at B.B.N. Printers, New Delhi

For
Swarajya Prakash Gupta,
and
to the memory of
Shashi Prabha Asthana (1947-1997)

Preface and Acknowledgements

The fieldwork, on which the present book is based, was done in December-January of 2000-2001 jointly with Dr C.J. Scarre, Deputy Director of the McDonald Institute for Archaeological Research of Cambridge University, and his wife Dr Judith Roberts, a senior archaeologist of Cambridgeshire. Dr Scarre received a grant from the McDonald Institute for Archaeological Research to do this fieldwork.

The basic thrust of the work was to explore the possibility of conducting archaeological excavations in Surat where the Europeans including the British were most likely to have left behind the material traces of their presence between the 16th and the 18th centuries. However, before undertaking such excavations, one has to have an understanding of the historical frame within which the relevant archaeological issues can be contextualized. The purpose of this book is to put forward this frame and advance the general concept of 'the archaeology of European expansion' in South Asian archaeology.

As the details of the economic history of Surat and its adjoining region are not within the scope of our study, I have refrained from using any archival source in this matter. References to these archival sources occur extensively in the writings of the historians who have specialized in the economic history of Surat during this period. Voluminous 'factory records' are also available in published form. What has become reasonably clear to me is that they do not throw any significant light on the actual material basis of life of the European residents of Surat in the 16th-18th centuries AD.

The published records of European travellers in Mughal India are also voluminous. I have used them as much I could, although I am aware that I have been able to use only a portion of them. At the same time I may find it difficult to accept that any significant material detail related to the Europeans in Gujarat has been left out here. In any case, if this leads to the emergence of the archaeology of European expansion in India as a distinct area of interest in South Asian archaeology, I shall consider this historical exercise of mine a success. Theoretically this has tried to portray the early European presence in Gujarat as part of its long-term trade interaction from the east coast of Africa to the Strait of Malacca.

This volume was researched and written in the academic year 2001-2002. My first and foremost sense of indebtedness is to Dr C.J. Scarre who invited me to join his fieldwork and gave me the go-ahead to write and publish this monograph. In India we received warm cooperation from everybody we met. In Bombay I begin by thanking my brother Mr Ajay Kumar Chakrabarti of Nuclear Power Corporation and my sister-in-law, Dr (Mrs) Mahua Chakrabarti of Victoria Jubilee Training Institute, Dadar. They took care of the details of our stay and transport in Bombay. Among the professional friends in Bombay Dr Savia Viegas of K.C. College was exceptionally helpful. The authorities of the K.C. College, Bombay, invited us for a discussion which was also joined, among others, by Dr Devangana Desai of the Asiatic Society of Bombay, Dr A.P. Jamkhedkar, a former Director of the Maharashtra State Government Department of Archaeology and Mr Vikash Dilawari, a conservation architect. In Surat, Dr M.B. Meghani was our anchor-point. His enthusiasm for the past of his native city is infectious, and we greatly enjoyed meeting him. We also discussed Mughal Surat with Mr Jolly Wellington Christie. We benefited from meeting the headman of Sually village. Mr S.H. Sayed of Bharuch helped us to understand its monuments and ruins. Professor V.H. Sonawane, Dr Kuldeep Bhan and Dr K.K. Krishnan held discussions with us in Vadodara (Baroda). Dr Kiran Dimri showed us around the museum of the Department of Ancient Indian History, Culture and Archaeology of Baroda University. In the Archaeological Survey of India complex in Vadodara we met Mr Vikash Rawat (currently Director of Gujarat State Archaeology) and Dr (Mrs) Subhra Pramanik, the Superintending Archaeologist of the Vadodara Excavation Branch. The Superintending Archaeologist of the Vadodara Circle, Mr Gehlot, was then on tour. In Ahmedabad, thanks are due to Professor A.K. Singhvi of the Physical Research Laboratory and Mr Debasish Nayak, a conservation architect. It was also a great pleasure for me personally to meet Professor D.P. Agrawal in Ahmedabad. I thank Mrs Agrawal for her warm hospitality. Mr Y.M. Chitalwala of the Gujarat State Department of Archaeology and his colleagues, Mr Makwana and Mr Shah warmly extended their cooperation to us in Ahmedabad. Mr Chitalwala, who was my student in Calcutta University, was then officiating as the Director of his department. In a true Indian fashion he put up with the demands on his time by an old *masterji*. In Daman we have to thank Mr V. Pillai of the Daman Sub-Circle of the Archaeological Survey of India. In Diu Mr A. Parmar, Caretaker of the Diu fort, was very helpful. In Cambridge I thank Ms Dora Kemp for help with some illustrations.

Contents

List of Illustrations

1

Introduction

I. ARCHAEOLOGY OF EUROPEAN EXPANSION

I.1 A Brief Outline of Development

The study of early European expansion in various parts of the world is now a well-accepted component of archaeological research. In a vast segment of the world where the first European contacts ushered in the historical era, it is accorded the status of Historical Archaeology. In North and South America, Australasia and South Africa, Historical Archaeology means exclusively the archaeology of the period from their first European contact to the recent times, incorporating within it the strands of industrial archaeology and maritime archaeology or the archaeology of shipwrecks. In Europe this phase is roughly, though not strictly, synonymous with post-mediaeval archaeology. In India, the term 'colonial archaeology' is no doubt apt from the mid-18th century onwards, but for about 150 years before that, it is not a particularly suitable term because, except the Portuguese possessions of Goa, Diu and Daman on the west coast, the European settlements of the period cannot be technically termed colonial settlements. In the Indian context, the term "archaeology of European expansion" seems to be more apt to denote a particular component of the archaeology of the period from the landing of Vasco da Gama in Calicut in 1498 to the mid-18th century which witnessed the positive steps towards British paramountcy in India. It must be noted that this is only a component of the archaeology of this broad period, which otherwise remains basically the archaeology of the Mughal era. The archaeology of the period between the mid-18th century and 1947 is properly the archaeology of the colonial period in India.

'Historical Archaeology' in the United States (Schuyler 2001) and Canada (Trigger 2001) dealt initially with settlements which were either

American Indian sites showing evidence of European contact or those with the archaeological record of European settlers alone. Miscellaneous excavations were done at both these categories of sites as early as the 17th and 18th centuries. Professionalisation of this area of archaeological study occurred on a significant scale in the United States only in the 1930s when the numerous programmes to combat the Great Depression and the associated Historic Sites Act of 1935 led to a significant increase in federal funding for the excavation and preservation of 'historic' remains. In Canada, the Historic Sites and Monuments Board was created by the federal government in 1919 but the first related excavation took place only in 1941-43 when the site of a 17th century Jesuit mission in Ontario was excavated by Kenneth Kidd of the Royal Ontario Museum. In 1961, Canada created the Historic Parks Service (now renamed as Archaeology Division of the Canadian Parks Service) with the intention of both excavating and preserving historic period sites. In the United States, the creation of a National Park Service in 1916 was preceded by the Antiquities Act of 1906. The major excavation of the 1930s and 1940s was conducted by J.C. Harrington at Jamestown, the 17th century colonial capital (1607-1698) of Virginia. One of the important offshoots was a refinement of the typology and chronology of historic artefacts, including a study of clay pipes which has universal application for the dating of 17th and 18th century sites with European contacts. Founded in 1607, Jamestown was intermittently excavated till 1997 and has served as a major focus of American historic period archaeology. The pace of development in this field increased manifold in the 1960s, with various federal funding agencies outside the National Park Service and some States and universities picking up its cause. A major figure of this period was J. Deetz whose book on the archaeology of early American life (Deetz 1977) was able to excite popular imagination in this regard. One of his important field-projects was at Flowerdew Hundred Plantation (1617) in Virginia, which he used as a case-study (Deetz 1993) to examine 'the emergence of a distinct American culture from a British colony' (Beaudry 2001). Another major project of the period was at Williamsburg, the 18th century capital of Virginia, under the direction of I.N. Hume (1969). This was also the time when a book on the method and theory in American historical archaeology was published by Stanley South (1977). Meanwhile, an extra dimension, that of African-American life with special reference to slavery, was added to its scope of investigations. With Charles Fairbanks (cf. 1984) the plantation labour became a separate focus of archaeological investigation. The Society for Historical Archaeology, as distinct from the Society for American Archaeology, was established in

1967 and gained further importance when the National Register of Historic Places and State Historic Prevention Office were created on the state level due to the enactment of National Historic Preservation Act of 1966, Executive Order 11593 of 1971 and the Archaeological and Historical Conservation Act of 1977 by the U.S. Congress.

Apparently a little separate from this tradition but very much a part of the overall framework of America's historic period archaeology is the archaeological investigation of the Spanish period remains in Florida where St. Augustine, the oldest European settlement in the United States, was excavated first in 1935-37. It has been excavated intermittently till the present day, contributing to the archaeology of a colonial Creole community. Other Spanish frontier forts and towns have also been archaeologically investigated in Florida.

Spanish forts and towns formed the staple of historic period archaeology in the Caribbean basin—the islands of the Caribbean Sea and the lands bordering it. Here the history of identifying and investigating Spanish sites goes back to the 18th century. An early archaeological attempt to study Christopher Columbus was made by the U.S. navy vessel *Enterprise* which was sent to the Dominican Republic to study the site of La Isabela, the first settlement intentionally established by Columbus in the Americas (Deagan 2001). La Isabela was also excavated later. The effort of William Goodwin between 1911 and 1937 to map and excavate colonial sites in Jamaica (Goodwin 1946) led to a consolidation of interest in the archaeology of this period in the Caribbean. The interaction between the Spaniards and indigenous American inhabitants of the region was one of the major thrusts of historic period research in Cuba. Similarly, underwater archaeology, which in this case is dominated by Spanish and other shipwrecks, was another special focus of the Caribbean basin historical archaeology. In the case of Spanish–American town sites, long-term research programmes were undertaken to study "cultural interaction among Spanish, American Indian, and African residents and the resulting syncretic and newly developed *criollo* forms" (Deagan 2001).

> The archaeological record suggests that this admixture included the incorporation of Amerindian elements in non-socially visible, infra-structural areas, such as diet and food preparation, while visible symbols of social identification remained rigidly Spanish. Even after the extinction of the native Taino and related Amerindian people in the Caribbean, Spanish colonists continued to incorporate non-European traits into their households, replacing Indian contributions with African (Deagan 2001: 510).

Further, both slave and non-slave black settlements came in for archaeological attention throughout the Caribbean, with much attention being given to the theme of African influence on the colonial Caribbean, mostly in the form of Afro-American ceramic traditions. On a different level, the 1992 Quincentenary of Columbus's first voyage is said to have generated an enormous amount of support for historic period archaeology in the Caribbean region.

Elsewhere in Central and South America, the focus on the archaeology of post-Columbus period does not seem to be particularly focussed. Even in the case of Mexico this is said to be a 'relatively new field' (Cobean and Flores 2001). In Brazil, the major trend seemed to have been an architectural interest in old buildings, although fieldwork at the colonial period sites was not wholly neglected (Funari 2001).

There is a much sharper concern with historic period archaeology in South Africa and Australia. In South Africa there was an early concern to excavate the outposts of Dutch East India Company at such places as Posthuys (Post House) in Cape Town and Paradijs (Paradise) in the Newlands Forest, south of Cape Town. The Paradise work took place between 1980 and 1983 whereas the Post-House work was done in the 1970s. Historical archaeology as a sub-discipline emerged under Martin Hall in Cape Town University where in the late 1980s the Historical Archaeology Research Group was formed. Hall re-excavated Paradise between 1985 and 1989, throwing light on the development of 'Cape Dutch architecture', on which further light was thrown by the excavations at an 18th century site in Stellenbosch. Following the Dutch East India Company listing of people in its employment by their clearly defined ranks, Hall traced the archaeological manifestation of this ranking in his excavations at 91 Bree Street of Cape Town. The issues of space and architecture figure prominently in this kind of research in South Africa. There has also been a distinct search for archaeological traces of slavery, and although there is a general lack of artefactual evidence to prove slave identity, an interesting study using isotopic analysis and ethnography identified some skeletons found near the old Company battery at Fort Knokke as those of slaves. The Portuguese ship which was wrecked in Table Bay in 1818, while carrying them to Brazil, could also be identified on the basis of archival sources. South African archaeologists who are interested in this period have also been interested in tracing 'contact situations' between the indigenous hunter-gatherers and pastoralists and colonists. Although the initial concern was with the period of the Dutch Company, there is now an increasing interest in the archaeology of the British period of the 19th and 20th centuries as well. Yvonne Brink (2001) observes that a great deal of work remains to be done on 'mission stations, the Boer War, industrial archaeology, and indigenous African–European contact'.

Citing R.I. Jack (1985), Susan Lawrence (2001) argues that the increasing importance of the study of 'local history' and associated physical remains in the history departments of Australian universities, and the cheaper option of organizing training digs for students in Australia itself for the university departments offering courses in the archaeology of West Asia or the Mediterranean led to an increasing interest in the archaeology of the post-'contact' period or what is called 'historical archaeology'/'contact archaeology'/'aboriginal historical archaeology' in this continent. The turning point seems to have been the 1960s when a number of Ph.D theses were undertaken in this field in Canberra, Sydney and Melbourne. Maritime archaeology, or rather, the archaeology of shipwrecks soon became part of the scene. The Australian (now Australasian) Society for Historical Archaeology was established in 1971 and followed by the Australian Institute of Maritime Archaeology in 1982. With the acceptance of the idea of cultural resource management, the field developed rapidly in the 1970s, and by the early 1980s there emerged an organized body of literature throwing light on the life of the early European settlers in Australia. Excavation reports and artefact studies were both parts of this literature which culminated in Graham Connah's synthesis *The Archaeology of Australia's History* (Connah 1988) in 1988. Rapid urban development of the 1980s led to a sharper awareness of the heritage dating from the post-contact period and led to archaeological projects in the major cities like Sydney and Melbourne. In the 1990s this interest seems to have spread well in the countryside, taking in the issues of the location and character of mining, whaling and missionary activities and industrial archaeology in general. The contact archaeology in relation to the aboriginals had developed a special character in Australia. In addition to the traditional rock-shelters and shell midden sites showing signs of European contacts in the form of artefacts, there were places which were initially occupied by the European shepherds but later reoccupied by the aborigines after the Europeans deserted those camps. Besides, there were early missionary stations employing aborigines as servants. It is worth noting that the British settlements in Australia are mainly of the 19th century, with the first penal settlement in Sydney dating only from 1788. However, European exploration began with the Dutch in the 17th century, and in the 18th century there was an extensive trading system with fishermen from Southeast Asia. If one leaves aside the issue of maritime archaeology, there have been three main concerns of the Australian archaeologists dealing with this period: contact situations and early settlers, extractive economic activities of the day, and urban archaeology. Another important focus is the light which the archaeology of the period can throw on the aboriginal communities themselves. The archaeology of the present-day aboriginal Australia is increasingly becoming a part of this research, and although,

> it is frequently difficult to identify Aboriginal people in the absence of identifiably Aboriginal material culture (such as stone tools), but archaeologists are developing approaches that integrate oral histories, archaeological investigation, and documentary evidence... to overcome this 'invisibility' factor (Murray 2001: 125-126).

The Australian situation finds a close parallel in the development of historic period archaeology in New Zealand where European exploration dates from 1769 and the first European settlement from 1792. The first focus was on the sites of wars between the Maoris and the colonists, the related stockades and embankments being the focus of attention. In the 1960s when the first excavations took place, the emphasiz was on the 19th century Maori sites, although a British army barrack of the mid-19th century was also investigated. In the 1970s attention shifted to European mission stations, whaling stations, early farmhouses and sites of the forest industry. The Historic Place Act of 1975 was passed to protect all archaeological sites dating from one hundred or more years. Urban historical archaeology, especially in places like Auckland, came in for attention in the 1980s. Among the major projects undertaken in the historical archaeology of New Zealand, Ian Smith (2001) reports a programme of survey and excavation of fortifications associated with the Taranaki wars of the 1860s and 1870s and an investigation focussed, among other sites in the Clutha valley, on the archaeological remains of the Chinese gold miners of the area.

It is, on the whole, apparent that the development of archaeology of the colonial period—or what has come to pass as 'historical archaeology', or, as we have written here, 'historic period archaeology'—has developed only in a few major regions of the world: Canada and the United States of America, the Caribbean region, South Africa, Australia and New Zealand. In each case, the native population could be marginalised and the new settlers could in no way consider the history and archaeology of the native people as their own. This seems to provide a clear reason for the development of archaeological interest in the early European settlements and diverse aspects of their material remains and history in these regions. There is an immediacy of contact between the excavators and the ruins they are excavating or the relics they are unearthing. To some extent the current interest seems to have branched off to include categories of people other than European settlers, but still, the main motivation is to study the people to whom the excavators themselves can trace their descent. However, this does not detract from the inherent academic value of this interest in the history of archaeology as an area of study.

This value is, in fact, being increasingly realized even outside the core areas of its development in North America, Australia and South Africa. Since the 1980s there has been an increasing interest in historical archaeology in Latin America. As Daniel Schavelzon (2000) points out, 20 archaeological projects had been conducted in Buenos Aires since 1985. The first South American Conference in Historical Archaeology took place in Uruguay in 1993. The importance of archaeology in understanding the structure of the Ottoman empire which lasted from December 1516 to 1917 has also been clearly acknowledged (Baram and Carroll 2000).

I.2 Research Dimensions

I.2.1 *The Americas*

When James Hall, a descendant of Miles Standish who arrived in America aboard the *Mayflower* in 1620, began to excavate the ruins of the Standish house in Duxbury, Massachusetts in 1853 he was mainly interested in knowing about his own past—interested in forging a direct link between the Pilgrim fathers and himself. When the site of Ste. Marie Georgian Bay in Ontario—a mission site set up by the Jesuits in 1639 and destroyed by the Iroquois in 1648-49—began to be investigated by a Jesuit priest from Montreal in 1855, the obvious concern was to make the history of Jesuit missionary activities in this part of Canada better known and better deserving of attention. In each case, the documented past provided the key to the archaeological endeavour. The life of Miles Standish was well documented in the records, and so was the brief history of the Jesuit mission of Ste. Marie Georgian Bay. Archaeology brought these not-too-distant slices of the past closer to historical reality, providing an immediacy of contact between that past and the descendants of the people who made that past. In these cases, archaeology served the purpose of only an 'auxiliary science' to history. This, in fact, was the way historical archaeologists viewed their subject—a 'handmaiden to history'—for a long time.

The modern historical archaeologists' attitude is considerably different and puts emphasiz on the material record as a point of departure, seeking explanation of their data in terms of the known history of the relevant period and region, and using that explanation, again, to frame further questions of the archaeological data and look for further explanations in the relevant documents. The importance of archaeological research even in the context of such recent pasts is twofold. First, the written record does not include a whole host of people—the people, we know, existed: slaves, indentured servants, poor tenant farmers and modest freeholders who formed the majority of the population of pre-industrial America. Even if these people were mentioned in historical records, they were in all likelihood reported either very incompletely or with bias. Secondly, documents usually do not describe the items of ordinary daily life, the items which are taken for granted by the writers of historical documents. By producing a rich corpus of closely dated material evidence, archaeology makes possible detailed insights into the life of the period (Deetz 1993: 12-13).

I.2.1.1 Chesapeake Bay

The eastern shores of the Chesapeake Bay, roughly between Baltimore and Richmond on the eastern coast of the USA, mark a major and representative area where the discipline of American historial archaeology has taken its present shape through decades of work. In *Historical Archaeology of the Chesapeake,* the editors, P.A. Shackel and Barbara J. Little (1994) adopt a thematic organization for the volume's articles: early European settlement, plantation and landscape studies, 18th century life, and 19th century life. It is important to recall at the outset their observations on the early European settlements:

> European settlers did not simply transplant culture, but had to create it anew. Decisions and challenges concerning subsistence ranged from where to locate settlements to the methods of raising crops, to strategies for raising stock. Trade, warfare, governance, and relations with the mother country were of constant concern in this frontier society (Shackel and Little 1994: 6).

Among such sites in the Chesapeake region they have taken up Martin's Hundred, Suffolk Fort and Flowerdew Hundred. Martin's Hundred, a 20,000-thousand-acre plantation created in 1619 on the banks of the James river, had its administrative centre at Wolstenholme Towne which was a palisaded fort with some domestic buildings around it. This was burnt down during an Indian attack in 1622, which meant that a time capsule of early 17th century plantation life was preserved. Suffolk

Fort is a possibly contemporary site on the bank of the Nansemond river in Suffolk. The plantation of Flowerdew Hundred (Deetz 1993) was founded in the James river valley in 1619 by G. Yeardley, the first governor of Virginia, in the name of his wife, Temperance Flowerdew Yeardley. 'Hundred' was possibly a demographic-geographic division, larger than a parish but smaller than a county. It was at this site that the chronology based on the bore diameter of clay smoking pipes was perfected and based in turn on the realization that "the progressive reduction in bore diameter proceeded at a reasonably constant rate". J.C. Harrington, an early excavator of Flowerdew, offered six bore diameters with the following time-segments: 9/64 inch=1590-1620; 8/64 inch=1620-1650; 7/64 inch=1650-1680; 6/64=1680-1710; 5/64 inch=1710-1750; 4/64 inch=1750=1800. The shift towards more 'American' categories of material was clear with time: colourful dishes preferred to those of blue and white by 1760; marble as the preferred gravestone in place of slate by the end of the century; epitaphs on the graves stressing more secular themes and being written in the third person by this period; and the household trash being deposited in lined pits in about the same time. Deetz's summing up of the archaeology of Flowerdew Hundred is worth quoting:

> Archaeology at Flowerdew Hundred has indeed been a rewarding effort. The work of hundreds of people over nearly quarter of a century has detailed the development and change of a Virginia plantation, an unbroken sequence from Yeardley's first tiny settlement on the banks of the James through to the establishment of Willcox's rather ambitious plantation in the mid-19th century. The cast of characters is long and includes people whose names are known—George Yeardley, Abraham Piersey, Elizabeth Stephen, the Barkers and the Limbreys, the Taylor sisters, John Hood, the Poythress clan, the Wilkinses and Willcoxes, and finally General Ulysses S. Grant. But by far the majority of people who lived at Flowerdew Hundred and were responsible for learning the record for the archaeologist to ponder were anonymous. Tenant farmers, native-Americans, indentured servants, and slaves all have contributed to a story of everyday people doing commonplace things (Deetz 1993: 151).

Further, archaeological surveys in the area have revealed 60 settlements, half of which were European settlements. A late-17th-century iron-smelting industry has also been located in the area, and one of the project's goals was to study the early relationships between Europeans and African-Americans. There are also 'contact sites' and 17th century Anglo-American-African sites, an example of which is the site of Jordan's Point. At Bermuda Hundred which was designated a port town in 1691 there was a project to map the 1613 two-mile-long palisade fortification. At St. Mary's City the focus was on the excavations of the town centre and a Jesuit chapel. The plantation at King's Reach dates from 1690-1715 and an earth-fast structure of the turn of the 18th century was called Harmony Hall.

Under the category of 'plantation and landscape archaeology' of the Chesapeake Bay the following sites are mentioned: Jefferson's poplar forest, Mount Vernon, Enchanted Castle (a plantation complex), Cliff's Plantation and Stratford Plantation, Pohoke and Portici (battlefield), Annapolis (manipulation and design of space for ideological purposes), Oxon Hill (late 17th century–early 18th century structure), Locust Grave (tobacco farm), and Baltimore (18th century residence of a barrister).

The sites mainly dealing with the '18th century life' of the region are Williamsburg, Annapolis, and Free Blacks in Maryland. The examples of its '19th century life' are derived from Alexandria (Quaker buildings), Annapolis, Baltimore, Washington D.C., Manassas National Battlefield, Harper's Ferry, and west Virginia which has yielded many charcoal hearths, 19th century domestic farms, and civil war fortifications and encampments.

Although somewhat detailed, the preceding enumeration of the major components of the Chesapeake Bay archaeology serves the purpose of demonstrating the scope and extent of historical archaeology pursued in only a single region of North America. The analysis of the American lifeways over the past 400 years or more was no doubt one of the main objectives, but still, many other issues—some entirely theoretical—were involved. Two of the Chesapeake sites where the interplay of these objectives can be studied in detail are Williamsburg of Virginia and Annapolis of Maryland.

Williamsburg was the capital of the colonial Virginia in the 18th century. The basic initial purpose was—and still is—to reconstruct the colonial buildings and reconstruct them, and eventually preserve the site as a museum of living history. Research is organized under the auspicies of the Colonial Williamsburg Foundation which also took in its care the restoration of the neighbouring settlement of Wolstenholme Towne in the plantation of Martin's Hundred. The restoration and reconstruction work at Williamsburg began in 1928 and has continued since then. More than 500 buildings have either been restored or reconstructed, the number of the originals restored to their 18th century conditions being 88. More than 4 million people visit the site every year, and the importance of the site as a museum of the life of 18th century America needs no emphasiz. As the Williamsburg Foundation website proclaims "Think of the Williamsburg Area... and the images that come to mind are... 'Small Town' Colonial Life... the Search for American Independence...

the Model for Democracy used throughout the world".

Archaeology has gone much beyond any website declaration. One of the salient points is that:

> ... stratigraphic units are now painstakingly reconstructed and correlated with the property ownership and occupation sequences of sites, blocks, and neighbourhoods that have been drawn together from historical sources.... Archaeological evidence is linked with the data in the master biographical files created from historical records by reconstituting historical households and placing them in time and space (Brown III and Samford 1994: 233).

Another concern was with gardening, and apparently a clear division has been obtained between the formal garden spaces of the houses of the gentry and the more utilitarian 'kitchen gardens' of such excavated eating establishment as Shield's Tavern. The flora actually growing in those gardens has been reconstructed on the basis of botanical data found not merely in wells but also in various trash-pits. The growth of the town from a small 17th-century locus of dispersed farmsteads to the planned community of the 18th century has drawn considerable attention, and excavations in Block 29 may be taken up as a case study. In 1713 the first lots of this block show a mixed commercial and residential character but from about the middle of the 18th century it grew into an upper-class residential area. With the transfer of the capital of Virginia from Williamsburg to the nearby Richmond during the governorship of Thomas Jefferson in 1780, the block changed again, with its former importance being greatly reduced. Among the research conducted on the individual households, mention may be made of the intensive study of the household of John Brush, an early 18th-century gunsmith. A considerable amount of data on him came in the late 1980s and 1990s from the household and shop debris found in a privy constructed by him in the 1720s. At the plantation site of Carter's Grove owned by the colonial Williamsburg, archaeologists have excavated 18th-century farm quarters, leading to the reconstructions of slave dwellings and the analysis of issues like master-slave relationship, African and English acculturation and the development of slave communities by the mid-18th century. On the whole, what is remarkably interesting in the case of Williamsburg is the fact that "archaeological research has played a prominent role in defining the scope and character of landscape alterations, at various levels, from the individual house-lot to the town as a whole" (Brown III and Samford 1994: 242).

Another well-known archaeological site in the Chesapeake region is Annapolis, founded in 1650. It has been the capital of Maryland since

1795. Historic Annapolis Foundation was incorporated in 1952 and has been running, among other things, a programme of archaeological excavations in the city. The most famous site seems to be the two-acre garden associated with the house of William Paca, which was built in 1763-65. The garden survived till the early 20th century when it was replaced by a hotel building. When the hotel was pulled down in 1968, historical archaeological investigations have led to the restoration of the original features of the ground, with the palaeobotanical samples supplying the details of what grew in the garden. The layout of the garden has fuelled discussions on how power was exercised in Paca's time through an ostentatious display of wealth (Thomas 1998: 521-528).

I.2.1.2 Elsewhere in the Americas

The Chesapeake region is perhaps the single most important region where the scope of the archaeological sub-discipline of historical archaeology has matured over the years in North America, adequately outlining its major types of sites and investigative aims. A good, although somewhat dated, source of locating the general categories of excavation problems that one encounters in North American historical archaeology is the two chapters on sites in Ivol N. Hume's excavation manual *Historical Archaeology* (Hume 1969): "sites: domestic and sepulchral" and "sites: manufacturing, military and marine". The importance of these chapters lies in the fact that examples have all been taken from historical sites and the issues related to their excavations adequately highlighted. The problems associated with the excavations of cellars, gutters, kitchens, dairies, smokehouses, privies, etc. do not usually form parts of other excavation manuals, but in this case these constitute essential knowledge for a field-investigator. What he frankly advised regarding the unearthing of human skeletons, i.e. his 'sepulchral' sites, as early as 1969 is interesting and throws light on an issue which has only become more problem-ridden since then: "Unless the circumstances are very special, I would advise quickly covering them over and forgetting that you ever saw them. But if you do decide to go ahead, be sure that you first have legal clearance" (Hume 1969: 160). His 'manufacturing' sites are mainly industrial sites devoted to cabinet-making, glass-making, pottery-making, pipe-kilns, brick-kilns, iron furnaces, blacksmith's shops, and so on. A good example of the archaeological study of the 18th century and later pottery-making is that of the important nucleus of craftsmen at the Moravian missionary settlement of Bethabara in North Carolina. The settlement dates from 1753 and the master potter Gottfried Aust arrived there in 1755 (South 1999). Regarding military sites Hume points out the distinctions between permanent forts, temporary camps and battlefields.

> Little can usefully be said about battlefield sites. If one had time to dig in, we may be left with the remains of fortifications ...; if not, the site will have little to distinguish it, except perhaps some graves and a scatter of hardware that can best be salvaged by using a metal detector. There can be no meaningful stratigraphy (as far as the battle is concerned), and the salvage of relics becomes the be- all and end- all (Hume 1969:188).

The study of historical archaeology in North America has certainly grown more complex since the 1960s. 'Gender, race and class' are certainly a major concern (cf. Scott 1994) but those interested in archaeology's contribution to the study of socio-economic history of the recent periods will find much that is interesting in Donna J. Seiffert's analysis of the material from the excavations in the locality known as Hooker's Division on Ohio Avenue of Washington D.C. (Seiffert 1994). Mrs Starr was an established Baltimore Madam who arrived in Washington D.C. in 1858 and ran her establishment at No. 62, Ohio Avenue in Hooker's Division. Excavations conducted here in 1989 sampled deposits from ten house-lots, with these deposits being put in the context of the census data from a larger number of lots. Archaeological material was sorted into four household types—early prostitute, early working class, late working class and late prostitute—and related to the basic stratigraphy of deposits in each household type. On this basis Seiffert writes,

> .... The prostitutes of Hooker's Division in the 1870s and 1880s were apparently women of limited means like their neighbours in working-class households. The neighbourhood changed to a redlight district during the 1890s, and the business of prostitution changed as well. The Madam-owned brothels were replaced by capitalist business with non-resident owners, madam-managers, and employee-prostitutes. The material culture of the brothel changed as well. Based on the archaeological evidence, brothel residents enjoyed some material comforts that their working-class neighbours did not. Expensive meat cuts and buttons from fancy cloths suggest that prostitutes ate better and dressed better than their neighbours (Seiffert 1994: 164)

A different focus may be observed in P.R. Huey's archaeological study of the 17th-century Dutch at Fort Orange near Albany in New York (Huey 1991). The fort was intended as a base to trade with the Indians. A little more than 5 per cent of the original fort area was excavated in 1970-71, and among the major discoveries was the find of a shallow cellar supported by timber in one of the houses. Further, an adequate idea was obtained of the general comfort and style of the contemporary Dutch houses. For instance, there was an abundance of tableware including Chinese porcelain, glassware for drinking, and clay pipes of different makes for smoking. Venison was the most common meat, suggesting an ease of procurement from the Indians. On the whole, excavations at Fort Orange provided the first extensive evidence of the Dutch material culture in the United States in the 17th century.

Another major dimension of North American archaeology is what has been described as 'mission archaeology' (McEwan 1996). Christian missions "were among the most powerful institutions of the Spanish Crown for converting and 'civilizing' the native populations, commandeering labour and provisions, and establishing a presence in the vast frontier territories of Spanish America" (McEwan 1996: 473). They began in the 16th century but properly developed in the 17th and 18th centuries, being concentrated in parts of Mexico and the southern United States from Florida to California. Archaeological research at these sites has thrown a flood of light on the nature of early Spanish interaction with the American Indian tribes which did not always change their architectural style because of the Spanish impact but had the material basis of their life irrevocably changed due to the introduction of iron implements, firearms and European plants and animals. Conversion of some Indians to Christianity meant that in some cases individual Indians were buried in European-style coffins. The blending of Spanish and Indian elements slowly led to the emergence of a new culture called the *Criollo* culture.

The archaeology of the Spanish contact period is a major area of research in the Caribbean and Florida (cf. Deagan 1988). A large number of sites of this period have been excavated throughout the Caribbean, including La Isabella in the Dominican Republic, which was the first intentionally established Spanish settlement in the Americas. Some amount of syncretisation between the Spanish and the indigenous elements seems to find expression in the pottery of the period, especially the colonno-ware', a thick, low-fired, dark, crude pottery manufactured by the Indian and/or African elements of the population. In such areas as diet and food-preparation, there was an incorporation of Amerindian elements whereas the social norms were rigidly Spanish. However, it is important to remember that the initial Spanish impact led to a very severe population decline and this has something to do with the archaeology of slavery of the post-Spanish contact period in the Caribbean.

Between 1492 and 1515, the Taino peoples, only one of the three major components of the Caribbean culture in 1492—the Guanahatabey, the Island-Carib and the Taino—declined from several millions, to fewer than 25,000. In Florida, the nature of the impact was the same but on a lesser scale. The major islands of the Caribbean including Cuba are known as the Greater Antilles:

> The disappearance of the native inhabitants of the Greater Antilles is perhaps the most striking feature of European-Amerindian contact. These population declines and the concomitant reduction in the labour force available to the Spaniards had a grave effect on the Native Americans in regions peripheral to the Caribbean. Even before colonization efforts began, slave raids were common in the Lesser Antilles, the Bahamas, Florida, the Yucatan Peninsula, the northern coast of South America, and Panama. ... By 1518, even these groups could not satisfy the Spanish demand for labour, and the large-scale importation to the Caribbean of African people as slaves began.... From this movement emerged demographic and racial composition patterns that persist in the region today. It was also at this date that the production of sugar and hides eclipsed precious metals as the primary economic activity in Hispaniola, and attention turned from the Caribbean to Mexico and Central and South America (Deagan 1988: 199).

In the context of 'Spanish Florida', i.e. coastal Georgia and northern Florida, C.S. Larsen *et al.* (2001) examine in detail the bioarchaeology of this period and conclude that "a number of lines of evidence reveal a pattern of population decline and reduced health and quality of life in the native populations living in the Spanish colony" (Larsen *et al.* 2001: 97).

The archaeology of slavery in the Americas is rooted in the preceding historical development. The walled enclosures or 'jail-like structures' of many Cuban coffee and sugar plantations where the slaves provided the labour force were a part of the contemporary slave-management practices and have been investigated by archaeologists (Singleton 2001). Interestingly, archaeologists have read signs of slave-resistance in their study of plantation-space—in such modifications of residential space as the digging of storage pits beneath the floorboards of their houses. Slave resistance is also a theme of Orser and Funari's study of Palmares, a runaway slaves' territory in a hilly and forested section of Brazil's eastern coast in the 17th century (Orser and Funari 2001). It has been said that "the archaeology of slave resistance and rebellion can play an important role in fostering empowerment and critical awareness" (Orser and Funari 2001: 69).

Slavery is not the only focus of historical archaeology in South America. Among other interesting examples, one may mention an archaeological study of the downtown Buenos Aires where, apart from the architectural details, all other things from a city—faunistic, ceramic, material culture, and the botanical and chemical evidence—have been taken into consideration. This is based on 20 archaeological projects carried out in Buenos Aires since 1985 (Schavelzon 2000) and aided by a mass of archival evidence.

I.2.1.3 African American Archaeology as a Component of the American Historical Archaeology

This is one of the most important areas of research in North American historical archaeology (cf. Singleton 1985, 1999) and aimed at understanding not merely the material presence of African slaves but also their position in the contemporary social landscape and their interactions with their white owners. From this point of view, the archaeology of slavery has always been intertwined with the more orthodox concerns of historical archaeology in the USA and elsewhere, its ramifications being researched even at such classical Chesapeake sites as Williamsburg. However, as a separate sub-discipline its growth is apparently recent. There is no mention of this in Hume's 1969 manual, for instance. But the study of African American archaeology extends beyond the study of slavery and includes the related burial grounds, and settlements of free Africans in certain areas, especially in the Spanish-dominated enclaves such as Florida. The approach to Thomas Jefferson's plantation at Monticello in Virginia was lined by 19 buildings allotted to his slaves, hired labourers, artisans and indentured servants (Thomas 1998: 535). Excavations in the 1980s revealed the differences in the lifestyle of the different categories of these people. Some slaves lived in small log cabins whereas there were others living in stone houses with some amenities including better food and tableware. More diversities have been noted among the slave communities of the coastal Georgia and northern Florida (Thomas 1998: 538-539). More prominent discoveries in this field are perhaps those of slaves' skeletons and burial grounds, the discovery of the bones of 427 enslaved Africans beneath a parking lot of the downtown New York being an important example (Thomas 1998: 544-552). Its significance can best be expressed in the words of Michael Blakey, an African American anthropologist:

> The very existence of an African Burial Ground in colonial New York raised the issue of false historical representation. The vast majority of educated Americans had learned that there was little if any African presence in New York during the colonial period, and that the northern American colonies had not engaged in the practice of slavery. The Burial Ground helped show that these notions comprised a kind of national myth. Africans arrived in New York and

its Dutch predecessor, New Amsterdam, from the beginning; they had represented 15 to 40 per cent of these colonies and had laboured in most aspects of the building of the city and its economy. The majority of these people had been enslaved until Emancipation Day in 1827 (cited in Thomas 1998: 546).

The research on these remains was conducted by the African American scholars and showed evidence of high infant and childhood mortality along with the general evidence of malnutrition and heavy workload. This is a classic case where the conditions of a group of people about whom the documentary records are very incomplete in detail have been worked out by archaeology. Also, this is a case where the close ties between the contemporary political and social issues, and historical archaeology was well demonstrated. The strong involvement of the New York African American community was the catalytic factor which led to the study, preservation and National Historic Landmark status of this site. Four issues have been said to characterise African American archaeology in the United States: living conditions under slavery; status differences within the plantation community; interplay of planter dominance and slave resistance; and formation of African American cultural identity (Thomas 1998: 552).

I.2.2 Australia

In their review of the Australian historical archaeology which they see "as the archaeology of the modern world", A. Paterson and A. Wilson (2001) identify the following key areas.

Artefact studies: This includes objects—normally of glass and metal—modified by the aboriginals after their contact with the Europeans: usually glass artefacts from shipwreck and surface sites; leather and textile as preserved in the archaeological contexts; the material culture as an indicator of class, gender and ethnicity; butchery patterns; the building materials and household furnishings (both for preservation and possibility of dating); the presence of traded goods, such as ceramics, clay pipes and clothing, in historical contexts; craft related to ships and boats; and the formation of shell middens during historical periods.

Industrial archaeology: Mining has been said to be "unparalleled in its effect on the Australian landscape, and in scale and scope of traces left behind" and traces of logging, pastoralism and water management also fall in this category. In each case there are settlements associated with these activities, which make them the focus of archaeological studies. The locations of factories of different kinds—salt works, brickworks, lime production, oil distilleries, textile manufactures, ceramics, etc.—have been subject to detailed analyses with reference to their visible impact on the landscape, technology, and economy as a whole. Settlements related to transport infrastructure which may range from the first convict roads to railway lines are a form of study, and so is the archaeological research on the traces of extensive, industrial-scale farming and related signatures in the landscape. In the same vein, one can talk about the archaeology of Australian penal history, defence infrastructure and maritime sites.

Aboriginal interaction with others after the arrival of the Europeans: On the one hand this has studied specific places such as missions, and has adopted a regional approach on the other. The themes include contextual studies of historical events, analysis of the documentary sources on the aboriginal people, changes in indigenous life and institutions, and the evidence for fire, disease, exchange and historic period art in the aboriginal contexts. Among the regional approaches, mention may be made of such issues as the archaeology of colonisation and the study of how the aboriginal peoples came to be incorporated in the colonial system.

Paterson and Wilson (2001: 87)) also argue that "the fact that Australia was established as a penal colony and was largely settled initially through forced migration offers unique research potential".

Between 1788 when the first convict colony was established in New South Wales and 1868, 1,60,000 convicts or more were transported to Australia and employed basically as unpaid labourers in government and private projects with the status of 'assigned servants'. Graham Connah (2001) studied the house of a colonial aristocrat, A.C. Innes, settled near Port Macquarie, north of Sydney in the 1830s, to find out about the life of both a 19th century Australian aristocrat and his 'assigned servants'. The house was derelict by the end of the 19th century and destroyed by the end of the 20th, suffering "badly from the attention of both vandals and amateur antiquarians but particularly from the theft of building materials, made valuable by the morbid fascination of many modern Australians with anything remotely related to early colonial convictism" (Connah 2001: 143). In 1999 Connah began his excavations at the site. The outline of a large aristocratic house of the period soon emerged, complete with a system of running water and proper plumbing, but what was also found, in a gully out of the sight of the main house, was the remains of a small wooden building with a brick fireplace and sundry evidence of frugal living conditions. As Connah points out, the picture comprised "at one end of the scale the luxury of the latest development in sanitation, at the other a damp wooden hut with an earth floor" (Connah 2001: 151).

The brutality and the finality of the colonisation process of Australia are well-known, but Lesley Head and Richard Fullagar (1997) in their study of the contact situation in the Keep river catchment area of the northwest corner of the Northern Territory show how "even this most extreme 'contact' is characterized by layers of complexity and changes of direction" (Head and Fullagar 1997: 425). For instance, stone tools for wood-working were replaced by metal tools but stone was retained to pound plants and grind ochre. Also, some beautifully flaked tools, products of pressure-flaking, were incorporated into exchange networks as beautiful objects given as prestigious gifts.

The significance of historical archaeology from the point of view of the study of Australia's past has been best expressed by Connah (1996):

> ... the historical archaeologist in Australia is able to study the evolution of the Australian house and other buildings, the growth of cities and towns, the failure and disappearance of some settlements, the prisons in which the convicts lived and the public works that they laboured on, the impact of pastoral and arable agriculture on the varied landscapes, the depredations of past mining, the remnants of defunct secondary industries, the development of communications, the achievements of engineers, and the countless movable artefacts of iron, glass, ceramic, and other materials that litter the surface of the continent as witness to the burgeoning production of British, European, American, and Australian factories. Study of this huge variety of physical evidence can shed light on those aspects of Australia's historical past that are neglected in the documents and beyond the reach of living memory (Connah 1996: 75)

Connah (1996) also claims that in the archaeological record it is possible to "trace the gradual emergence of Australian culture as something distinct and different from the cultures of the settlers' homelands".

In the context of Australia, one may also think of the Pacific islands where the phase of European discovery is said to span 338 years from 1521 to 1859. The population collapse with the introduction of the previously unknown diseases in the islands and the role of European contact in social and political change (as amplified by the introduction of firearms and European ships in the inter-island warfare) are among the issues making the study of historical archaeology of the region.

I.2.3 South Africa

Historical archaeology in South Africa has been clearly labelled by M. Hall and A. Markell (1993) as 'the archaeology of colonialism'—'the archaeology of European colonial expansion into southern Africa and the archaeology of the impact of this expansion on the communities long-established here'. They point out that the basis of the current work was laid down in the 1970s and 1980s and underline two major themes: the study of the archaeology of impact (i.e. impact of European contact and settlers on the local inhabitants, cf. Schrire 1991) and the archaeology of the underclass, especially servants, slaves and the like. In addition, attention may be drawn to the special significance of the archaeology of shipwrecks in this context in South Africa because there is a rich collection of wrecks on her dangerous coastline.

The archaeology of impact is based around a few historical facts. Although the Table Bay near Cape Town was frequently used in the 16th and early 17th centuries as an anchorage by European ships sailing around the Cape of Good Hope for the East, there was no colony at all before 1615. The wreck of the Dutch East India ship *Haarlem* on the shores of the Bay in 1647 and the subsequent interaction of the shipwrecked crew with the local Khokoi led to the establishment of a small Dutch garrison at the site of modern Cape Town. In 1657, some of its residents were allowed to farm inland, and the process of expansion may be said to have begun.

Since the beginning of historical archaeology in South Africa, Cape Town and other areas in the western Cape have remained a major focus of research. The early Dutch East India Company (VOC) base had a number of outposts in the adjacent areas, and Paradise, one such outpost located on the slopes of the Table Mountain, drew archaeological attention from Hall *et al.* (1993). It has provided the architectural history of a single dwelling through the 18th century, inventory of the contemporary material culture and evidence of status difference between the house of the person-in-charge and the outbuildings occupied by the VOC soldiers and labourers. Excavations of the North Wharf of Cape Town's waterfront discovered the original iron and wooden framework of the jetty and the water pipe used to service the ships, confirming the available archival records of the 19th century (Saitowitz, Seeman and Hall 1993). The archaeology of the wreck site of the VOC ship *Oosterland* (1697) in the Table Bay is a famous example of the archaeological interest in such sites of the Cape Town area. Similarly, the 'Amsterdam battery', a late 18th century Dutch military installation in the same Bay area has been excavated, again verifying and complementing the archival evidence (Seeman 1992, Miller 1997). A remarkable analysis of the archaeology of the underclass in Cape Town comes from investigations in the Cobern Street burial ground (*c.* 1755-*c.* 1840) which was meant for people who worked as manual labourers. Fifty-three burials were excavated and various indices, including the results of stable carbon and nitrogen isotopic analyses, were taken into consideration to know the types of people buried in the cemetery.

> The isotopic analysis of the Cobern Street graves provides strong confirmatory evidence for the presence of both first-generation slaves from Africa and the East and locally born people. The cultural association of Western elements in the graves of both patent foreigners and local folk points to the swift incorporation of strangers into the existing cultural world at the Cape. This was the world of the underclass, whose stamp is echoed in cemeteries in the New World, where coffins, shrouds, trade beads, pipes, as well as objects for making fire, sewing and cutting, speak to aspects of leisure and necessity in daily life. Over and above the details of teeth and age, sex, race and gender, our isotopic work confirms the association of people from widely different parts of the world—Muslims from the East, Africans from the North, slaves and possible freemen from the Cape, innocents and a felon—all united in death in a common yard. It is a picture that is emerging clearly in slave contexts elsewhere (Cox *et al.* 2001: 91).

There has been plenty of historical archaeology outside the Cape Town region too. Excavations at Vergelegen (Markell 1993), a Dutch estate of the 18th century have thrown light on how the Dutch vernacular architectural tradition was transferred to a frontier colonial situation.

Research has been extensive even outside Cape Town. The 19th century water supply system of Praetoria in eastern South Africa was the topic of an archaeological enquiry (Schalkwyk, Naude and Vollenhoven 1995). Fort Daspoortrand, one of the 30 military fortifications erected within the municipal boundaries of Praetoria between 1880 and 1902, was investigated with reference to its western ammunition tunnel, storeroom, entrance, and miscellaneous artefacts (Vollenhoven 1994). Cartridge cases dating from the Second Anglo-Boer War (1899-1902) were excavated in what has been called a Late Iron Age settlement near Winberg in Orange Free State, throwing light on the continuity of such settlements (Dreyer 1994). Nineteen imported vessels which are examples of European and Oriental ceramics, and two clay pipes were excavated in six rock-shelters of the upper Seacow river valley in the northern Cape Province. All but one of these examples were acquired in 1840-1880 by indigenous retainers employed in the farms which appeared in the valley during that period (Moir and Sampson 1993). Rorke's Drift, a battlefield of the Anglo-Zulu War of 1879 was archaeologically investigated, leading to the locations of the British Commissariat store and the hospital burnt down by the Zulus (Webley 1993). Features of archaeological interest were traced in the Wagon-making area (1880-1930) of the Lovedale Mission Station in the eastern Cape Province (Nogwaza 1992). Livestock remains associated with European artefacts were found in the excavations of the rock-shelters of the upper Seacow valley, and archaeo-zoological analysis suggests how slaughtered meat was distributed to the farm-labourers who lived in those rock-shelters (Vogt, Plug and Sampson 1992). In the context of the South African hunter-gatherers of the colonial period, an important, perhaps pathbreaking, study is by A.D. Mazel (1992) on the archaeology and history of San hunter-gatherers over the last 150 years in Natal Drakensberg.

I.2.4 Miscellaneous Areas and Themes

The slave trade closely touched Africa's west coast, and it is not surprising that the archaeological implications of this trade would be examined in that area. For instance, there has been archaeological research at the site of the town of Savi on the coast of Benin since 1991. As the capital of the Hueda kingdom, Savi was a place of great importance in the trans-Atlantic slave trade. Archaeological research has demonstrated that significant values and meanings were assigned to the trade items which were incorporated into the Savi society. Excavated material from excavations both from the elite and commoners' areas, and the documentary evidence from eyewitness accounts, demonstrate distinct and multifaceted motivations and strategies involved in establishing trade relations with Europeans (Kelly 1997).

The arrival of Europeans on the southern coast of Madagascar in the 16th-18th centuries has formed the basis of a study by M.P. Pearson (1997). Three groups of the local population—the Tandroy, Karembola and Mahafaly—imported guns but avoided otherwise contact with the outsiders. In the 16th and 17th centuries there was a discontinuity in their settlement patterns: river valley habitations were discarded for defensive locations in the waterless southern plain. There were European colonies at Fort Dauphine and St. Augustine. Excavations of a Portuguese stone house of the 16th century revealed imported artefacts—Chinese porcelain, celadon and fine Islamic glass, none of which could be dated prior to the 17th century.

A somewhat novel but aparently gaining in importance is the theme of transnational cross-currents of larger political entities which spanned the period of European expansion but were themselves located outside Europe. The Ottoman empire lasted from the late 13th century to the end of the First World War, and ranged from modern Croatia to Iraq and Yemen, including much of north Africa. The date of the incorporation of the various geographical segments in the fold of the empire differed—in Crete, for instance it is not earlier than AD 1669—but the claim of the Ottoman empire as a specific unit of archaeological study has been pushed in a publication edited by Uzi Baram and Lynda Carroll (2000). The model, of course, is the well-acknowledged theme of Roman empire as a coherent archaeological area to be studied within its own framework (cf. Richmond 1957), but in the case of the Ottoman empire, the idea has been applied to a period almost overlapping with the contemporary world. In the New World, the archaeology of the Spanish empire as a colonial experience was viewed within a single framework by R.P. Schadel (1992), and T.D. Dillehay and K. Deagan (1992) established its broad theme as 'the Spanish quest for empire'. The archaeology of empires as a research theme (Sinopoli 1994) may not be unknown, but whether it can be more than a pragmatic device to incorporate the whole spectrum of archaeological data from disparate geographical regions, which were under a single political control for sometime, in the overall framework of historical knowledge of those regions, still remains to be seen. Baram and Carroll (2000) offer four main ingredients of the archaeology of the Ottoman empire: interaction with the forces of the global European expansion and identity as components of the archaeology of Islam, the Middle Eastern studies, ethno-archaeology of the relevant regions and the present political and other attitudes to the historical entity of the Ottoman empire.

I.2.5. An Overview

The preceding review, although brief and to some extent disjointed, was aimed at driving home the points of both depth and diversity of the post-European-contact archaeological research in North and South America, Australia, parts of Africa and elsewhere. In Europe, the archaeology of this period is consigned to 'post-mediaeval archaeology' which, in the context of Britain, "is generally understood as the period of the unification of the British Isles, the establishment of Britain upon the path of maritime colonial expansion and the initial stages of industrial growth" (editorial of the first volume of the journal *Post-medieval Archaeology* in 1967). The divide between the mediaeval and the post-mediaeval is taken to be 1609 in Scotland (Crawford 1967). Whatever may be the precise chronological confines of post-mediaeval archaeology in Britain and Europe, there is no confusion about the dates of the beginning of 'historical archaeology' in the Americas, Australia and

South Africa and elsewhere where the first footsteps of the Europeans mark the beginning of this particular phase of archaeology in those areas. Again, the logic is not the same everywhere. In North America, Australia and South Africa, the European expansion literally stands for the dividing line between prehistory and history, but there is no justification of relegating the complex societies of Central and South America, which the Spanish conquistadors destroyed, to the realm of prehistory and making the historical period of these areas begin with this destruction. The fact that even the previous existence of the Aztec writing system was ignored to make way for the beginning of 'history' in the New World only with its discovery by Columbus is interesting in itself.

However, the point which is more relevant to the present context is that in each of these areas, the tradition of historical archaeological research can be taken back to the 19th century and is in this sense deep-rooted. The proper efflorescence of research had naturally to wait till the modern period when the possible contributions of archaeology to the history of this comparatively recent past could, in the light of the development of archaeology as a discipline, be properly appreciated. The overriding considerations of this research are easy to understand: the material basis of early European life and its impact on, and interaction with, the indigenous inhabitants, the physical character and various geographical issues of the European settlements of this period, the archaeological evidence of slave trade and the plantations run with slave labour, and the emergence of regional modern identities as opposed to the European identities of the original settlers. Added to these are the archaeology of shipwrecks and the many-sided details of industrial archaeology, and running through them all, is a concern with how the global factors acted on these regional scenes and vice versa. If this adequately sums up the American side, the Australian and South African cases have certain peculiarities of their own. Where else outside South Africa would cartridge cases of the 19th century be used to date 'Late Iron Age' settlements? The overwhelming concerns with things like mining, large-scale pastoralism, convict settlements, etc. give historical archaeology in Australia an added flavour.

If there has been a distinct development by the beginning of the 21st century, that has been in the increased focus on the material developments of this period in different regions as parts of a global network. This is what Orser (1996) writes in his *A Historical Archaeology of the Modern World*, and this is what P.L. Kohl means by his "globally conceived, regionally specific historical archaeology" (Kohl 2000). Orser's summing–up is that historical archaeology is "a multi- and interdisciplinary field that shares a special relationship with the formal disciplines of anthropology and history and seeks to understand the global nature of modern life" (Orser 1996: 27). Later, he puts more emphasiz on its goals to establish closer links with anthropology:

> Archaeologists who tend to see historical archaeology as a critical pursuit generally believe that it can have a distinct impact on our understanding of the historical roots of today's world, including capitalism. This understanding is linked to a critically informed anthropology that seeks to be active and engaged in the problem of today's world (Orser 1999: 625).

In a sense, the study of historical archaeology has come round a full circle. The immediacy of the past from the present viewpoint was the motive-force of early excavations, and at the turn of the century it has been supposed to play a role in the study of global capitalism. The latter approach is fast becoming a major force, well-reflected in such publications as *The Archaeology of Urban Landscapes* (Mayne and Murray 2002) where the focus is on the historical archaeology of urban slums. C.J. Donnelly and A.J. Horning (2002) point out that the post-mediaeval archaeology of Ireland began with the study of those 16th and 17th century sites which were associated with a major influx of British settlers in Ireland. However, they conclude by claiming that the post-mediaeval archaeology of Ireland and elsewhere must look beyond its national and disciplinary boundaries and be based on its global context.

To seek the global links of regional traits and trends is one thing but to harp on 'the global nature of modern life' as the starting point of investigations is quite another. To some extent, the current theoretical occupation of 'historical archaeology' is reminiscent of the situation of general archaeology as a discipline in the 1960s. What is also interesting is that the concern seems to be limited so far only to North American academics. It is interesting to reflect that all the contributions to the Baram-Carroll volume on the historical archaeology of the Ottoman empire came, with one exception, from people based in the U.S. universities (the exception is N.A. Silberman who calls himself a historian of archaeology and is based in an institution in Belgium). What the protagonists of the globally networked historical archaeology or the archaeology of the modern world do not seem to appreciate is the fact that the primary and the most detailed evidence of the global interrelationship during this period is the written record kept in archives in various places and various languages. Archaeologists can certainly use the secondary sources, i.e. the products of this archival research by historians, but it is doubtful if they can be credited with originality in this sphere. They can make solid contributions of their own by making the history of this period more real and by throwing light on the life of the people neglected in the historical sources.

Further, it may not be forgotten that the historical archaeology of the Americas, South Africa and Australasia is essentially a Western quest to know more of the Western history in these areas. There has always been a strong element of nationalism running through it. This urge on the part of the Western settlers in the vast Amercian, Australian and African continents to find the material evidence of their early struggles and seek the emergence of an archaeological identity for themselves is quite natural and has been echoed well in an article on William Kelso's discovery of James Fort in Jamestown, Virginia (Lange 2002). This fort was the nucleus out of which Jamestown grew.

"In this spot the first General Assembly met", Kelso says. "It was the first representative body, the origin of the American form of government". Kelso's team had located a national shrine (Lange 2002: 77).

II. SCOPE OF RESEARCH ON THE ARCHAEOLOGY OF EUROPEAN EXPANSION IN INDIA

We have argued in the beginning that in the Indian context there is a distinction between colonial archaeology, the starting point of which may be taken as the mid-18th century, and the archaeology of the period before that, going back to 1498 when the Portuguese arrived. Whereas the archaeology of colonial India marks a separate phase of India's archaeological history, the archaeology of the period of European expansion must be considered only a component, however distinct, of the overall archaeology of the Mughal period.

Whatever may be its general position in the scheme of Indian archaeological studies, the problem is that it has not yet been the subject of any focussed archaeological research. It has long formed a major staple of Indian historical studies, but in the domain of archaeology it has been completely neglected. Apparently, the archaeologists did not think that it might be important to try to offer a coherent archaeological perspective of a phase of Indian history about which so much was already known from the historical sources. This neglect notwithstanding, the threads of archaeological research on this period are clear enough.

What would require actual investigations on the ground is the physical evidence of the European trading establishments, including the places where they landed with their goods. Although their locations are mostly clear, one is not sure if they have been properly identified in all cases. The two questions which may immediately be asked on this basis are: the extent to which they were integral parts of the already existing Mughal port framework, and what do they tell us about the organization of their trade and the ways in which it was conducted. Further, the European presence was not limited only to the major Mughal ports where the merchants with goods from Europe landed. The Mughal courts of Delhi and Agra were important places to travel to, and for an efficient and economical collection of the goods to be bought in India for the European market, a close familiarity with the Indian countryside where things like indigo were produced and cloth woven, was necessary too. The European merchants in Mughal India did not lead isolated lives; they had to interact closely both with the people and the land, and it is good archaeology to trace this contact network.

The scale of this network is not always appreciated. It covered virtually the entire length of the Indian coast which was intermittently dotted by European presence between the 16th and 18th centuries: the commercial premises or, as they put in the contemporary records, "factories" of the English, French, Dutch, and the Danes, which flourished from the 17th century onwards, and the Portuguese forts and commercial and military enclaves going back to the 16th century. Intimately related with this distribution is a series of questions regarding their locational geography: how do they relate to the physical and other geographical features of the land and what light do they throw on the thrusts of European penetration of India? There were also a few churches (invariably Portuguese) and miscellaneous burial grounds.

In view of the extensive literature that we have cited on the historical archaeology of the New World, South Africa and elsewhere and its increasing significance in the general scheme of archaeological studies, it is indeed surprising that no systematic archaeological attention has yet been devoted to these remains and their associated geographical and historical issues. Meanwhile, we attempt to make a beginning with Gujarat. However, in a significant way, this attempt will differ from the way in which the study of historical archaeology is generally approached in the Americas, Australia and South Africa. Here our emphasiz is on visualising the early modern European presence in Gujarat as a part of a long historical continuum.

2

Gujarat's Maritime Trade Till *c.* 1600

The early European expansion in Gujarat in the 16th-18th centuries took place in the context of the maritime trade of this province.

The purpose of this chapter is to offer an outline of Gujarat's maritime trade till *c.* 1600 and draw attention to the nature of the available published sources and also the fact that Europeans of this period were here as a part of a long historical continuum. The Portuguese presence became increasingly visible all along the west coast after 1498, and if we have carried our story to *c.* 1600, roughly the period when other Europeans—mostly the Dutch, French, Danes and British (only the British, Dutch and French in the case of Gujarat)—begin to feel interested in the scene, that is because in the 16th century the Portuguese sources introduce an element of coherence and vividness which were by and large lacking in the sources relevant to the earlier periods.

I. TRADITIONAL PORTS AND TRADE LINKS OF THE GUJARAT COAST

I.1 Geographical Prelude

The long coastline of the province, which is framed by the Great and Little Ranns of Kutch, the Gulfs of Kutch and Cambay, and the Narmada and Tapti estuaries, and its position on the Indian coast in relation to the Gulf, the Arabian coast, the mouth of the Red Sea, and the Horn of Africa down to Ethiopia, have ensured its maritime significance throughout the course of Indian history. The fall of Diu on the southern coast of the Kathiawar peninsula to Portuguese in 1535 and the first arrival of British ships at the mouth of the Tapti at Surat in 1607 were only parts of a long-drawn continuum of its overseas contacts and geographical role in the struggle for the mastery of the Indian Ocean.

Of the three main geographical divisions of Gujarat, Kutch and Kathiawar/Saurashtra are peninsulas, both with central hills, long coastal plains and radial drainage patterns. The Gujarat mainland, divided into the northern plains or *Anartta* and the southern plains or *Lata,* has its major rivers—the Sabarmati, Mahi, Narmada and Tapti—flowing into the Gulf of Cambay and is oriented, as far as the internal routes are concerned, towards Rajasthan, Malwa (central India) and Maharashtra. The Great Rann, an area of about 18,000 square km which frequently remains flooded to the depth of up to a little less than a metre between April and October, separates Kutch from Sind and has four islands arranged from east to west on its southern shore. The flood occurs as the water of the Kori creek at its western end is driven up by the monsoon winds and combines with the rains and the flooding of the minor rivers.

> The floodwaters ... leave a hard, flat surface covered with stone, shingle and salt. As the season wears on, and the heat grows greater, the ground baked and blistered by the sun, shines over large tracts of salt with dazzling whiteness, and the air, dim and quivering, mocks all distances by an almost ceaseless mirage. Only on some raised rocky lands is water found, and only near water is there brushwood, grass, or any sign of growth. Except a chance bird, or herd of wild asses, a stray antelope, or an occasional camel caravan, no sign of life breaks the weary loneliness (Campbell 1880: 12).

There are three main routes, all easily negotiable by camels, across the Great Rann to the Indus delta and the Thar-Parkar area of Sind. The Little Rann (*c.* 5000 sq. km) separates Kutch from the Gujarat mainland but there are well-defined cart-tracks across it to places like Palanpur and Ahmedabad and through them, Marwar (Rajasthan) and Malwa.

Much of the surface water of Kutch is salty but can be avoided by digging wells into the groundwater which was available at the depth of between *c.* 4 m and *c.* 14 m in the 19th century. An area called Banni, which juts into the northern Rann like a peninsula, is a rich pasture land, and Kutch in general is noted for its breed of horses and cattle. Agriculture is pursued mostly in the coastal plain and the valleys of the central hills, but as the mean annual rainfall is about 12.62 inches (*c.* 32 cm) with a high variability, Kutch has never been famous for its agriculture.

In the Kathiawar peninsula which is separated from Kutch by the Gulf of Kutch, the annual mean rainfall is about 23 inches (*c.* 58.4 cm) but as its variability is high, agriculture is not a strong point of Kathiawar either. It has been said that as late as the 19th century or a little earlier, an arm of the Little Rann came down to touch the Gulf of Cambay and thus kept the Kathiawar peninsula separate from the mainland Gujarat.

This section of the province has a better rainfall than Kathiawar, but even then it is below 100 cm annually in most of the areas except a small coastal patch south of Ahmedabad.

I.2 The 19th-Century Evidence

The basic evidence is available for the two peninsulas and suggests that the old pre-industrial maritime tradition of Gujarat certainly continued till the end of the 19th century, which in turn can serve as a baseline to understand the related archaeological and historical evidence enumerated below.

I.2.1 Kutch

For Kutch our source is J.M. Campbell's *Gazetteer of the Bombay Presidency, vol. 5. Cutch, Palanpur and Mahikantha* (Campbell 1880) and J. Macmurdo's 'An account of the province of Cutch' in *Transactions of the Literary Society of Bombay* (Macmurdo 1820). Macmurdo's report is dated 25 June 1818. The substantive evidence comes from the gazetteer.

I.2.1.1 Boats

When the gazetteer was compiled, perhaps in the 1870s, there were six types of deep-sea trading vessels in the traditional ports of Kutch: *Padav, Navdi, Kotia, Ganjo, Batela* and *Bagela*.

Padav was 8.22 m to 11.4 m long, 3.2 m to 3.8 m broad and had 2 masts, 3 sails, 28.5 to 62.5 tons, and a crew of 4 to 7 men. It was engaged in trade with the ports of Kathiawar, Konkan and Malabar.

Navdi was 8.22 m to 12.34 m long, 3.2 m to 3.8 m broad and had 1 mast, 3 sails, 28 to 80 tons and a crew of 4 to 12 men. It was engaged in trade with Basrah, Zanzibar and Maskat.

Kotia was 8.22 m to 12.34 m long, 3.2 m to 5.02 m broad and had 3 masts, 2 sails, 28 to 80 tons and a crew of 4 to 12 men. It was engaged in trade with Zanzibar, Maskat and other ports and the chief trading vessel of Kutch of the time.

Ganjo was 11.43 m to 14.63 m long, 4.57 m to 5.94 m broad, and had 3 masts, 3 sails, 62.5 to 125 tons and a crew of 8 to 15 men. It was engaged in trade with Zanzibar, Maskat and other distant ports.

Batela was 12.8 m to 13.71 m long, 3.2 m to 5.48 m broad, and had 2 masts, 3 sails, 28 to 125 tons and a crew of 4 to 12 men. It was engaged in trade with Zanzibar, Maskat and other distant ports.

Bagela was 12.8 m to 17.37 m long, 5.02 m to 5.94 m broad, and had

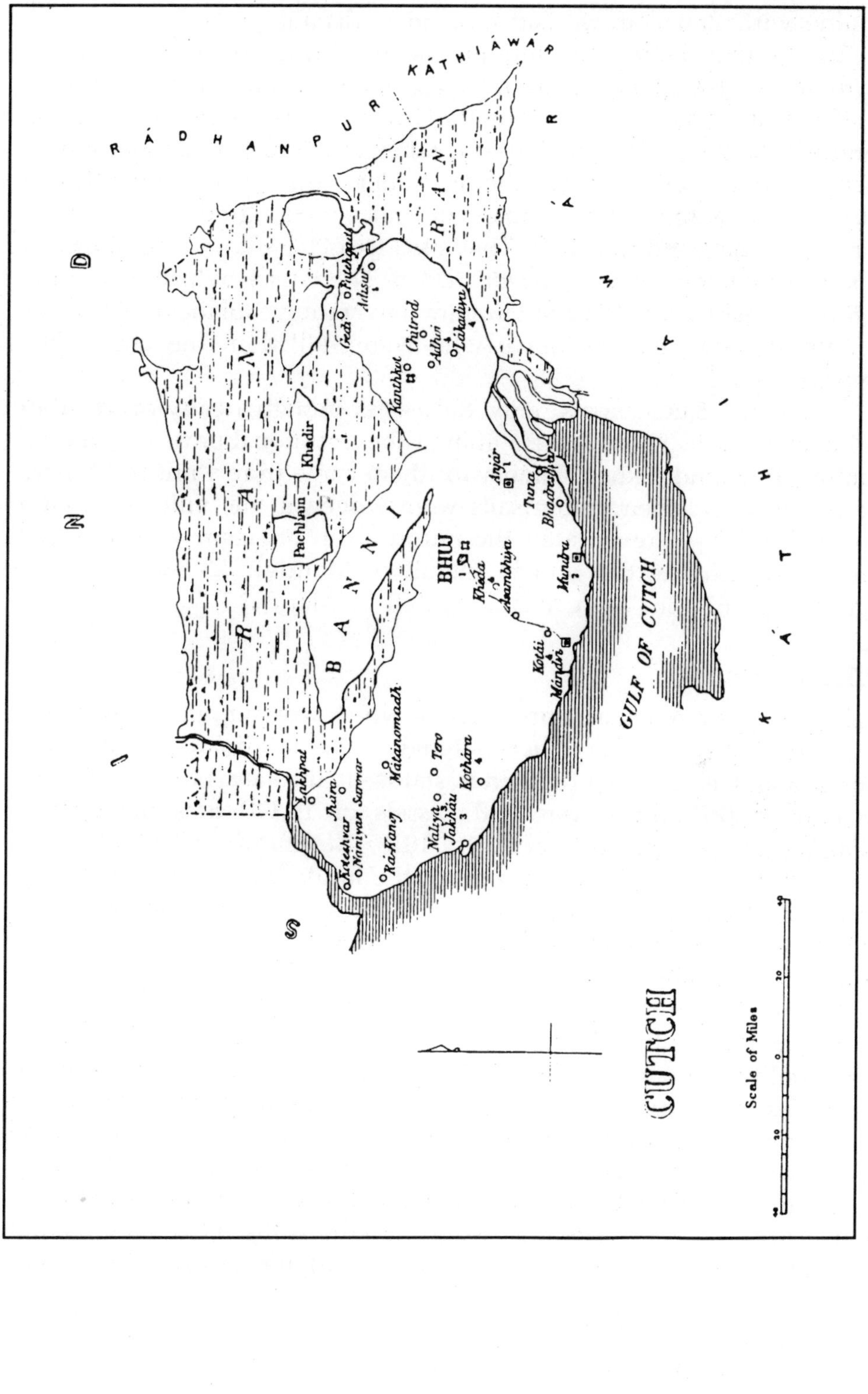

Fig. 1. Kutch (after Campbell 1880)

2 masts, 3 sails, 90 to 285 tons and a crew of 10 to 24 men. It was engaged in trade with Zanzibar, Maskat and other distant ports.

In addition, there were dug-out canoes (*Hodi*), rowed by paddles and used for fishing and carrying passengers to and from boats.

There are also references to the Kutch boats sailing to Calcutta (Campbell 1880: 116). The small boats belonged to the sailors themselves, whereas the large ones belonged to the traders. The captains of the Kutch boats knew how to use the compass and calculate longitude and latitude from a quadrant and pikestaff. They also had charts and a pre-modern book on navigation, called *Captain's Tables*. The vessels which went only up to the Malabar coast did not employ navigating captains or *Muallims* but only commanders or *Nakvo* who were skilled in the use of the compass.

Of all the Kutch boats, only *Kotia* was brought ready-made from the Malabar coast. The rest were built at the traditional ports of Mandvi, Mundra, Tuna and Jakhau. Timber for them came from Konkan, Kanara and Malabar and their cotton sails were woven in the villages around Mandvi. In 1878-79, even after the introduction of steam vessels in the Bombay-Karachi sector which included Mandvi, 23 new vessels aggregating 761 tons were manufactured at Mandvi.

I.2.1.2 Harbours

In all, there were nine harbours, three of which were important: Mandvi, Tuna and Mundra. The others—Rohar, Vavania, Jinjuda, Koteshvar, Jakhau and Lakhpat—had a minor status in the late 19th century. At the end of 1877 there were 260 vessels of 15,140 tons (aggregate), belonging to the Mandvi port. In 1818, Macmurdo (1820: 217-218) reported that more than 800 vessels of the individual 'candies' tonnage (local weightage, 1 modern nautical 'ton' being about 2.8 'candies' ton) from 40 to 500 used to operate out of Mandvi, carrying on a brisk trade with Arabia, Bombay and the Malabar coast. It lay at the mouth of a small river, and although the small boats, even when loaded, could cross the bar at its mouth at high tides, boats with tonnage of about 36 or more could not do so and were unloaded in the roadstead. Of Mundra which lies to the east of Mandvi on the Gulf of Kutch, it has been said that it offers 'safe and sheltered harbour' during the stormy season (June to October). Of the rest, Lakhpat is interesting because of its location at the northwestern extremity of the peninsula at the mouth of the Kori creek. This creek represents the eastern mouth of the Indus. Until about AD 1000 this was, in fact, the chief mouth of the Indus. After about

AD 1,000 the main Indus stream turned towards the west. "Still, as late as the middle of the 18th century, the eastern or Kori branch continued to bring water enough to irrigate a large area of rice-land to the north of Lakhpat" (Campbell 1880: 10). Kutch and Sind fought over the Kori water and in 1764 Kutch lost this battle. Since then Lakhpat declined, but even at the dawn of the 19th century it was 'a great seat of commerce' which fast lost its importance because of the development of Karachi port and shoaling at the mouth of the Kori creek.

In June-July there was no traffic; things stood at standstill. During the rest of the year there was a steady schedule. Boats bound for Sind, Kathiawar and Konkan, i.e. places within easy distance, sailed in August. Boats leaving for areas further south, such as Bombay and Malabar, sailed in September. The boats bound for the Arab ports and Zanzibar sailed in November.

I.2.1.3 Trade Items

On a general level the exports from Kutch were cotton, silk product, cotton thread, piece-goods of coarse varieties, alum and clarified butter or *ghee*. The imports were bullion from Mocha (a little north of Aden in Yemen), ivory, rhinoceros horn and hide from east Africa, date, coconuts, grains of all kind and timber from the Malabar and Konkan coasts including Daman. In the context of 1835, the following was written about Mandvi which in that year had about 250 vessels (25 to 200 tons each) carrying a large lateen sail with two masts.

> A maritime communication was kept up with Zanzibar and the whole coast of Africa, with the Red Sea and Arabia, with the Persian Gulf, Makran, Sind and with India as far as Ceylon. The most valuable branch of traffic was with the eastern coast of Africa or 'Swally' as it was called in Cutch, the chief exports being cotton cloth, and the imports ivory, rhinoceros hides, and dollars (Campbell 1880: 117).

From Daman came timber, teak, *Acacia catechu* (*Khair*) and a fine cloth called *Basti*. Timber was the chief article of trade, and every year 50-60 vessels came from Daman to Mandvi. From Cochin or north Malabar came mostly timber—teak, blackwood *Sisam*, *Punai* and *Dhupla* (masts and yards of boats). Kutch exported to Sind iron, steel, lead, tin, Malabar spices and rice. About 40-50 boats were engaged in trade with the Makran coast every year. The Kutch exports to Makran comprised teak, blackwood, jackwood, boxes with locks, shields made of rhinoceros and elephant hides from Zanzibar, etc. The Makran imports to Kutch were clarified butter, rapeseed, wheat and pulse.

Only 4-5 boats were employed annually in the African coast trade. The major export was about 500 bales of cloth of different kinds. The imports included *Babul* (*Mimosa arabica*), gum (*Kher*) and aloes (*Eriya*), used to adulterate opium and as a dye. From Mocha came raisins, coffee, etc. and the exports to Mocha every year included about 10,000 bales of cotton and cloth, 400 bales of thread, 200 boxes of snuff, 200 bales of sal ammoniac, 200 *Maunds* (1 *Maund* being less than 20 kg) of borax, 250 *Maunds* of shellac, lotus seeds, dried rice cakes, and about 10,000 wooden or ivory combs. Hemp or *Ganja* (nearly 300 *Maunds* every year) and toddy (local Kutch and Malabar varieties; 150 casks, each cask containing from 500 to 1,000 bottles), sesamum and grain were also exported to Mocha.

Zanzibar supplied Cutch with ivory, rhinoceros skins, coconuts, Indian millet, sometimes a rice called *sohili*, cakes of wax, sesamum oil, lemon pickle, cloves, mats *Chandroz* raisin from the *Pinus sylvestris*, and ox hides. There were about six vessels employed in this trade. They made one trip a year, starting in November-December, *Pos*, and coming back in April-May, *Vaisakh*. They took from Cutch, cloth, iron nails, anchors, cumin seed, and boxes with locks, twine for sewing sails, brass wire and brass bars for amulets and anklets, opium, shoes and leather buckets. (Campbell 1880: 119).

There was also considerable internal trade in Kutch, by means of carriers, with Marwar and Malwa (Macmurdo 1820: 118).

I.2.2 Kathiawar

For Kathiawar our main source is J.W. Watson's *Gazetteer of the Bombay Presidency, Vol. VIII, Kathiawar* (Watson 1884).

I.2.2.1 Boats

The vessels were not given their Indian names but simply classified into large, medium and small categories with their tonnage given in modern terms. The large vessels were about 11m to 14.63m long and had 2 masts and 2 sails, and 148 tons. They used to run to Bombay, Karachi, Calcutta, Basrah, Aden and Zanzibar. It took them 1.5 months to complete their return journey to and from Bombay. It took them 1 month to do the same for Karachi, 4 months for Calcutta, 3.5 months for Basrah, 4.5 months for Aden and 6 months for Zanzibar. The trips to Bombay and Karachi were taken between September and June, to Basrah between September and December, to Calcutta in September-October and to the Malabar coast between September and March.

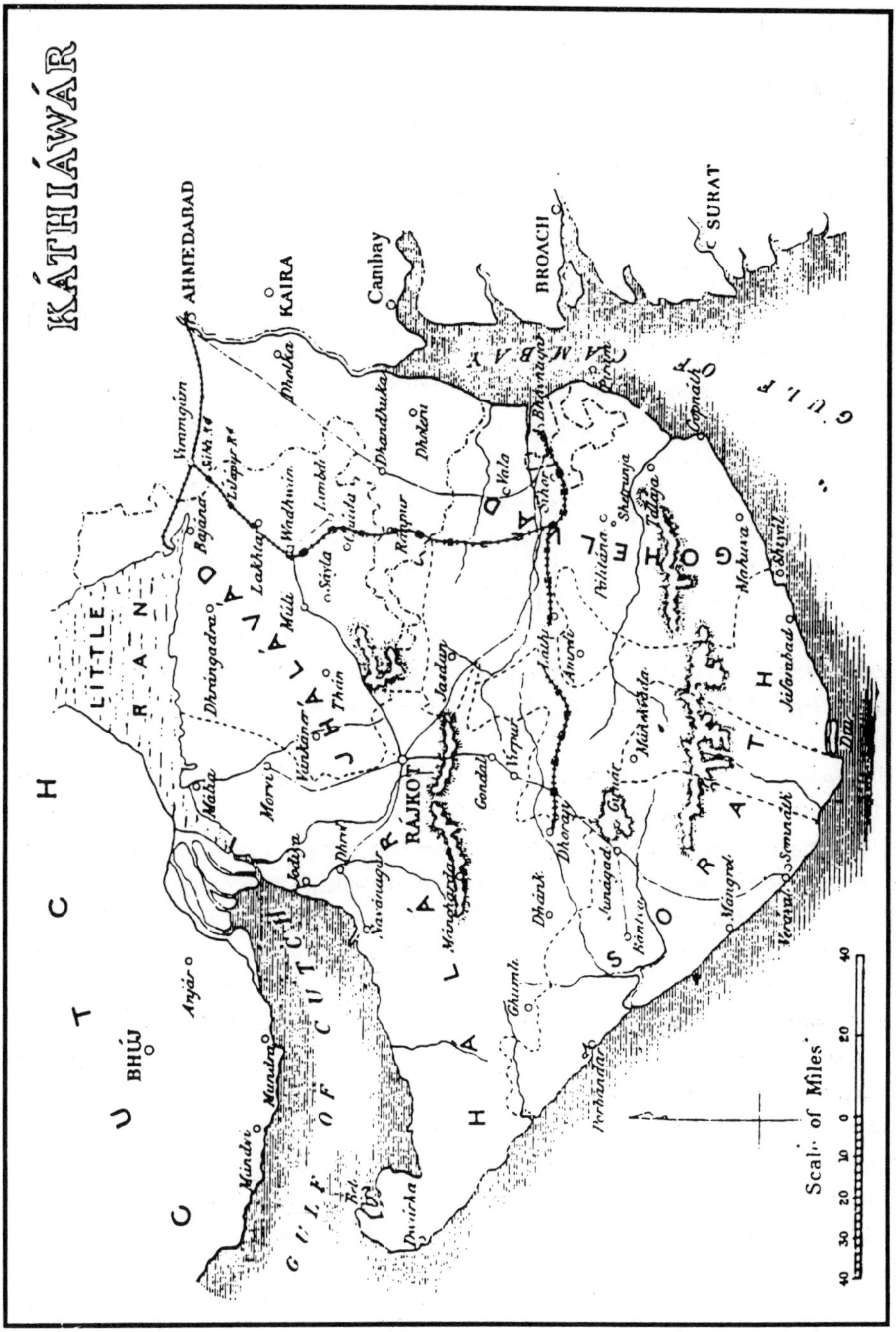

Fig. 2. Kathiawar (after Watson 1884)

The medium-sized vessels were 5.48 m to 6.7 m long and had 37 tons. They could be used for trade with Karachi, Bombay and the Malabar coast. The small vessels were from 2.74 m to 3.96 m long and had 11 tons. They were used only in the Gulf of Kutch.

In 1882, there were 45 vessels of all categories at Jodia, 50 at Bedi and 55 at Salaya, all in the area of the Gulf of Kutch.

I.2.2.2 Harbours

In 1842 the number of traditional ports mentioned in the context of Kathiawar was 62: (1) Vavania, (2) Jodia, (3) Hadiana, (4) Balachadi, (5) Khiri, (6) Navabandar, (7) Nagna, (8) Rojhibara, (9) Bedi, (10) Sarmat, (11) Salaya, (12) Pindara, (13) Rajpara, (14) Poshitra, (15) Arambhda, (16) Bet, (17) Kachhigad, (18) Rupan, (19) Madhi, (20) Bhogat, (21) Miani, (22) Porbandar, (23) Navi, (24) Madhavpur, (25) Sil, (26) Mangrol, (27) Chorvad, (28) Veraval, (29) Hirakot, (30) Sutrapada, (31) Dhamlej, (32) Kodinar, (33) Velan, (34) Vanagburu, (35) Ghogla, (36) Diu, (37) Navabandar, (38) Jafarabad, (39) Bherari, (40) Rampara, (41) Kathivadar, (42) Shial Bet, (43) Chanch, (44) Devalia, (45) Mahuva, (46) Katpur, (47) Kalsar, (48) Kotda, (49) Gadhula, (50) Sultanpur, (51) Nahana Gopnath, (52) Mithivirdi, (53) Kuda, (54) Gogha, (55) Evania, (56) Akvada, (57) Bhavnagar, (58) Adheli, (59) Gundalu, (60) Kala Talav, (61) Bavaliali, and (62) Dholera.

Of these 62 centres strewn along the entire Kathiawar coastline where "every little creek provides a means of access and has its trade centre" (Watson 1884: 236), 12 were closed in 1842, some owing to the silting of channels and others to their unfitness for modern trade. Of the fifty remaining centres, only 12—Jodia, Bedi, Salaya, Porbandar, Navabandar, Mangrol, Veraval, Jafarabad, Mahuva, Gogha, Bhavnagar and Dholera—had an extensive trade. The chief historic ports of Kathiawar have been said (Watson 1884: 237) to be Gogha, Diu, Somnath-Patan, Mongrel and Porbandar. Mangrol was reputedly Ptolemy's (mid-2nd century AD) *Monoglossum Emporium* and that is where ships came from Malabar for horses. Somnath-Patan was the embarking port for Persia and Mecca. Diu in the 16th century was the port of call of all ships bound to and from Gujarat, the Red Sea and the Gulf. Gogha, Patan, Mangrol and Porbandar were flourishing ports up to the end of Aurangzeb's reign in 1707.

Further comments have been made on some of these ports. Bhavnagar lay on the Bhavnagar creek, 9.65 km from its mouth and 12.06 km above Gogha. The landing place was at the mouth of the creek.

Mahuva was on the bank of the Malan river and the boats of 110 tons could enter the creek at high tide. Veraval had considerable trade with Maskat, Karachi, Bombay and nearer ports. At Bedi vessels could come up the creek. At Jodia there was some silting and at Porbandar the coasting craft could anchor near the town where they were sheltered from the northwesterly storms by a rocky spit. There was very scant anchorage at Mangrol but Salaya was a valuable natural harbour. Jafarabad was convenient for the coasting craft. Vavania, a small port on the Little Rann, was once a port for large vessels. Navabandar lay at the mouth of the Bhadar and for Bherai and Kathivadar there was a common entrance by the Mota Pat creek. Talaiya/Sultanpur lay at the mouth of the Shetrunji and Sundrai was an insignificant port for grains of the Bhal area.

I.2.2.3 Trade Items

For Bombay the vessels took cotton, grain, wool and sesamum, bringing back groceries, cloth, chinaware, metals and drugs. For Karachi they took clarified butter and sesamum, to bring back rice and dates. For Zanzibar they took earthen pots, silk and shoes and brought back timber, coconut, wax, ivory and grain. The vessels generally went empty to Calcutta, Basrah and Malabar and brought rice from Calcutta, dates from Basrah and timber, coconut, ginger, tamarind and pepper from Malabar. There was a form of indigenous marine insurance, called *Keel* or *Pathan* insurance. All deep-sea vessels had a compass and in some cases, even charts.

I.3 Observations on the 19th-Century Evidence

It is apparent that the gazetteers of Kutch and Kathiawar, on the basis of which the summaries of the preceding sections have been made, deal with the evidence only in its barest outline. There must still be scope to work out the details on the basis of local fieldwork and investigation of the oral traditions. The fieldwork may be focussed on the boat-building tradition, the continuity—if any—of the traditional trade practices, and the location of archaeological sites in relation to the traditional ports mentioned in the gazetteers. It is learnt (Shahani 1997) that this trade still continues, although in boats which are fitted with modern engines to supplement the sails.

Secondly, whatever data the gazetteers offer on trade items should convince anybody that they were in no case limited only to the luxury goods. In fact, apart from the import of gold from Mocha on the Arabian side of the Red Sea and unspecified but presumably United States dollars (as bullion) from Zanzibar, there is hardly any luxury item mentioned in the long lists of Kutch and Kathiawar's trade goods. Even with the far-off places like Zanzibar, the emphasiz is on the procurement of what was easily available and what could be sold profitably in their trade network. The mention of such items as lime–pickle and rice as imports from Zanzibar to Kutch is revealing in this connection. We also find it interesting that 10,000 wooden and ivory combs and many bottles of toddy went annually from Kutch to Mocha. By the end of the 19th century, the importance of cotton and cloth as traditional exports of Gujarat was not as important as before, but still, they occur as export items again and again in the gazetteer lists. Teak and other varieties of wood were staple imports from the Konkan coast beginning with Daman and from Malabar down south. On the whole, there is a strong degree of eclecticism regarding the traded goods, the main emphasiz being on the commodities which would sell easily in the network.

Thirdly, the trade items also make clear the fact that none of these traded items, especially those which were imported to Gujarat, were likely to have left behind imprints in the archaeological record. The Gujarati exports too, except in rare cases (cf. ivory combs), would not leave behind a direct archaeological trace. This is an important point to consider when we try to assess the relevant archaeological evidence.

Fourthly, the relative significance of Gujarat and Sind in the trading network of the northern part of India's west coast needs some assessment in the present context. The position of Lakhpat at the mouth of the Kori creek which represents the old eastern mouth of the Indus and its reputation as an old centre of commerce imply that this was one of the major places through which the Indus delta could be accessed from the point of view of maritime trade. Considering that there is only one major reported early historic site of the pre-Christian era from the Indus delta in Sind (i.e. Brahminabad), and considering that the development of Karachi as a major harbour is only a recent development, we suspect that from the point of view of India's ancient maritime trade, Gujarat was more important than Sind.

Fourthly, it is important to note that the gazetteer data pinpoint Gujarat as a component of a vast trade network extending to Calcutta/ the Bengal delta on the east, Malabar on the south, the entire Canara, Konkan and Makran coastline, the Indus delta and the Makran coast, the Gulf, the mouth of the Red Sea and the east African coast as far south as Zanzibar. There is no scope to doubt, even in the context of the 19th century, the familiarity of the traditional sailors of Gujarat with the entire Indian coastline between Makran and Calcutta, the entire Gulf region and the Arabian coast and east Africa from Zanzibar northwards. The fact that this pattern continued till the end of the 19th century is an incontrovertible argument in favour of the premise that the northern end of the Indian Ocean was a single economic interaction zone. The sequence of archaeological and historical evidence of this interaction will bear us out.

II. THE SEQUENCE OF ARCHAEOLOGICAL AND HISTORICAL EVIDENCE

II.1 The Indus Civilization

There is only a single piece of positive evidence in Gujarat as proof of its contact with the Gulf region during the period of the Indus civilization. However, there are two other finds which may be interpreted to suggest such a contact. In the Gulf region itself, and in the general area between Mesoptamia and Afghanistan, there are 'Indus' finds but none, except perhaps one, relates specifically to Gujarat.

A round 'Persian Gulf seal'—4.82 cm in diameter and made of steatite, showing a two-headed reptile or dragon flanked by two jumping goats or gazelle-like animals—was reported from the surface of the 'Indus' site of Lothal (Rao 1963). This was a direct import from the Gulf area. Among the two suggestive pieces of evidence is a rectangular (20 mm by 18 mm) seal of conchshell, showing a design where the necks of a short-horned bull, a unicorn and a goat are joined together in a wheel-like design. The rectangular seal as a type is 'Indus' but the whorl-motif occurs in Mesoptamia, the Gulf and Central Asia. In this case, the exaggerated eyes and the outlines of the animal bodies suggest the manufacturing tradition of the Gulf. This piece comes from a context of the Late Harappan submerged structures at Bet Dwarka (Rao 1987) and has been dated 1570 BC (TL). The second indirect piece is a fragment of a chlorite vessel with mat design found in the 'Indus' context of Dholavira (personal information from R.S. Bisht). It is difficult to be more detailed about this unpublished find.

Although it has been claimed that the Harappan coastal sites of Nageshwar and Bagasra were seaports (Shahani 1997), the exercise of some caution is necessary in these cases. Nageshwar (17 km northeast of Dwarka) is located at the edge of a perennial sweet-water lake, from where access could be had to the shell resources of the Gulf of Kutch. This was certainly a manufacturing centre of objects made of *Turbinella pyrum*, but this does not necessarily mean that Nageshwar was a seaport. The claim of Bagasra, which is located about 1 km away from the southeastern shores of the Gulf of Kutch in the Rajkot district and like Nageshwar a manufacturing centre of *Turbinella pyrum* objects, is perhaps stronger, mainly because the Indus civilization centre here is a fortified one. Some traditional ports on the Gulf of Kutch (cf. Jodia and Navnagar) had fortifications near them. However, the fact that black-slipped Harappan jars have been found both at Bagasra and in Oman (Sonawane, in press) does not specifically make Bagasra a port. It was once inferred that a particular type of 'Indus'-level pottery which is common in Gujarat, i.e. 'Reserved Slip Ware' was an import from Mesoptamia, but a detailed study of its distribution and the contexts of that distribution has shown the premise to be wrong (Chakrabarti 1990: 53-61).

If one thinks of the locations of Bet Dwarka (the northwestern tip of the Kathiawar peninsula), Dholavira (the island of Khadir in the Great Rann) and Lothal (Dholka area of the mainland Gujarat; in the Bhal region between the Bhogavo and Sabarmati rivers), one gets an interesting pattern. First, Bet Dwarka is the site of a traditional port on the southern shore of the Gulf of Kutch, and the fact that it was located there, suggests that the Harappans were familiar with some of the traditional harbours of the Gulf of Kutch. The interpretation of Kuntasi at the eastern end of this gulf as a Harappan port has much to recommend it. Secondly, Dholavira seems to lie on a straight route across the Great Rann to Sind. The argument was put forward by J.P. Joshi (1990: 410), and in view of the orientation of routes to Sind across the Rann, as described in the Kutch gazetteer, we accept this hypothesis. Incidentally, the chlorite vessel fragment with mat design, which has been found at Dholavira, had a parallel find at Mohenjodaro. A close link between Dholavira and Sind is probable, and Dholavira need not be interpreted as a maritime port. Thirdly, the location of Lothal in the Bhal area shows that the Gulf of Cambay was well used in the maritime traffic of the Indus civilization. The fact that the Gulf of Kutch and Cambay were both used for trade with the Gulf during the Indus civilization period of Gujarat, shows how deeply rooted is the tradition of Kutch-Kathiawar contact with the world of the Gulf.

None of the Indus material found in the Gulf can be specifically tied to Gujarat. At Ras al-Junayz in the Ras al-Hadd area of the Oman peninsula at the mouth of the Gulf, an 'Indus' ivory comb was found in association with an Indus copper seal and painted pottery. The excavations here also yielded many lumps of bitumen which were possibly stripped from a boat (Cleuziou and Tosi 1994). The point is the ivory comb. In the light of the 19th-century evidence that 10,000 wooden and ivory combs used to be annually exported to the Red Sea area from Kutch, the Indus ivory comb from Ras al-Junayz may be interpreted as a Gujarati export. Further, the Ras al-Hadd area was "the natural landfall" of ships coming from India (Chaudhuri 1985: 129) especially from Gujarat. This lends an extra support to the view that the Ras al-Junayz Indus finds went from Gujarat. It has also been pointed out (Chaudhuri 1985: 129) that Ras al-Hadd lay at the junction of two sea-routes coming out of the Gulf: one aligned towards India and the other aligned towards the Red Sea. The fact that there is evidence of Harappan trade in this area suggests that the Harappans were probably familiar with the southern coast of Arabia and the Red Sea (Chakrabarti 1998). No positive evidence is forthcoming in this area, but in view of the perishability of the traditional trade items we cited before, it is not illogical to infer that there was indeed contact between the Indus civilization and the Red Sea region including the southern Arabian coast. On a different point, however, one can be reasonably certain. The Ras al-Hadd Harappan material proves that the Harappans were familiar with the wind system that took them to the Gulf from Gujarat—"The understanding of the winds associated with the monsoon-cycle over the Indian Ocean goes back at least to the closing centuries of the 3rd millennium BC" (Chakrabarti 1998).

II.2 Early Historic Period: The Evidence of the Periplus

In Gujarat's maritime history there is a major gap till the mid-1st century AD when in the text called *The Periplus Maris Erythraei* and written by an Egyptian Greek in the mid-1st century AD (Casson 1989; for a more recent discussion on date and other implications for Indian history, Robin 1997, Fussman 1997) a number of Gujarat ports have been mentioned with some details about the navigability of their harbours and imports and exports. In a rich and vibrant article by J. Kennedy (original 1898, reprinted in Allchin and Chakrabarti 1997) on 'the early commerce of Babylon with India, 700-300 BC' there are references to the finds of Indian cedar and teak in the Assyrian Babylonia, dating from the times of Nebuchadnezzar (604-562 BC) and Nabonidus (555-538 BC). A beam of Indian cedar was found at Birs Nimrud in the palace of Nebuchadnezzar and two rough logs of Indian teak were found embedded in the masonry of the period of Nebuchadnezzar and Nabonidus in the temple of the moon-god at Ur. Considering the fact that Kutch played a role in the trade of teak and other timbers as late as the 19th century it is possible that the teak in Assyrian Babylonia was traded from Gujarat. Although no direct archaeological evidence is forthcoming, one may assume that in the Mauryan period Gujarat was an integral part of the network which extended from the Mauryan empire in India to north Africa and the Mediterranean. The Asokan inscriptions which contain direct references to the kingdoms of this region are its most direct testimony. A mid-second-century AD inscription from the Girnar hill of Kathiawar specifies that the governor of Gujarat under Asoka was a 'Yavana king' called Tusaspha—a distinctly Iranian-sounding name.

Perhaps no discussion on early Indian trade can be complete without a reference to the biblical Ophir from where the Phoenicians brought 420 talents of gold for the king Solomon. According to G.F. Hourani (1995: 9) the list of merchandise from Ophir—gold, silver, jewels, *almug* wood, ivory, apes and peacock—"smacks of India, etymologically and economically". However, J. Carswell in his editorial notes (Hourani 1995: 130) argues that Ophir was probably not India but southern Arabia.

Of all the classical sources it is the nautical almanack of the Periplus which is most important from our point of view. In the 2nd century AD. Ptolemy was no doubt familiar with Gujarat, and he certainly mentions the Junagarh belt and its coastline (*Syrestrine*) and Barygaza at the Narmada mouth, including a small harbour called Ammoni (Sastri 1927), but very little else. On the other hand, the Periplus in the 1st century AD confronts us with an Indian Ocean trading world which was already fully developed from the Red Sea to Southeast Asia. This world lay oriented along a few lines. The first line extended from the mouth of the Nile to the ports on the Red Sea, Berenike (modern Ras Banas) and Myos Hormos (modern Abu Sha'r) being the two most famous of them. The second line extended to the Horn of Africa down to Aksum in Ethiopia, and Rhapta in the vicinity of Dar-es-Salaam in Tanzania (Rhapta located in Zanzibar as well, according to some scholars, cf. Casson 1989: 141). Zanzibar was on the way, its location being a little north of Dar-es-Salaam. A major port in this sector was Adulis (Massawa or Annesley Bay, cf. Casson 1989: 102-106) on the Ethiopian shore of the Red Sea. Avalites was the Ethiopian port on the shores of the Bab-el-Mandeb. The third line extended along the Arabian coast to the Gulf, roughly between Aden and Ras al-Hadd. The major ports here were Muza (Mocha or al-Mukha) on the Bab-el-Mandeb, the strait between the Gulf of Aden and the Red Sea, Okelis (the lagoon of Shaykh Sai'd to the west of Aden, where the southern Arabian coast turns north, cf. Casson 1989: 157-158) and Kane, east of Aden and on the south coast of Arabia (cape of Husn al Ghurab., some 205 nautical miles east from Aden). There were also ports on the shores of the Gulf (cf. Omana, the identification of which is uncertain–Casson 1989: 180). The fourth line was that of the entire Indian coast beginning with the mouth of the Indus and continuing up to the mouth of the Ganga. The fourth line extended up to Southeast Asia and included, possibly somewhat later, China. The interconnection of these lines in various ways led to an intricate maritime world when the ships sailed straight to the Malabar coast from Africa or hugged the coast all along the way to Gujarat and the areas further south. Was the establishment of this maritime world only due to the discovery of the monsoon winds by Hippalos a little earlier? We have previously pointed out that the Indus civilization trade with the Gulf from Gujarat depended on a knowledge of the monsoon winds. It has further been noticed that trade with the Mediterranean basin was at its height at Arikamedu on the eastern seaboard of south India by 50 BC (Begley *et al.* 1996: 39), at least a hundred years before the Periplus. On the whole, our assumption is that by the 3rd century BC, i.e. the heyday of the Mauryan empire, the maritime world of the Indian Ocean, to which we are introduced by the Periplus, was in place.

The testimony of the Periplus on the Gujarat coast is fairly accurate. He mentions a port called Barabarikon in the Indus delta, linked to the capital of the region called Minnagara. Immediately to the south of the Indus mouth he mentions "Eirinon, with the additional names Little and Big". The identification with the two Ranns of Kutch is beyond doubt, and the same may be said about the identification of 'the gulf called Barake' with the Gulf of Kutch. "Immediately after the gulf of Barake is the gulf of Barygaza": the latter has to be identified as the Gulf of Cambay and Barygaza as modern Broach or ancient *Bhrigukachchha*. His 'Syrastrene' coast is the coast of Saurashtra. The port of Barygaza was not easy of access and :

> For this reason local fishermen in the king's service come out with crews (sc. of rowers) and long ships, the kind called *trappaga* and *kotymba*, to the entrance as far as Syrastrene to meet vessels and guide them up to Barygaza. Through the crew's efforts, they manoeuver them right from the mouth of the gulf through the shoals and tow them to predetermined stopping places; they get them under way when the tide comes in and, when it goes out, bring them to anchor in certain harbours and basins. The basins are rather deep spots along the river up to Barygaza (Casson 1989: 79).

Goods came to Barygaza from the inland marts of Ujjayini or Ozene, Paithana and Tagara, the last two being in the Deccan or 'Dachinabades' or *Dakshinapatha*. Regarding Barygaza itself the following merchandise is mentioned:

> In this port of trade there is a market for: wine, principally Italian but also Laodicean and Arabian; copper, tin, and lead; coral and peridot (?); all kinds of clothing with no adornment or of printed fabric; multi-coloured girdles, eighteen inches wide; storax; yellow sweet clover (?); raw glass; realgar; sulphide of antimony; Roman money, gold and silver, which commands an exchange at some profit against the local currency; unguent, inexpensive and in limited quantity. For the king there was imported in those times precious silverware, slave musicians, beautiful girls for concubinage, fine wine, expensive clothing with no adornment, and choice unguent. The area exports: nard; costus; bdellium; ivory; onyx; agate (?); *lykion*; cotton cloth of all kinds; Chinese (sc. Silk) cloth; *molochinnon* cloth; (sc. Silk) yarn; long pepper; and items brought here from the (sc. Nearby) ports of trade (Casson 1989: 81).

From our present perspective we note three points about the character of trade at Barygaza: first, it is closely related to the inland marts of central India and the Deccan, receiving goods like nard even from the northwest; secondly, the boat-types *trappaga* and *kotymba* are mentioned in identical terms in later Indian texts (Casson 1989: 203), suggesting a continuity in the types of boats of the area; and thirdly, the Barygaza port lay away from the Narmada river mouth, just as Surat in later days lay away from the Tapti mouth.

The Periplus adds that for those who sailed to Barygaza from Egypt, the right time to set out was around the month of July. Casson (1989: 289-290) adds that they left around July "to take advantage of the summer northerlies in the Red Sea in order to get down to its exit at Bab-el-Mandeb and of the southwest monsoon in order to get out of the Gulf of Aden". To get down to the west coast of south India, they took about 20 days. The return was in December-January, taking advantage of the benign period of the northeast monsoon. In any case, the ships sailed from Egypt in July because they wanted to reach the Indian coast not before September when the southeast monsoon would begin to quiet down. An arrival in October would expose them to the contrary winds of the northeast monsoon. Casson (1989: 290) points out that the Arab sailors of the late 15th and early 16th centuries preferred to sail towards the end of August and the beginning of September when the southeast monsoon had begun to slacken, because by then the boats were technically improved to reach the Indian coast in a shorter time.

The attribution of the discovery of monsoon to Hipalus/Hippalus has been discussed recently by Mazzarino (1997) and Tchernia (1997), and the general current opinion is to associate this 'discovery' with Eudoxus of Cyzicus towards the end of the 2nd century BC (cf. Karttunen 1997: 329-330). In any case, the 'discovery' means no more than acquiring the ability to sail straight from the Red Sea to the ports on the western coast of south India. As we have argued before, the advantage of the monsoon winds must have been known to the sailors of the Indus civilization.

The dependability of the *Periplus* as a text has gained seriously from the recent excavations at Berenike. The site was abandoned in the 6th century AD but before that there were two major phases of trade at the site, one at the beginning of the 2nd century AD and the other in the mid-late 4th century AD. There is some evidence of Indian contact with Berenike in the 2nd century AD (cf. Salomon 1991) but trade between Berenike and India is said to have increased dramatically during the second term. The Indian goods include abundant teakwood and black pepper, and in lesser quantities, stone beads, textiles, coconuts, rice, *Amalaka/Amalaki*, bamboo and Job's Tear (Sidebotham and Wendrich 1998). According to a summary provided by F.C. Wild and J.P. Wild,

> Evidence for trade with India and, indeed, for the presence of Indians on the site, has come in the form of of: a graffito on a 1st century AD amphora in Tamil-Brahmi; Indian and Sri Lankan beads; pottery of South Indian origin; and botanical remains such as coconut and, in particular, large quantities of black peppercorns. A high proportion of the wood remains from the site was of teak, including reused planks, possibly from dismantled ships (Wild and Wild 2001: 212).

The find of what is called Z-spun cotton and which is considered an import from India forms the subject of a special study by Wild and Wild (2001). Such cotton pieces have been interpreted as parts of sailcloth.

> The sailcloth, the webbing, the rope and sewing thread, even the patching materials, are uniformly Z-spun, indicating manufacture in India and/or the use of Indian materials for running repairs during the voyage (Wild and Wild 2001: 217).

It is interesting that the ships which used these sails manufactured of Indian cloth were Mediterranean ships with a single main mast and large, square, reinforced (by adding strips of cloth) sail, unlike the ships represented in Indian art with two or three main masts and apparently unreinforced sails. Whether the teakwood found as fragments of ship's body means that some of these ships were built in India is an issue which cannot be answered at present. One also cannot be sure if the teak went straight from south Indian ports or went via Gujarat. There is no reason why Barygaza could not play a role in trade with Berenike.

Miscellaneous Rome-inspired objects have been found in various places in Gujarat. First, Pratipal Bhatia (1997) underscores the presence of six Roman coin hoards from Gujarat: Junagarh (2 hoards), Mehsana (1 hoard), Palanpur (1 hoard), Surat (1 hoard) and Nagdhara (near Surat, 1 hoard). Secondly, there are a few pieces of cameos and bronze: cameos with female figure from Karvan, handle of a jug in bronze with the figure of a cupid from Akota (modern Baroda) and a figure of an Atlantis in bronze from Devnimori. According to Cimino (1994), a capital with a decoration of acanthus leaves at its base from Uparkot in Junagarh also suggests Roman influence. Thirdly, there are a few amphora fragments (cf. Raschke 1978: 1026-1027). There was a time when the 'red-polished ware' of the early centuries AD in Gujarat were taken to be imitations of the Samian ware of Rome (cf. Subbarao 1953: 56-64), but these days this pottery is taken to be purely Indian and its presence in the Gulf area has been taken as Indian imports (cf. Whitehouse and Williamson 1973; Kervran 1994: 37-58; Ray 1995: 104 for a distribution map of the red polished ware).

II.3 The Post-Periplus Phase Till c. AD 1300

The sources dealing with the maritime trade of India's west coast during this period are not always limited to Gujarat. They seem to focus more on the Konkan coast of Maharashtra (roughly from Thana downwards) and the coasts of Karnataka and Kerala. V.K. Jain (1990) who has offered a thriving picture of Gujarat's internal trade between *c.* AD 1000 and *c.* 1300 mainly on the basis of epigraphic references, could not back it up by citing many Gujarat-specific sources as far as the foreign trade was concerned. It appears that Gujarat's individual role has become somewhat blurred in the post-Periplus sources in between the significance of the Indus delta in the Sassanian and later contexts on the one hand and the ports of the Konkan coast on the other. This does not mean that Gujarat lost its significance in India's maritime trade during this period. Whatever indirect evidence is available suggests that Gujarat was still an important zone of maritime trade.

Politically the area passed from the control of the Kshatrapa power of western India in the early centuries AD to that of the Guptas of eastern

India in the 4th century. In the post-Gupta period, the king, Harsha (AD 606-646) of northern India was the suzerain, at least for some time. The regional dynasty of Gujarat of this period, beginning perhaps with the late 5th century AD when the Gupta power was weak, was the Maitraka dynasty with its capital at Valabhi near modern Bhavnagar. This dynasty became powerful towards the close of the 6th century AD. The next major focus of Gujarat's political history was provided by the Chalukyas. In the first half of the 10th century AD they were powerful and had their capital at Anhilwadapatan or modern Patan to the north of Ahmedabad. There were other minor dynasties in various pockets but by and large the Maitrakas of Valabhi and the Chalukyas of Anhilwadapatan impart a coherence to the political history of Gujarat till the establishment of the Muslim power. Gujarat was annexed to the Delhi Sultanate in AD 1297. The independent Sultanate of Gujarat was created in the early 15th century. It finally fell to Mughal power in 1572-73.

While picking up the thread of Indian Ocean maritime trade outside the Roman context, one has to remember the surge of the Sassanian power in Iran in the 3rd century AD. It has been claimed that Ardashir I (accession AD 224), the first Sassanian king, "made vigorous efforts to establish control on the Gulf" (Whitehouse and Williamson 1973). An important result of this effort was the establishment of the port of Siraf (near modern Bushair). The Sassanian Siraf measures more than a kilometre across and possesses a fort built perhaps by Shahpur II (310-379). The site was both a port and a naval base. Red polished ware of Gujarat has been found on the Iranian shore of the Gulf. By *c.* 800 Siraf was a wealthy international port.

> By the early 5th century, when Bahram V acquired Daibul, the Sassanians controlled the coast from the Persian Gulf to the Indus. In the 6th century, Iranian merchants dominated Indian and Sinhalese entrepots and the Sassanian government defended their activities as far afield as Aden and Ceylon (Whitehouse and Williamson 1973: 45).

It is unlikely to be a situation of 'domination' but their occupation of Debal in the Indus delta must have made the Sassanians an important partner in the coastal and oceanic trade of the Indian west coast, down the line from the Indus mouth to Malabar.

The end of the 8th century saw the inception of regular trade between the Gulf and China (Whitehouse and Williamson 1973: 49; Rougeulle 1996). The Chinese links of the Indian coast have not been worked out in detail, but the Chinese ceramics of the 13th-14th centuries in the Tamilnadu and Kerala coasts have been studied by Y. Subbarayalu (1996) who considers that "the ceramics form quite an impressive evidence" of the Chinese trade of the 13th and 14th centuries under the Southern Song and Yuan dynasties of China. The Ming emperors imposed an embargo on trade and the Chinese trade could revive only in the later part of the 16th century. It is inconceivable that, with the Chinese trade of the Gulf being fully operational from the 8th century onwards, the Indian coast did not develop Chinese links in about that period, although the sources seem to be silent on this point. On the Chinese side there is some interesting archaeological evidence of Chinese contact with Tamilnadu in the 13th century in the form of the ruins of a Hindu temple and a Tamil-Chinese inscription recording the installation of a Siva image in AD 1281 in the southeastern part of the city of Quanzhou at the mouth of the Jinjiang river in southern China (Pearson, Min and Guo 2002).

At this point it may be worthwhile to refer to Hourani's opinion on the possibility of direct sailing between the Persian Gulf and China in pre-Islamic times (Hourani 1995: 46-50). Although he finds some slight evidence of Persian commercial voyages to China under the Sassanids, there is nothing, according to him, to prove direct Chinese sailings to Mesopotamia before Islam and for many centuries after Islam. He feels that Quilon on the southern India's west coast, which was visited by Chinese junks in the 12th century, "was the furthest point west ever reached by Chinese ships till the Ming dynasty".

What the sources are definite about is the presence of Arab trading settlements in western India. The Arab conquest of Sind in AD 712 was certainly an important factor to reckon with in this connection. From the 9th-10th centuries AD the Indian epigraphic records seem to be copious on this point, along with the Arab records. One, however, is not quite sure if such settlements of non-Indian traders on the Indian west coast began only with the Islamic Arabs or the Arabs were preceded by the Nestorian Christians. Andre Wink (1990: 48) claims that there were Christian colonies by the 5th century AD on the Arabian coast, Indian west coast up to Malabar and to a lesser extent in Sri Lanka and beyond. One does not feel surprised because Cosmas Indicopleustes, the author of a text of the 6th century, puts India within its scope of Christian topography. He also suggests that spices from Southeast Asia used to reach India's west coast ports before being shipped to Iran, Arabia and Africa.

In AD 636 the governor of Bahrain in the Gulf sent attacking missions to Thana and Broach. They were not successful. In one sense this is a positive indication of the fact that Gujarat in general and Broach in particular continued to retain their maritime significance in the post-*Periplus* phase. It appears that the Arabs kept on invading the Gujarat coast, and in the later half of the 8th century they attacked Valabhi, the capital of the Maitrakas (cf. Singh 1990: 73). In the first half of the 7th century the Chinese pilgrim Hsuan Tsang found the Maitraka kingdom prosperous, and regarding southwest Kathiawar, he wrote that because of its position on 'the highway of the sea, all its inhabitants utilized the sea and were traders by profession' (Watters 1905: 248).

In the beginning of the 9th century we have an account of the travels of Soliman of Basrah, who was speaking of the lands and seas to be crossed before one could reach China. According to him Quilon on the Malabar coast was one month's sail from Muscat. He wrote of the Hindu king of Gujarat and added that "the Arabs enjoyed great favour in his dominions" (Major 1857: xxvii).

Under the Silahara dynasty (AD 810-1260) trading on the Konkan coast prospered, with the *Sresthis* or Indian merchants being engaged in coastal trade (Chakravarti 1986). This coastal trade and voyages in Konkan have been further highlighted with the help of the Arab sources (Chakravarti 1998). What is interesting is that Cambay is listed in these sources with three Konkanese ports—Saymur (Chaul), Subara (Sopara) and Thana, all in the Bombay region. Sindan in the Thana area is also mentioned in the same sources as having links with Cambay (Chakravarti 1990) and as being a place from where indigo used to be exported to the West in the 11th century (Chakravarti 1992/1996; for a further discussion on the ship-owning merchants of the Konkan coast, Chakravarti 2000).

The Arab traders were on the west coast on a regular basis from the 9th century AD, and by the 10th century there were many mosques in the land from Cambay to Chaul. A 10th century Arab ship-captain Buzurg bin Shahriyar found a large number of Arab and other Muslim merchants in Gujarat (for the details, Jain 1990: 74-75). A highly significant category of evidence in this regard is provided by some Arabic inscriptions, dated between AD 1218 and 1291 and found not merely in the coastal towns of Cambay and Somnath but also in the inland towns of Junagarh and Anhilwadapatan (for the details, Jain 1990: 74-81). One of these inscriptions found in Cambay refers to a merchant-chief and 'prince of shipmasters'—Haji Ibrahim—who dealt in betel nuts which do not grow in the Cambay area. This implies that this merchant had to import betel nuts from the coastal Konkan or Malabar or from Bengal/Assam. An inscription dated AD 1232 from Anhilwadapatan refers to the death of a merchant from Sharzur in north Iraq. According to an inscription dated 1286-1287 from Junagarh, a mosque was established there by one Abu'l Qasim, an important merchant and shipowner who also arranged for pilgrim visits to Mecca from Gujarat.

In the 11th century Alberuni (Sachau 1910: vol. 2,104) refers to Somnath:

> The reason why in particular Somnath has become so famous is that it was a harbour for seafaring people, and a station for those who went to and fro between Sufala in the country of the Zanj and China.

A stone inscription of AD 1264 from Somnath, which, although written in 'very bad Sanskrit', contains 'numerous Arabic and Persian words', is important regarding the presence of Arab merchants in Gujarat (Hultzsch 1882; Sircar 1961-62). The inscription introduces us to Nuruddin Firoz, a rich Muslim merchant who was originally from Hormuz.

> The purpose of the inscription is to grant the income from a piece of land covered with houses, from an oil mill, and from two shops to a Masjid built by the donor, a Muhammedan shipowner from Hurmuz.... The grant provides also for the expenses of particular religious festivals to be celebrated by the Shiaite sailors of Somnath Pathan. The eventual surplus is to be made over to the holy district of Makka and Madina. The Musalman congregation of Somnath Pathan are appointed trustees (Hultzsch 1882: 242).

The startling fact that there was even a Muslim governor/ruler under a Hindu king in the area of Sinjan in Thana on the Konkan coast is attested by a Sanskrit inscription dated AD 926 (Sircar 1957-1958). This Muslim governor was a *Tajika* (Arab) named *Madhumati* (Sanskritised form of Muhammad) who received the territorial division of *Samyana* (Sinjan) from the Rashtrakuta king Krishnaraja (AD 878-915). The inscription is dated in the reign of Krishna's successor Indra III (AD 915-928). Apparently, Muhammad continued to be a governor even under the successor king. What is interesting is that he is credited with the conquest of 'the chiefs of all the harbours of the neighbourhood'. Further, he is credited with the establishment of free ferries on two local streams and a "feeding house ... where Sali rice, curries and ghee were catered free of cost".

That by the 12th century, the northern half of the Indian Ocean acquired the character of a pond to be crossed and re-crossed at will is clear on the basis of whatever has been published of the documents or letters on the 'India trade' in the Cairo Geniza records. Although there are about 400 such letters in all (Goitien 1980), they are concerned with the southern west coast, especially modern Mangalore. The sender of the two letters analysed by S.D. Goitien in 1980 was Madmun b. Hasan b. Bundar, 'the representative of the merchants and Superintendent of the port of Aden and head of the Jewish communities of Yemen' and also a shipowner and middleman between the Jews of the Mediterranean and those on business in India. The recipient of these two letters was Abraham b. Perahya Ben Yiju, a Tunisian Jew whose mercantile and industrial work in Mangalore can be fixed between 1132 and 1149 but who possibly visited India even before (on Ben Yiju, also Ghosh 1992). He ran a brass factory there, employing the local Jews and non-Jews, In the words of Goitien.

> He exported iron, a commodity not handled by the Jews in the Mediterranean, but taking pride of place in India trade; spices, such as pepper and ginger, and betel nuts, and of course the products of his brass factory. Copper and lead were sent to him from the west.... Besides this, the west sent gold coins of various currencies and all those daily commodities which westerners out in India needed or desired: Spanish and Egyptian textiles, writing paper not to be had in India at all, sugar, raisin, and dates, and household goods of different descriptions (Goitien 1980: 46).

The correspondents of three more letters analysed by Goitien (1987) were Arus b. Joseph al-Arjawani al-Mahdawi, a Tunisian maker and seller of purple cloth and his sister's son Allan b. Hassun to whom he also married one of his daughters. For India Arus provided Allan with corals and storax. In the first of these three letters we find Allan proceeding to Sindabar (perhaps in the modern Ratnagiri district), the northern port of entry to the pepper country on the Malabar coast. In the second letter we find that Allan brought 72 bales of iron and 150 sacks of pepper and other spices from India to Aden. In the third letter he sails again to India from Aydhab on the west coast of the Red Sea.

Gujarat is not yet known to have been specifically mentioned in the Geniza records. However, these records bring home a hitherto unperceived texture of the 12th century trading world across the Indian Ocean, of which Gujarat was a major part. Also, Gujarat was not entirely ignored in the Jewish records. The route of ships from Mangalore to Aden in Ben Yiju's days was via Diu on the southern coast of the Kathiawar peninsula.

Ben Yiju was not alone, and that becomes clear from the account of the voyage of a Spanish Jew, Benjamin of Tudela, who went to south India from the Gulf in the early 1160s. His description of an island called Kish in the Persian Gulf is interesting for its reference to Indian traders:

It is ... a considerable market, being the point to which Indian merchants and those of the islands bring their commodities; while the traders of Mesopotamia, Yemen and Persia import all sorts of silk and purple cloths, flax, cotton, hemp, mash (a kind of pea), wheat, barley, millet, rye, and all sorts of comestibles and pulse, which articles form objects of exchange; those from India import great quantities of spices, and the inhabitants of the island live by what they gain in their capacity of brokers to both parties (Major 1857: xlvi).

An interesting part of Jain's analysis of Gujarat's maritime trade between *c.* AD 1000 and 1300 (Jain 1990: chapter 4) is that it has been put in the background of a thriving internal trade and a network of sea routes. The internal trade was part of a pan-Indian framework and involved not merely the transport of 'luxury' goods such as silk, cotton, spices and horses over long distances but also items such as foodgrains, sugar, oil, pottery, etc. over comparatively short distances. The internal routes linking Gujarat with the rest of India went to Sind, Rajasthan, Konkan coast and Malwa. Like Konkan towards the end of the 13th century, Gujarat too must have been an important reaching point of the transhipment of horses from the Gulf ports and Aden. It has been argued (Chakravarti 1991) on the basis of the testimony of Marco Polo and others that "practically every sea-going vessel to India carried considerable number of horses from Persian Gulf ports and Aden". An undated Sanskrit text cited by Jain (1990: 125) mentions that ships from Hormuz brought horses and other cargoes to Ghoga on the west shore of the Gulf of Cambay.

Jain (1990) also offers a list of Gujarat's imports and exports in this context. Although this list is not exclusive to Gujarat, he has compiled it in the chapter on 'foreign trade' of his book. Among the imports, he first mentions 'metals'—copper, *Tutia* or vitriol, tin, lead, silver and gold. In addition to Aden, Southeast Asia is considered a major source. Precious stones came from the Gulf and Sri Lanka. Silk came from China, possibly through Sri Lanka and Malabar "which appear to have been the extreme points of westward destination of the Chinese *Junks* during the early mediaeval period" (Jain 1990: 93). Spices and aromatics came both from Southeast Asia and south India, although the role of the former as a source-region was more important of the two. Ivory was dominantly African and miscellaneous things like rosewater, dates, asafoetida and saffron came from West Asia. Among the exports were textiles, iron and iron swords and other objects, leather and leather goods, timber, aromatics, spices and dyes, precious and semi-precious stones, sugar and foodgrains like rice and wheat, and miscellaneous items like birds, animal horns and slaves. A textual source cited by Jain (1990: 105) says that a minister of a 13th century king of Gujarat banned the abduction of men by seamen and thus acquired religious merit.

Some details have been offered by him (Jain 1990: 128-136) regarding the ports as well. The chief ports between AD 1000 and 1300 were Broach, Cambay and Somnath, Bhadresvara (Kutch), Mangrol and Ghogha (Kathiawar) and Kavi, Gandhar and Rander (south Gujarat coast) being the minor ones. As Barygaza Broach's importance is well-understood, but it retained its significance in much later contexts too. According to the Arab geographer Al-Idrisi (1099-1166) it was a port for people arriving from Sind and China. In about the same period Alberuni attaches significance to Broach and Rander as major cities of south Gujarat. A 10th-century Arab geographer says that Broach was known in the West as the centre of manufacture of iron and shafts of spears. According to an Indian text of the period, a merchant of Anahilwadapatan (the then capital of Gujarat) came to Broach with 55 merchants and 500 ships for trade. The same text says that the kings used to appoint persons to salvage the ships wrecked off the coast of Broach.

The earliest epigraphical reference to Cambay was in the 9th century but it began to be important only after the 10th century, being mentioned by various Arab writers and Marco Polo. It was one of the main ports where horses from the Arab world used to be brought in ships. This was also a place from where ships sailed for Mecca. Similarly, Somnath or Devapattana or Prabhasa, which, according to the Cintra eulogy of the reign of Sarangadeva (*c.* AD 1287) is mentioned as being located "where the river Sarasvati flows into the ocean", drew attention from the Arab writers including Alberuni and Marco Polo. According to an epigraphic reference Mangrol or *Sri-Mangalapura* was an important centre of trade in grains, betel leaves and salt. It could also be a staging station for Mecca. There is epigraphical testimony regarding the use of Porbandar as a harbour in the 10th century AD. In the Bhavnagar area Hathav was important up to the 8th century but later Ghogha was important, receiving horses and other goods from Hormuz in the Gulf. By the 12th century Diu was well-known (cf. Geniza records). There is an inscription of the 12th century to support the idea that Bhadresvar in Kutch was the most important port of the Kutch area. Kavi was located almost opposite the port of Cambay and Gandhara in the eastern corner of the Gulf of Cambay was the place where Ibn Batuta (Travels: 1325-54) left on his voyage to south India.

It may be useful at this point to have a detailed look at the evidence furnished by Al-Idrisi who was born in Morocco towards the end of the 11th century and the Venetian Marco Polo who passed through this region towards the end of the 13th century. Al-Idrisi found vessels from Oman, China and the rest of India at Debal in the Indus mouth (Dowson 1867: 77). Merchandise of every country was found in Cambay which was three miles from the sea and 'placed at the extremity of a bay, where vessels can enter and cast anchor' (Dowson 1867: 84). Broach was a port for the vessels coming from China and Sind (Dowson 1867: 87). The capital of Gujarat, Anhilwada Patan, was 'frequented by large numbers of Musulman traders'. They were 'honourably received by the king and his ministers, and find protection and safety' (Dowson 1867: 88). Marco Polo found indigo and cotton, among other things, in Gujarat which also turned out enough dressed skins 'to load a number of ships for Arabia and other quarters' (Yule 1875: 383). Cambaet/Cambay produced indigo, cotton and dressed hides in abundance and attracted merchants with many ships and cargoes of chiefly gold, silver and copper (Yule 1875: 388-389). He found Semenat/Somnath 'a place of very great trade' (Yule 1875: 389) and the king of Aden, according to him, received 'a large amount of duties' from the ships plying between his kingdom and India and carrying to India 'a very large number of Arab chargers, and palfreys, and stout nags adapted for all work' (Yule 1875: 434).

II.4 AD 1300–1600: Gujarat Under Delhi Sultans, Independent Sultans and the Mughals

In his survey of Muslim communities in Gujarat, S.C. Misra (1964: 13) writes that there was a "considerable Muslim population of all shades and sects, as Rajput rule drew to a close in Gujarat". The fact that these kings had Muslim subjects including rich merchants and offered patronage to the construction of mosques in their domain did not, however, prevent the conquest of Gujarat (1297) in the name of Islam by the Delhi Sultanate under Alauddin Khilji. As *Mirat-i-Ahmadi*, an early 18th century Persian history of Gujarat, puts it,

> He sent an army for the conquest of Gujarat under the command of Ulugh Khan … and Nusrat Khan…. These Khans subjected Naharwala, that is Pattan, and the whole of that dominion to plunder and pillage…. Raja Karan Baghela…. His women, daughters, treasure and elephants fell in the hands of religious warriors of Islam. They obtained lot of wealth and jewels from rich men of Khambayat. They broke the idol of Somnat… and sent riches, treasure, elephants, women and daughters of Raja Karan to the Sultan of Dihli (Lokhandwala 1965: 28).

The scale of political change was vast, and it is the political history of the succeeding periods which has kept the historians busy (cf. Misra 1963—for the sources of the period from 1298 to 1442, pp. 5-16; Chaube 1975; Watson 1983 reprint). Except M.N. Pearson's *Merchants and Rulers in Gujarat, the Response to the Portuguese in the 16th Century* (Pearson 1976) there is not much concern with Gujarat's sea-trade of this period in historical literature. The sources apparently increase greatly in quantity, but these are mostly Arabic and Persian sources, referring only to the Muslim merchants in the rather rare cases where such references are actually available. Pearson's discussion is overwhelmingly based on the Portuguese and other European sources, and what he calls 'other local sources' consists of only Persian chronicles aided by a very limited Arabic accounts. The picture is very lopsided, as is bound to be the case where indigenous Gujarati sources are either unexplored or unused. The section on trade in M.R. Majumdar's *Cultural History of Gujarat* (Majumdar 1965: 63-78), for instance, does little to bring to light the little-known or unknown Gujarati material.

For the 14th century Ibn Batuta provides a clear, although limited, account. The 15th century is illuminated by the records of Abd-er-Razzak who set out for India from Herat via Hormuz in 1442, the Venetian Nicolo de' Conti whose 25 years of absence from Venice (1419-1444) took him as far as China, Athanasius Nikitin, a Russian who visited India in 1468-1470, and the Genoese merchant Santo Stefano who visited India at the close of the century. For the situation which persisted in the early 16th century after the advent of the Portuguese, Duarte Barbosa whose account was completed in 1518 provides a clear and detailed description of the contemporary sea-lanes to Gujarat and elsewhere. For the 16th century other European records are available (for a brief list, Pearson 1976:108), and if we have chosen Barbosa's account, that is because he tried to be most comprehensive.

However, at the outset it should be worthwhile to put some emphasiz on the fact that Gujarat's economy did not depend on sea-trade alone. J.W. Watson (1983 reprint: 14) calculated that during the latter part of the 15th and the first quarter of the 16th century when the independent Sultans of Gujarat with their capital in Ahmedabad were at the height of their power, they derived land revenue of Rs. 5,84,00,000/- from their 25 administrative divisions (some outside modern Gujarat), which amounted to a little more than half of their total revenue of Rs. 11,46,00,000/-. Of the remaining Rs. 56,62,00,000/- about one-fifth part was derived as tribute from the Deccan and the rest came from the custom dues of ports—"custom-dues from 25 ports on the western coast of India, and 26 foreign marts, some of them in India, and others in the Persian Gulf and along the Arabian coast" (Watson 1983 reprint: 14). One is not sure how the Gujarat Sultans derived custom-dues from ports outside their kingdom but apparently they did, possibly from the ships of their subjects trading with those ports. In any case, according to Watson's calculation, the revenue which Gujarat's maritime trade yielded in the late 14th and early 15th centuries, i.e. in a period before the Portuguese could exert serious influence in this field, was Rs. 44,96,00,000/- or £ 4,49,60,000 (Rs. 10 = £1, according to Watson's conversion). Watson's calculation markedly differs from the calculation offered by Pearson (1976: 23-24) who puts Gujarat's revenue of this period at much less, showing basically the shakiness of the sources on which such calculations are based. What is important is that revenue from maritime trade was a major component of the revenue structure of the Gujarat Sultans.

Ibn Batuta's description of Cambay or 'Kinbaya' is evocative:

> ... situated on an arm of the sea resembling a river, it is navigable for ships and its waters ebb and flow. I myself saw the ships lying on the mud at ebb-tide and floating on the water at high tide. The city is one of the finest there is in regard to the excellence of its construction and the architecture of its mosques. The reason is that the majority of its inhabitants are foreign merchants (Gibbs 1994: 797).

He mentions a few rich Muslim ship-owning merchants of the place. There was apparently a substantive number of Iranians living and trading at the place: a chief merchant was Najm al-Din of Jilan (one of the provinces of Iran on the Caspian coast) and the Deputy Governor of the place was Shaikh-Zada of Isfahan. From Cambay he went to Kavi/ Kawi, then a mile from the sea and also on a tidal bay, and from Kavi to Qandahar or Gandhar. There were important ship-owning Muslim merchants in the court of the 'infidel king' of Gandhar, one of them—Ibrahim—owning six vessels. Batuta embarked on a ship with horses at Gandhar and mentions an island called Piram at the mouth of the Gulf of Cambay. He found Ghogha/'Quqa' a large town with an important market but the ships had to be anchored 4 miles away from the shore on account of the low tide. From Ghogha he went to Goa.

Although he does not discuss much of trade, the record of John Mandeville, a native of St. Albans (England), whose travels began in 1332 and the book completed in 1366, cannot be passed over in silence. It has been argued (Letts 1953: xxxii) that his *Travels* was a compilation, but at the same time was "in many ways the most important record of overland travel in the Far East". He does not say much about India

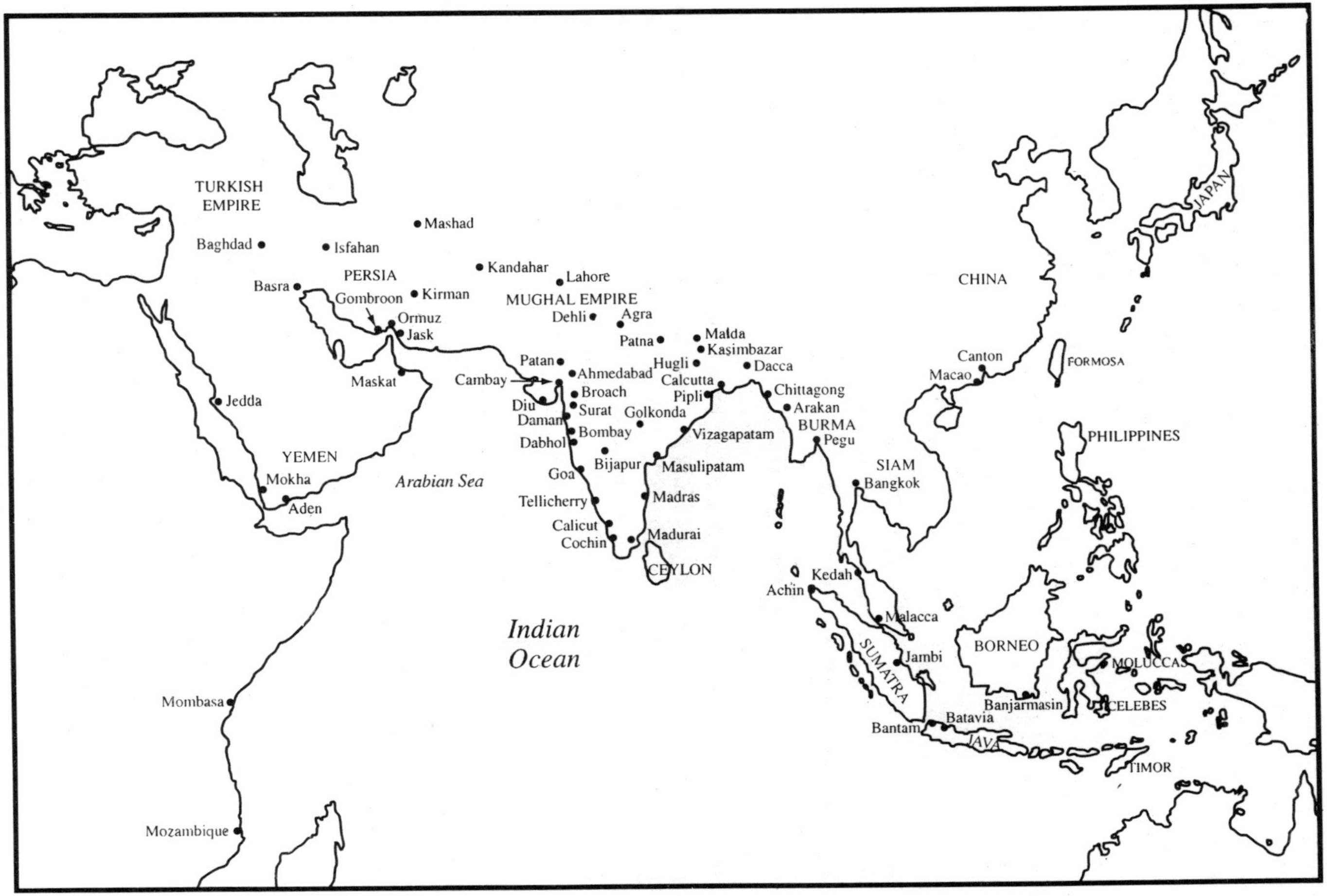

Fig. 3. Some Indian Ocean Ports and Trading Marts, 16th-18th Centuries

but the very fact that a 14th century Englishman from St. Albans was discoursing about the geography of India and referring to the ports of Thana and Broach (Sarchie/Paroche) and the pepper-growing area of "Lombe' or Quilon is significant in itself, showing that the later appearance of East India Company ships off the coast of Gujarat was not historically a fortuitous event. He also referred to Hormuz "whither merchants of Venice, of Genoa, and of many countries come to buy merchandise" (Letts 1953, vol. I, p. 117). In the context of Bharuch or Broach he called it a fair and good city which had 'many good Christian men'. From here men journeyed to the pepper-growing land of Lombe by sea.

That there were travellers in the 15th century is proved by R.H. Major's compilation of a few sources (Major 1857)—mainly Abd-er-Razzak, Nicolo Conti and Santo Stefano.

Abd-er-Razzak's account is important for the description of Calicut and Vijayanagara, but he highlights the importance of Hormuz:

> The merchants of seven climates, from Egypt, Syria, the country of Roum, Azerbijan, Irak-Arabi, and Irak-Adjemi, the provinces of Fars, Khorassan, Ma-wara-amahar, Turkistan, the kingdom of Deschti-Kaptchack, the countries inhabited by the Kalamucks, the whole of the kingdoms of Tschin and Matchin, and the city of Khanbalik, all make their way to this port; the inhabitants of the seacoasts arrive here from the countries of Tchin, Java, Bengal, the cities of Zirbad, Tenasserim, Sokotra, Schahrinou, the islands of Diwah-Mahall, the countries of Malabar, Abyssinia, Zanguebar, the ports of Bidjanagar, Kalbergah, Gudjarat, Kanbait, the coasts of Arabia, which extend as far as Aden, Jiddah, and Yembo ... (Major 1857: 5-6).

Nicolo Conti also came via Hormuz. He first went to Cambay which he referred to as a "very noble city" where precious stones were found. Athanasius Nikitin travelled via Hormuz too and mentioned Gujarat and Cambay as the areas where indigo grew (Major 1857: 8):

> Hormuz is a vast emporium of all the world; you find there people and goods of every description, and whatever thing is produced on earth you find it in Hormuz. ... Cambayat (Cambai) is a port of the whole Indian sea, and a manufacturing place for every sort of goods; as talach, damask, khan, kiota, and there they prepare the blue stone colour (Thomas 1857: 19).

The Genoese Santo Stefano sailed straight from Aden to Calicut, which took him about 35 days. On his return journey he went to Cambay where he found some merchants of Alexandria and Damascus. According to him lac and indigo were procured in Cambay.

Duarte Barbosa's account which was completed in 1538 (Barbosa

1918) is greatly detailed and brings before us, for the first time, the canvas of Indian Ocean trade covering all its three shores.

He begins by giving a methodical description of the Portuguese and general European approaches to India after their ships rounded the Cape of Good Hope and the Cape of Sam Sebastiam and passed by a group of islands which he called the Great and Lesser Hucicas. The first port of call was Sofala in the Zambezi delta (modern southern Mozambique) where he found the Arab merchants buying cotton cloth, silk and beads from the ships which came from "the great kingdom of Cambaya" and trading them with gold and ivory from the interior. Moving up the coast they reached Angoya, an island where he found merchants dealing in "gold, ivory, silk and cotton cloths and Cambay beads". Further up the coast there was the town of Mozambique with a Portuguese fort which had objects coming to it both from Portugal and India. An island called Quiloa (modern Kilwa) was passed on the way to Mombasa which had ships from Cambay. Still "journeying along the coast towards India", they came upon Melinde/Malindi from where Vasco da Gama obtained a Hindu pilot to take him straight across the ocean to Calicut in 1498. Here Barbosa expressly mentions the "heathen of the great kingdom of Cambaya", coming every year with many ships full of merchandise including rice, millet and wheat. They collected in return gold and ivory and made 'great profits'. On the way to Cape Guardafui (Horn of Africa) there was the Arab town of Magadoxo/Mogadishu where many ships came from Cambay bringing cloth and spices and carrying away "much gold, ivory, wax and many other things, whereby they make exceeding great profits in their dealings". Cape Guardafui drew ships from Cambay, Chaul, Dabul and ports further south, the Bengal coast, Southeast Asia and China. Portuguese pirates lay in wait here. Among the ports of the Red Sea was the port of Cues where the Arabs brought Indian 'spices, drugs and other rich wares' from Jeddah, the port of Mecca. They first put them in small vessels, crossed the sea, and then loaded them on camels to take them to Cairo and then Alexandria where they were bought by the Venetians. The Portuguese inroads did much to destroy this trade. Jeddah too was a port where every year ships from India carried spices and drugs, taking back to Calicut "much copper, quicksilver, verdegris, saffron, rosewater, scarlet cloth, silks, camlets, taffetas and diverse other goods... also... much gold and silver".

Eventually Barbosa mentions 'the city of Adem' or modern Aden.

> To the harbour of this city come ships from all parts, more specially from the port of Juda, whence they bring copper, quicksilver, vermilion, coral and woollen

and silken cloths, and they take thither on their return great store of spices and drugs, cotton cloths and other wares of the great kingdom of Cambaya. From Zeila and Barbora too come many ships with food-stuffs in abundance; (in return they take back Cambay cloth and beads both large and small ...) and those of Cambay come laden with cloth of many kinds; so great is the number of them that it seems an astonishing thing ! And, as I have already said, they bring cotton, drugs (great quantity), gems, seed pearl in abundance, *alaquequas*, and to the same kingdom of Cambay they take back madder, opium, raisins of the sun, copper, quicksilver, vermillion and great store of rosewater, which is made here. They also take much woollen cloth, coloured Meca velvets, gold in ingots, coined and to be coined (and also some in strings), and camlets, and it seems an impossible thing that they should use so much cotton cloth as these ships bring from Cambaya. They come to this city from Ormuz, from Chaul, Dabul, Baticala and Calecut (whence most of the spices are wont to come) with great store of rice, sugar, and cocoanuts; and many ships come also from Bangala, Camatra and Malaca, which bring as well abundance of spices, drugs, silk, benzoin, lac, sanders-wood, aloes-wood, rhubarb in plenty, musk, thin Bengala cloths and sugar (great store); so much so that this place has a greater and richer trade than any other in the world, and also this trade is in the most valuable commodities (Dames 1918: 55-57).

Zeila and Barbora are in modern Somalia, whereas *alaquequas* of Barbosa has been interpreted as carnelian. As a record of the trade of Aden in the early 16th century Barbosa's description must be considered invaluable. East of Aden, the Hadramut coast was important too, where the "moors of Cambaya, Chaul, Dabul, Baticala and Malabar" came with ships

laden with great plenty of cotton cloths, both coarse and fine, ... many perforated garnets and other gems of inferior kinds, rice, sugar, spices of all sorts and other wares which they sell to the country dealers, who purchase them at good prices, and take them to Aden; and so to the whole of this part of Arabia (Dames 1918: 64).

Horses of Hadramut were considered better than those of Hormuz, and Indian traders took horses and frankincense in return. Barbosa mentions Masquate/Muscat as a place which has 'great trade' and many fisheries. In the Gulf he refers to pearl-fisheries as well and from there "the Moors of Ormus" bought them to "carry them to India and many other lands". Many ships sailed to Barbosa's Bacora or modern Basrah "with great abundance of merchandize and spices and cotton cloths, and there they obtain plenty of wheat, and great store of butter, gingelly oil, barley, camlets and diverse other wares".

Ormus/Hormuz was described at great length.

> In this city are many merchants of substance, and many very great ships. It has a right good harbour where many sorts of goods are handled which come hither from many lands, and from here they barter them with many parts of India. They bring hither spices of all sorts, and divers kinds, to wit, pepper, cloves, ginger, cardamoms, eagle-wood, sandal-wood, brasil-wood, myrobalans, tamarinds, saffron, indigo, wax, iron, sugar, rice (great store) and cocoanuts, as well as great abundance of precious stones, porcelain and benozoin, by all of which they gain much money. They have also great plenty of Cambaya, Chaul and Dabul cloths, and from Bengala they bring many *synbafos*, which are a sort of very thin cotton cloth greatly prized among them and highly valued for turbans and shirts. For which they use them (Dames 1918: 92-93).

Hormuz received goods also from Aden and other parts of the Gulf, including horses from Arabia which then were carried to India, one or two thousands of them every year. By the time Barbosa visited Hormuz, the Portuguese under Alfonso D'Albuquerque built a fort there.

Barbosa's "kingdom of Guzerate" comes into view after his description of the port of Debal or Diul in Sind, which received rice, sugar, spices, timber and planks from elsewhere in the subcontinent and sending in return "great store of cotton, horses and cloth". In Gujarat there were "many seaports with much sea-trade" and he found "many great heathen merchants too" along with the 'Moors'. There were people from many lands in the kingdom of Cambay: the Arabs, Turks, Mamluks, Khorasanis, southern Persians and Turcomans. The identification of a port which he calls Patanexy has been debated but it appears that it was Somnath. He described it as having 'a good harbour, rich and with much trade' (abundance of silks and cotton, worn 'throughout India, Malaca and Bengal'). Ships from the southern coast came here with coconuts, jaggery and spices and took away 'much cloth, cotton, horses and wheat', the whole voyage lasting about four months. Porbandar and Mangrol had 'good harbours and much trade', again the Malabarese coming here with coconuts, emery, wax and cardamoms and returning with many horses, wheat, rice, cotton cloth and other stuff. The trade network of Diu was extensive:

> It is on a small island, hard by the main, and has a right good harbour, a trading port used by many ships, with exceedingly great traffic and commerce with Malabar, Baticala, Guoa, Chaul, and Dabul. Ships also sail hence to Mecca, Adem, Zeila, Barbora, Magadoxo, Melinde, Brava, Mombaca and Ormus with the kingdom thereof. The articles of merchandize brought hither by the Malabares are as follows: cocoanuts (great store), areca, jagra, emery, wax, iron, Baticala

Sugar, pepper, ginger, cloves, cinnamon, mace, nutmegs, sandalwood, brasil-wood, long peppers, and besides these, many silks and other wares which come from China and Malaca. From Chaul and Dabul they bring thither great store of woven cottons and linens, and take them away again to Arabia and Persia. The traders who bring these goods take in return much silk cloth and country cotton, many horses, wheat, gingelly (and the oil got from it), cotton, opium, both that brought from Aden and that which they make in Cambay, which is not so fine as the former. They also take many of the common silk camlets made in Cambaya, which are good and cheap. From India also they bring many large carpets, taffety, cloth of scarlet-in-grain and other colours, spices and other things, and all these goods are carried by the folk of this country to Meca, Adem, Ormus and other parts of Arabia and Persia, to such a degree that this town now has the greatest trade of any found in these regions; and yields such a sum of money that it is an astonishing thing, by reason of the bulky and precious goods that are here laden and unladen. Thus from Meca and Adem alone they bring hither coral, copper, quicksilver, vermillion, lead, alum, madder, rosewater, saffron, gold, silver (coined and bullion) in such abundance that it cannot be reckoned (Dames 1918: 128-130).

Gogha was also a place which had ships from Malabar and other parts of India and also from Mecca and Aden. Barbasy or Broach (most probably) was another 'good port with much shipping'. Guindarim or Gandhar attracted ships from Malabar. 'The best workmen in every kind of work' were found in the city of Cambay with 'many fair houses'. A reference is made to carnelian mines near Cambay, from where they were taken to the Red Sea coast Cairo, Alexandria, Arabia in general and Persia. Reynel/Rander was rich place trading in its 'own ships' with Malaca, Bengal, Tenasserim, Pegu, Martaban and Sumatra.

Those who dwell here have many great and fair vessels, which carry on this trade, and whosoever would have at his disposal things from Malaca and China, let him go to this place, where he will find them in greater perfection than in any other place soever (Dames 1918: 146-147).

Surat comes in for a passing mention: "Hither sail ships in great numbers from Malabar and other parts". From Surat he passed on to Daman or some place near it and from there he moved on to the Konkan coast.

Indigo is not mentioned specifically in his list of exports and imports of the Gujarati ports by Barbosa but 'fine indigo in cakes and another coarser kind' figure in his list of commodities or merchandise found in the kingdom of Gujarat during his time (Dames 1918: 154).

There are other sources dating from Barbosa's period, i.e. the 16th century, and it would be invidious not to mention Pedro Alvares Cabral,

Tome Pires and Ludovico Varthema at this point. Cabral (Greenlee 1938) set sail for Calicut from Melindi (2 August, 1500) on the coast of Africa by hiring a Gujarati pilot. He reached Calicut on 13 September. In Melindi he found 3 ships from Cambay and later on waxed eloquent about the productivity and wealth of this land. The Cambay city was then known as "Cairo of India" which was walled and had great merchants trading in their own ships with the Red Sea, Ethiopia, the Gulf and other parts of India. According to Tome Pires (Travels: 1512-1515), the kingdom of Cambay was both rich and thickly populated, with mercenaries from the Middle East and Abyssinia. Its principal cities were Surat, Rander and Diu, the other port-cities being Daman, Gogha and Bharuch. He also mentioned the inland city of Champaner (Cortesao 1944, vol. I, pp. 33 onwards). Ludovico Varthema (Travels: 1503–1508) went up to Borneo and Malacca, and according to him Cambay was 3 miles inland and could not be reached by large or middle-sized ships except at high water. The tide here flew up 3 or 4 miles. The city was walled. The immense quantity of cotton produced in the area was loaded every year in 40/50 ships and carried to different countries. Further, he says that the ships of Cambay—about 300 ships of different countries—supplied "all Persia, Tartary, Turkey, Syria, Barbary, that is Africa, Arabia Felix, Ethiopia, India and a multitude of inhabited islands with silk and cotton stuffs" (Badger 1863: 111). Jan van Linschoten (Parr 1964) has been called the Dutch Marco Polo and his *Itinerario* was published in 1595, but he was concerned only with Goa. He does not mention Gujarat at all.

If one steps aside from such 16th century Portuguese and other European narratives and looks at their historical settings, one immediately realizes that a new and very important political factor was then added to this whole scenario, i.e. the presence of the Portuguese who were rapaciously hungry to control everything in the Indian Ocean sea-lanes from Mozambique to Malacca. The scale on which they introduced brigandage, arson, murder and pillage to these sea-lanes and the bordering shores was unprecedented, even though one makes allowance for the fact that the kings and Sultans were no paragons of virtue when it came to acquiring wealth and power. According to Pearson (1976: 31), "By 1600 Portugal had some fifty ports or defended areas in Asia, stretching from Sofala to Macao", the most important of them in the Gujarat littoral being their forts at Diu and Daman. Off the Indian coast at least—Pearson (1976: 41) speaks of "all ships trading in Asian waters"—this coastal apparatus of dominance was supported by the system of *Cartaz* or 'pass' which had to be taken by every trading ship—

irrespective of any native power it belonged to—from a competent Portuguese authority, deposit a cash security against the payment of 'duties' on homeward journey, and accept restrictions on what it could contain and what it could not. The fact that such passes "were issued from at least 1502 onward" (Pearson 1976: 41)—only four years after the arrival of Vasco da Gama in Calicut–speaks a good deal of the naval superiority of the Portuguese in the Indian Ocean, the ruthlessness of their intent to make use of it, and the abject surrender of the land-powers around this ocean to this hitherto unthought-of repression in the high seas.

Even the Great Mughals, who owned Gujarat after 1573, did not try to change the situation, and thus by 1607 when William Hawkins arrived in Surat by the British ship *Hector* he found the Portuguese the major hindrance in the pursuit of British interests, especially in the sea. We are not in a position to assess if Gujarat's inclusion in the Mughal empire led to any fundamental shift in its productions or both inland and maritime trade. We suspect that the basic pattern laid down through centuries of agriculture, crafts, and inland and overseas trade was possibly unchanged, except perhaps on matters of scale.

III. SUMMARY OF THE ARGUMENT

The basic purpose of the present chapter was to put the European advent in Gujarat in its proper long-term historical context. An exhaustive discussion of the pre-1600 sources was not within its scope; the aim was only to bring out the nature of contacts Gujarat had, both as a traditional focus of Indian Ocean trade and in terms of the basic geography of its long coastline and traditional harbours.

The point of beginning was certainly the Indus civilization. Considering that there is no settlement of this civilization in the present-day Indus mouth in Sind, that the Indus mouth itself then lay in the region of the Great Rann of Kutch where the combined flow of the Indus and the ancient Saraswati met the sea, and that there are Indus sites in the Kathiawar peninsula, which make sense as ports in view of the location of the traditional harbours of the region, we would argue that Gujarat was the primary region through which the overseas contacts of the Indus civilization were negotiated. We would further emphasize, especially in view of the Indus find at Ras al-Junayz in the Ras al-Hadd area of Oman, which was the landfall for ships coming from the direction of India, that the sailing advantage of the seasonal monsoon winds was appreciated by the sailors of this civilization. This find also lays open the possibility that the Indus ships could have known the southern Arabian coast as well. Even if they did not actually sail along that coast themselves, they must have met people who knew that area in Ras al-Hadd. Further, considering that the Indus ivory combs figured in the Ras al-Junayz find and that both wooden and ivory combs have been among the traditional exports of Gujarat to that and other Arabian regions, we would infer that there is a thread of continuity in the nature of basic commodities exported from Gujarat, right from the period of the Indus civilization. We would unhesitatingly give cotton and cotton cloth the pride of place in this matter.

The Indus civilization's contact with the Gulf area through Gujarat lasted till *c.* 1400/*c.* 1300 BC, and if the find of Indian teak in 7th-6th century BC. Babylonia is to be taken seriously, the Gujarati contact with this region continued through the post-Indus period up to the threshold of India's early historic urban growth. As a part of the Mauryan empire of the 3rd century BC, which was familiar with kingdoms as far as Greece and north Africa, Gujarat was possibly a part of the maritime network covering the Red Sea, the south Arabian coast, the Gulf, and the entire western line of the Indian coast by then. By the 1st century BC, if not earlier, the Mediterranean ships were sailing straight, with the help of the monsoon, from the mouth of the Red Sea to the southern stretch of India's west coast and established trading stations on the east coast as well. The Indian east coast's southeast Asiatic contacts across the Bay of Bengal, possibly both from the Ganga delta of Bengal and the Kaveri-Krishna-Godavari-Mahanadi mouths of Tamilnadu, Andhra and Orissa are, in all likelihood, earlier than the 1st century BC. On the whole, the 1st century BC was roughly the period when the trading worlds of the Arabian Sea and the Bay of Bengal combined to form the large Indian Ocean trading world stretching from the Red Sea to the Strait of Malacca, with important ramifications on the other sides of these points. One can safely imagine that Gujarat was one of the nodal points of this vast trading world.

When does it get linked to the African east coast from the Cape Guardafui to Mozambique and Zanzibar? The find of Kushan period coins in Ethiopia is a pointer in this direction, and the find of Axumite coins in south India (Nawartmal 1999) bring home the fact that this link continued from the first two/three centuries AD to the first half of the 4th century AD, the latter being the date of Axumite coins in India. No direct evidence is forthcoming from Gujarat, but it appears that the kind of picture Barbosa offers—that is, the picture of Cambay ships sailing into the east African ports—had its first stage in the early centuries of the Christian era. R.K. Mookerji (1912: 189) cited some source to the effect that the "Gupta (AD 319-500) and White Huna (AD 500-580) coins were said to have been in use in Madagascar", thus giving an idea of the time by which the world of Indian Ocean trade depicted by Barbosa in the early 16th century was fully in place.

Another important point in this connection is to know when Gujarat had developed its direct links with Southeast Asia. As Pearson (1976: 101) puts it, "In the 15th century Gujarat stretched out two arms: to Aden and the Red Sea, and to Malacca". Hard archaeological evidence is not forthcoming but we suspect that the latter link goes back to the late centuries BC when the two trading worlds of the Arabian Sea and the Bay of Bengal combined. By the early centuries AD this must have been firmly in place, because, if the Sassanians based on the shores of the Gulf were looking into a trading world stretching as far as China, Gujarat could not be out of this world.

The evidence of the Periplus is interesting in two major ways. His list of the trade goods passing through Barygaza makes it abundantly clear that, despite the presence of the exotica like fine wine and beautiful girls for concubinage, it was not fundamentally different than the goods passing through Gujarat's harbours till the 19th century. Further, the mention of Chinese (silk) cloth in this context drives home the point of Gujarat's maritime links to the East by the 1st century AD. Secondly, we can also learn from the Periplus that Gujarati ports like Barygaza were drawing goods from a wide hinterland stretching as far as the northwest, central India and the Deccan.

The settlements of the Jewish merchants and Nestorian Christians on India's west coast, possibly from the time when the Sassanians were powerful on the high seas were a natural concomitant of the Indian Ocean's trading world just as the presence of the Muslim traders from the Gulf area and beyond along the entire line of India's west coast from the 8th-9th century onwards was a part of this trading world too. In the early 15th century Nicolo Conti found Nestorian Christians "spread over the whole of India". At 'Malepur' or modern Mylapuram in Chennai he reported the body of Saint Thomas "honourably buried in a very large and beautiful church" which was worshipped by Nestorians who numbered about a thousand in that city. In about this period Santo Stefano had noticed in Calicut "as many as a thousand houses inhabited by Christians". In about 1442 according to Abd-er-Razzak's testimony, there was a Christian councillor called Nimeh-pezir in the royal council of Vijayanagara (for Conti, Stefano and Razzak, Major 1857). The point is that Nestorian Christianity in India is solidly pre-modern in origin, and can best be appreciated in the light of the Sassanian influence on the trade of the Indian west coast as early as the 3rd century AD.

Although it has been customary among the historians to observe that "the long-distance 'international' trade of Asia around 1500 was ... largely handled by Muslims of various origins" (Pearson 1976: 14), the truth may be more complex. The kind of written material that one has from the Islamic world is not yet known to exist for the indigenous non-Islamic boat-builders, sailors and ship-owning merchants of Gujarat and elsewhere in the Indian littoral. On the whole, what Ashin Dasgupta wrote about the Indian merchants in general, without looking into their religions, may be closer to the truth:

> Upon the whole the trade in the Indian Ocean remained firmly in the hands of the Indian ship-owning merchants with only an occasional flutter, especially in the early 16th and early 17th century, when the Europeans threatened to cut in (Dasgupta 1982: 417).

This was written obviously about a time when the days of the Indian shipping were in a sense numbered, but there is no special reason why the Indian sailors and merchants could not hold their own in the early contexts too.

Whatever it was, the British ships which anchored off Swally at the mouth of the Tapti in 1608 came as a part of a trading world which stretched back to the 3rd millennium BC.

The abundant European accounts of India from the 15th century onward have the added significance of demonstrating that India, from the European point of view, was never a 'lost continent'. It was not something which was discovered anew after the decline of the classical world. There was a steady continuity of European knowledge of India. In fact, many observations on the Indian life and customs, that one comes across in these European accounts, are remarkably like the classical observations on the land–the observations of the Greek ambassador in the Mauryan court of Pataliputra, for example. Further, by the 15th and 16th centuries, the European geographical knowledge of India was remarkably detailed in the context of the time. As far as Indians are concerned, this knowledge extended to the essentials of non-Islamic religious life, including a brief listing of Hindu religious texts such as *Vedas*. Apparently, texts such as these were not 'forgotten' texts to be 'discovered' by the Orientalists of the late 18th and 19th centuries, who only applied to them the norms of European scholarship of the period. Kate Teltscher (1995) has tried to link these writings to the later genres of European representations of India, without always making clear the relationship between such representations and the different phases of the growth of European power in the subcontinent. It is also entirely logical to perceive the first phase of European writings on India (15th-17th centuries) as a continuation of the earlier classical tradition and also as an external source of the fact that the non-Islamic religious tradition of India continued uninterrupted. There was no lost text for the Orientalists to 'discover'. This puts the much-trumpeted Orientalist scholarship on India in its true light, making it basically a story of translating these texts into European languages and of interpreting them according to the conventions of European linguistic, philosophical and historical scholarship. For the Indians themselves, outside the ambit of a small group of English-educated 19th century elite, there was no 'Oriental renaissance'.

3

Surat

We arrived in our port of Surat at the beginning of September and have there established a factory, with much benefit to the Worshipful Company and all the English nation, if we may continue to trade in peace; for the land is very healthful and fertile, and abounds in rich commodities. It seems like another Egypt, or, to say better, a terrestrial paradise; such is the abundance in all earthly things.

The Rev. Patrick Copland at Swally Road to the Rev. John Randall in London, 14 January 1613 (Foster 1934: 239).

Now, I let your Worship know that, by the special favour of God, we have set up our factory in the city of Surat. I hope that it will subsist many years, and I pray God that such may be the case, for I think that in all India there is no place so suitable for the commodities that come from England.

Thomas Kerridge in Surat to Sir Thomas Smythe in London, 25 January 1613 (Foster 1934: 252).

INTRODUCTION: THE PURPOSE OF THE CHAPTER AND THE SOURCES USED

The purpose of this chapter is to discuss the basic history of Surat up to the late 18th or early 19th century and investigate its major issues related to the places associated with the Europeans. We then try to understand these issues in relation to the contemporary topographic and settlement features. This approach will also be adopted in the next chapter where we examine the cases of Bharuch, Cambay, Ahmedabad, Daman and Diu.

The sources of the history of European trade with Mughal and post-Mughal India are legion, mostly the day-to-day records kept by the European merchants and 'factors' and the correspondence they had with their superiors in Britain, Netherlands, France and elsewhere. We are not in a position to assess if these archival sources, some of which are published, have been fully or even adequately mined, but apparently there is no lack of historical literature on this and related themes (for a current review based on this literature, Prakash 1998). The main, if not exclusive, concern of these sources is with the companies' administrative and economic affairs and they do not throw light on the details of the material sphere of life. The documentary sources used by us are different in the sense that we use only the descriptions of the major trading places of Gujarat, which were left behind by various European travellers in the region between the 16th and 18th centuries AD. Compared to the range of indigenous sources on Mughal India, which were restricted mostly to the enumeration of political events, statecraft, battles and courtly intrigues, these European sources go a long way to open up our horizon of understanding India of that period. Even if Indian sources of other kinds had come down to us from this period, very little research headway seems to have been made in this regard except some isolated attempts (cf. Desai 1994, for an authoritative review of the mostly untapped Persian language sources on the history of Gujarat; Singh and Rajshirke 1992, trying to use the letters, account sheets, ledger books, and bills of exchange of the Gujarati business community in the second half of the 18th century). In addition to the descriptions of her inland and maritime trade, minerals, manufacturing and agricultural products, wealth, religious and philosophical attitudes and even the details of political events, in the European travellers' records we get observations on such little things as the daily halting places along communication routes, ordinary peoples' behaviour, different communities, physical features of various cities they visited, etc. The tone varies from period to period and from author to author but on the whole these records are invaluable from our point of view in the sense that they help us to properly locate the relevant European establishments and other features.

Most of them knew Gujarat, especially Surat which was the point of entry to India for many of them. For the 16th century our major sources for this chapter have been the accounts of J.H. Van Licschoten (Burnell 1885), Tome Pires (Cortesao 1944), Francois Pyrard (Gray 1888), Ludovico Varthema (Badger 1863), Pedro Alvares Cabral (Greenlee 1938), Joannes De Laet (Hoyland and Banerjee 1928) and Father Monserrate (Hoyland and Banerjee 1922). Among them Pyrard's and Monserrate's accounts belong to the late 16th century. The early 17th century records which are relevant to Gujarat and/or Surat are those by William Hawkins (Markham 1878), Thomas Roe (Foster 1899), Thomas Coryat (Purchas 1905, vol. 9), Thomas Best (Foster 1914), T. Herbert (1638), Nicholas

Downton (Foster 1939), John Lancaster (Markham 1877), Edward Terry (Purchas 1905), John Jourdain (Foster 1905), Nicholas Withington (Prasad 1980), William Finch (Nath 1990) and Pieter van den Broeke (Moreland 1931, 1932). Well into the 17th century, we have the accounts of Francisco Pelsaert (Moreland and Geyl 1925), Johan van Twist (Moreland n.d.) and J.A. De Mandelslo (Commissariat 1931). For the middle to the late 17th century there are the writings of Peter Mundy (Temple 1914, 1936), Francois Bernier (1968 rep.), Jean-Baptise Tavernier (Ball 1925), Niccolao Manucci (Irvine 1907), John Freyer (Crooke 1909, 1912), Abbe Carre (Fawcett 1948), J. Olafsson (Temple 1923), A. Hamilton (Foster 1930), Streynsham Master (Temple 1911), William Hedges (Yule 1888), John Ovington (Guha 1979 a), J. de Thevenot (Guha 1979b), G.F.G. Careri (Guha 1979b), Manuel Godinho (Moraes 1952) Francois Martin (Varadarajan 1984) and Johan van Twist (Moreland 1937). For the 18th century we may turn to J.S. Stavorinus (1798), A. Parsons 1808) and William Milburn (1813). Our sources are unlikely to be exhaustive or even fully comprehensive, but one can be sure that they cover between themselves all the important issues which are relevant to our discussion. Further, although these sources belong to the different phases of Surat's history from the 16th to the 18th centuries, one is not sure if a phase-wise development of Surat's history can be attempted in detail only on their basis. In any case, we have not made such an attempt, our basic focus being to understand Surat in its historical context and in the context of some of its major physical features.

I. A BRIEF GEOGRAPHICAL SKETCH

The British took over the administration of the city of Surat in 1800, after about 200 years of familiarity with the place. The first gazetteer of the district (Campbell 1877) puts its size at 1,669 square miles (*c.* 4324 sq. km) which were divided into eight administrative subdivisions—Olpad, Mandvi, Chorasi, Bardoli, Jalalpur, Chikhli, Balsar and Pardi. The Surat city was included in the Chorasi subdivision. The district, with a wedge-shaped slice of the princely Baroda state cutting it in the middle, lay between the Kim river on the north and the Damanganga river on the south. The sea was its western boundary, whereas the line of the eastern boundary was irregularly shaped and bordered by a number of princely states including Baroda which was under the ruling house of the Gaikwads.

Three geographical elements of the area are worth taking into account: the coastline, the rivers and their alluvial belts, and the communication lines. Between the Kim and the Tapti, the coastline bulges out, but to the south of the Tapti estuary it takes an inward bend. All along the line, however, it possesses regularly spaced creeks, almost invariably the mouths of large or small rivers. The major ones which show up on the district-level maps are marked by the Kim, Sena, Tena and Tapti mouths in the northern section, whereas in the south we have, from the north to the south, the estuaries of the Mindhola, Purna, Ambika, Auranga, Par, Kolar and Damanganga rivers. The coastline is generally fringed by small hills of drifted sand but there are areas where springs of freshwater have helped the growth of creepers and palm trees. A distinct feature is the way in which the tidal waters pass beyond the limits of the heaped-up sand and leave the main creeks to flow in winding channels through extensive tracts of low-lying country. Another feature is the presence of salt marshes in the areas which are regularly overflown by tidal waters. A shallow film of salt water can also be found in the areas around springs. When the water of the marshes and around the springs and in the tidal channels outside the main streams dries up, the surface is soon reduced to flakes of earth and eventually to dust, the latter blowing across the land in hot weather months, blighting the crops and damaging the soil of cultivated fields. Water is brackish and scanty along the coast, except in a few isolated pockets. Cultivation along the coast is confined to small patches and the population is dominated by sailors and fishermen.

The belt of cultivated land beyond the coastal dunes, salt-marshes, tidal channels and springs is broad in the north and narrow in the south. In the north the Tapti, which originates at Multai in the Satpura hills and flows through the Khandesh region of Madhya Pradesh and Maharashtra before reaching Gujarat, has created the most important fertile and generally level alluvial tract of the district. In the south, the area covered by such alluvial tracts depends both on the nature of the stream and the nature of the country it flows through. The southern streams are smaller and generally marked only by pools in summer months. They also flow through a rocky surface. One finds cultivated lands fringed by trees in the hollows near the stream beds, but the land in between has only a thin soil cover and a scanty water supply. These tracts throw up mostly grass and hardy brushwood, and although serving as village grazing grounds, they have 'a somewhat rough and uncared-for look'. This 'look' extends, in fact, to large areas in the eastern parts of the district where the outliers of the Satpuras introduce a broken, upland topography which used to have large tracts of forest and a population of—in the language of the gazetteer published in 1877—'the

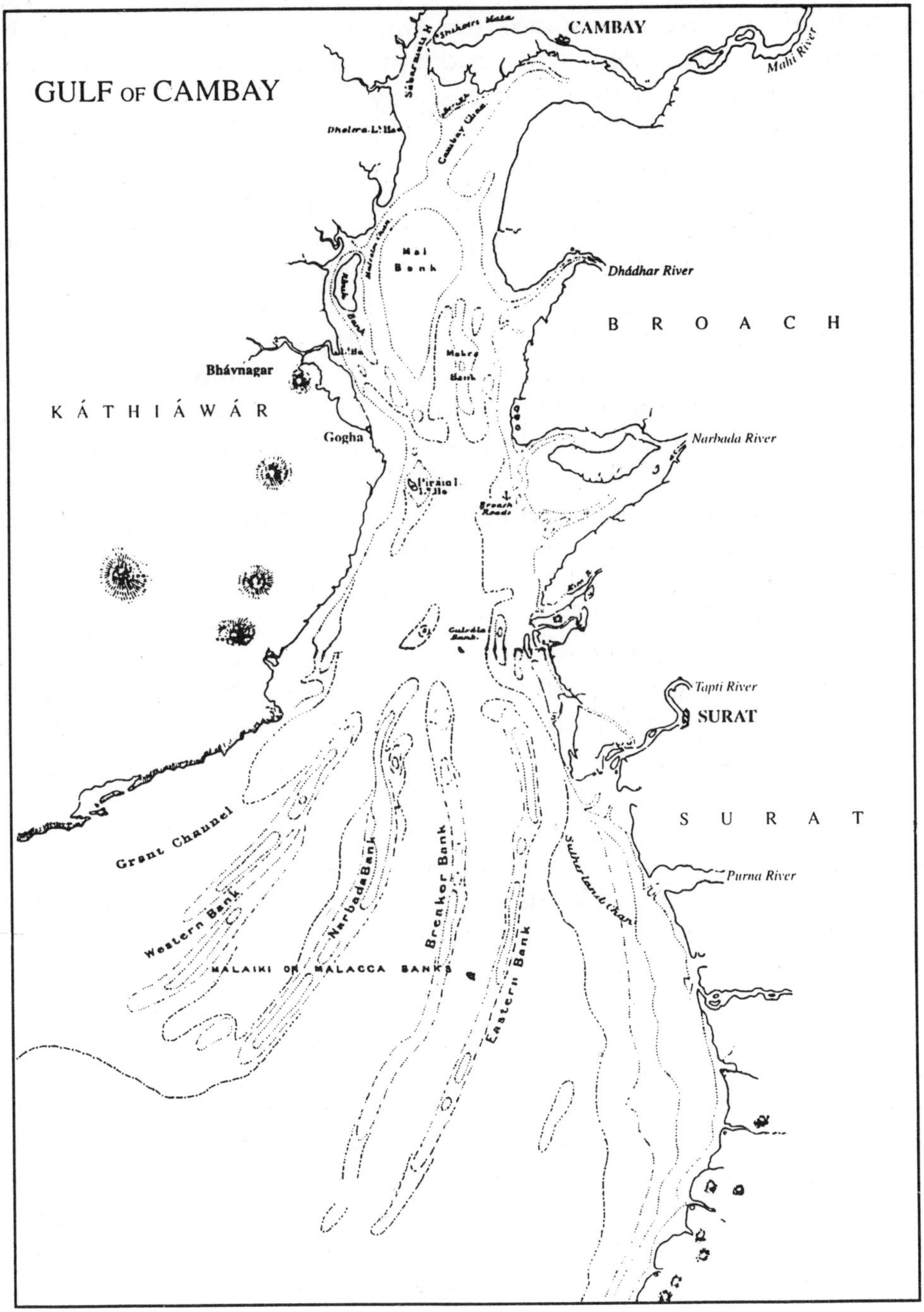

Fig. 4. Gulf of Cambay (after Campbell 1877)

rudest tribes'. This is the area of the Dang forests. In the Damanganga territory in the extreme south, the rugged surface is furrowed by watercourses and dotted with badlands where the poor soil and unwholesome water have led to a scanty population.

The Kim and the Tapti (or Tapi) valleys, thus constitute the bulk of the cultivated areas of the Surat district. The Kim which rises in the Rajpipla range is *c.* 112 km long and has a drainage area of *c.* 1,800 sq. km. In the dry months its flow peters down to a succession of pools, and although the tidal wave is felt for a large stretch up the channel, it cannot be used for navigation. The Tapti has a course of *c.* 725 km, with a drainage area of *c.* 78000 sq km. Its flow across the alluvial plain of Surat is for *c.* 113 km. Of this length, *c.* 50 km or more are subjected to the tidal impact. For the first 35 km or so in the eastern part of the district, the river flows through a less cultivated tract, but in the rest of the area the river banks have a high section of tough yellowish clay, interspersed by limestones and capped by a deposit of black soil. For the rest of its journey till it comes close to the sea, the Tapti flows through a richly cultivated plain where, aided by 60-70 inches (*c.* 150-180 cm) of annual rainfall, crops like wheat, rice, millet, sugarcane and cotton are grown. However, a point which should not be lost sight of—even in the context of the well-cultivated Tapti plain—is that the rivers here, including even the Tapti, are not particularly conducive to creating irrigation facilities, unless irrigation dams are created upstream in the rocky terrain in the east and water led away by canals from them. Traditional irrigation system based on wells and various lifting devices could not make the local agriculture free from its general dependence on the rains. This, and its location in the midst of a much larger stretch of poorly cultivated country, explain the many recorded instances of famine in this region. Peter Mundy's description of the famine of 1630-32 under the title 'The begininge of the great Famine' (Temple 1914: 38 and later; also appendix A under the title 'The famine of 1630-1632'), which he related, at least secondarily, to 'the want of rayne this last season' amply underlines one of the abiding historical realities of Indian agriculture. J. Mandelslo's explanation (Commissariat 1931: 7) of the same famine is clearer: the 'great drought' of 1630 and the 'continued rains' of the following year. He arrived in the province in 1638, and although he found the province 'well recovered' by that time, the marks of that famine could be seen everywhere. In December 1831, a Dutch factor wrote to the council in Batavia that out of about 260 families in Swally, only 10 or 11 families survived the famine, and in Surat, where the factor reports that the city and the fields were all under great flood,

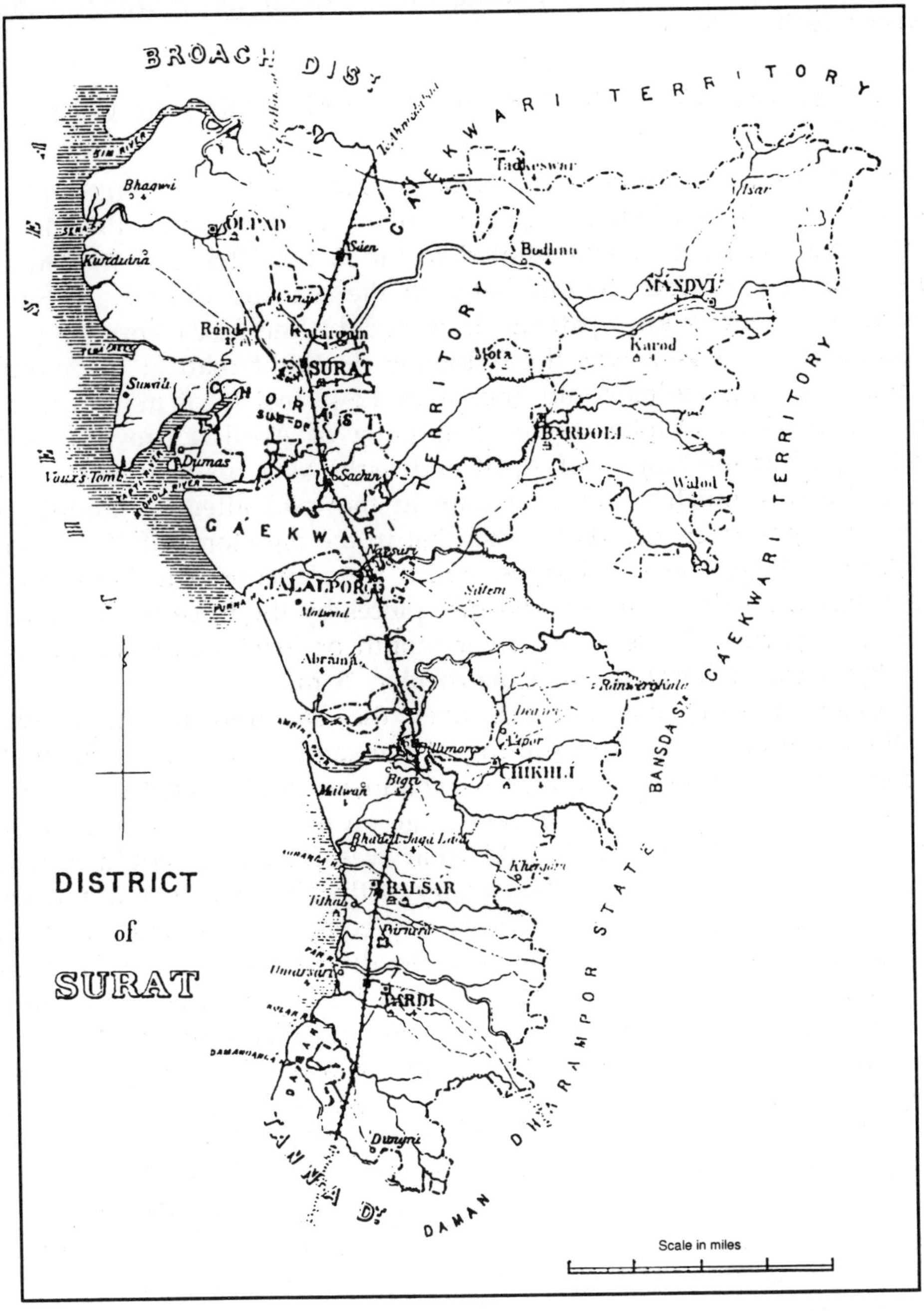

Fig. 5. Surat Area (after Campbell 1877)

about 30,000 people died, including 10/11 British and 3 Dutch factors (Foster 1910: 180-181).

II. THE SURAT BAR AND THE NAVIGABILITY OF THE TAPTI UP TO SURAT

Some details about the navigability of the Tapti will not be out of place here. In the 1870s when the first gazetteer of the Bombay Presidency was being compiled, it was limited to the last *c.* 32 km of its course. The state of the Tapti channel between the sea and the city of Surat which lies about 19 km upstream in a straight line (*c.* 24 km along the winding river course), was the following. In Surat road at the mouth of the Tapti large ships could anchor in 42-48 feet (12.8 m–14.6 m) at low water. From October to the beginning of April it provided safe anchorage but the storms of April and early May made it unsafe for ships drawing much water to remain in the road after the middle of April. The gazetteer records the fact that in the big storm of 20th April, 1782, some large and small ships, which were anchored in Surat road, were driven on shore and broken into pieces by the force of the storm. The average rise of tide at the river mouth or 'bar' was *c.* 4.6 m, but *c.* 6 km west of Surat it came down to *c.* 3 m.

Even in 1876, the entrance over the bar into the Tapti was continuously changing. The shifting of the sand opened new channels and closed the old ones. Before 1876 a channel called the Dumus channel (thus named after the name of the village on the left bank of the river) provided the entrance but in 1876 that was filled and could remain navigable only at high tide. The estuary of the river was *c.* 6 km across but the entrance passage was narrow and could be negotiated only by a properly experienced pilot. Between the dry sands near the bar there was not sufficient depth even for a small boat. For nearly two-thirds of the distance up to Surat, the sand-banks were continuous. Many of them were dry at half-tide. There were two major sand-banks, one near Magdala about 6 km and Umra, about 16 km, from the mouth of the river. There was deeper water in the river in Surat itself—at all times of the tide a depth of water not less than 3 m. Although boats could sometime pass up to Rander, about 5 km, and Amroli, about 18 km, above Surat, the ordinary limit of navigation in 1876 was the city of Surat itself. Country craft from 18 to 36 tons and light steamers were the only vessels which could ply from Surat in the months excluding the period from June to September.

While writing on the navigability of the Tapti, the gazetteer adds that "the character of its bed has changed but little since the days when Surat was one of the chief centres of commerce in Western India". In 1863 a steamship of 400 tons was stuck in the shoals and became a wreck, while trying to take a cargo of cotton near Magdala, about 6 km from the mouth of the river. In 1855, ships of 144-180 tons could come up as far as Surat and then there was over the bar at all times of the tide a depth of 4.5 m of water. In 1846, there were only two channels marking together a width of not more than 1.6 to 2.4 km. Boats, if stuck in the sand-banks, were often lost. In 1813 the navigation was equally difficult. In November 1774, the situation at the bar was better, but even then,

> Except when in want of repairs, ships engaged in the European trade remained at anchor on the roads, the merchants taking their goods to Surat either by land or in small boats (Campbell 1877: 14).

In the context of 1774-1775, the Dutch Rear Admiral J.S. Stavorinus (1798: vol. 2, p. 447) wrote that there was no more than three feet of water over the bar at the mouth of the river at low tide. Large ships could enter the river at high tide when the water rose to fifteen feet. What could happen to people trying to reach Surat by boat at low tide has been graphically expressed by Abraham Parsons who experienced this in early December, 1777. He left the parent ship by boat at 2 P.M. and it was a full hour before he could get over the bar. Then,

> We proceeded with oars up the river, making but little progress, the ebb tide being commenced, and at eight we ran on a shoal bank, but were soon got off again by the poor fellows jumping out naked, and pushing lustily; in an hour more we got on another bank; and, notwithstanding our endeavours, we were obliged to remain till two in the following morning, when the flood tide set us off again (Parsons 1808: 246).

Parsons agreed with Stavorinus in pointing out that the fully loaded large ships could not come over the bar till they partly unloaded and got about 'fifteen feet draught of water'. After that they could enter the river at high water and could go up to Surat. Even when the sea was rough, the ships which did not draw more than 12 feet of water might run safely run over the bar at high tide. William Milburn who published his book *Oriental Commerce* in 1813 on the basis of the material collected during a period of 25 years wrote that the navigation up the river to Surat was difficult, the frequently shifting sandbanks being the cause of trouble. "Near two-thirds of the distance from the bar to Surat, is a continued chain of banks, having but narrow channels between them" (Milburn 1813: 157).

Things could have been a little better in 1688-1689 when J. Ovington (Guha 1979b: 96) wrote that the river was "very commodius for the importation of foreign goods" which were "brought up to the city in hoys and yachts, and country boats, with great convenience and expedition". It is interesting to note that, despite Ovington's easy reference to the transportation of goods from the river mouth to Surat, he does not write that the goods could be unloaded from the ocean-going ships at Surat itself. In the context of about 1640, J-B Tavernier (Ball 1925, vol. I, p.5) wrote that the large vessels could not 'enter the river at Surat' until after they were unloaded. The same opinion has been voiced by Godinho (Moraes 1952: 124) who in addition refers to 'certain deep hollows' dug artificially into its bed for allowing heavy vessels to lie on the silt at low tide. In 1666, M. de Thevenot noted that even in a small boat the passage up the river took the time from 10 A.M. to 8 P.M. In 1638, according to Mandelslo (cited by Campbell 1880) who travelled from Swally to Surat by boat, even ships of 70-80 tons found it difficult to negotiate the journey from the river-mouth to Surat. When the Portuguese invaded Surat in 1530, the larger ships could not go over the bar because of the sands. The Portuguese troops came up in small vessels, but even then it took more than a day. This does not mean that large ships could never come up to Surat at its heyday: in suitable times of the year when the river was full, it was possible to bring ships of 1,000 tons as far up the river as Surat. This is a long cry from the present condition of the Tapti mouth, where the river looks absolutely stagnant at Hazira near the big refinery constructed by Reliance Corporation. However, we noticed this in January (2001) when there were no rains in the drainage area feeding the river. In the monsoon months, the situation would be somewhat better.

III. THE COMMUNICATION LINES FROM SURAT TO KHANDESH, KONKAN, MALWA AND RAJASTHAN

One particular aspect of the Tapti valley was not dependent on the river's navigability. Its alluvial corridor provided a straight and easy access from the Surat area to Burhanpur in Khandesh, from where one could join the long road to Rajasthan, Agra and Delhi across the Narmada and via Mandu and Dhar in Malwa and Ajmer in Rajasthan, and the much shorter route to the Deccan via Chalisgaon. These are among the time-honoured arterial routes of India and Surat was closely linked to them by the Tapti valley.

The route from Surat to Burhanpur has been described in detail, among others, by Thomas Roe who left Surat on 1 November 1615 and reached Burhanpur on the 14th of the same month, passing through 'Biarat' or Viara in the Navsari area, 'Mugher' or Mulher fort, 'Nanderpar' or Navapur in Pimpalner, 'Nimgul' or Nimgull, 'Sinchelly' or Sindkhera, 'Tolnere' or Thalner, 'Chapre' or Chopra, and Arawd (Foster 1899, vol. I, pp. 87-89).

The route to Ajmer from Burhanpur took, in the case of Roe, the following route: Burhanpur–Raipur–Borgaon–Bikangaon–Akbarpur (on the Narmada, a few miles south of Mandu)–Chitor–Ajmer. He departed from Burhanpur on 27 November and reached Ajmer on 23 December. From Burhanpur the Deccan was easily accessible. First, across the Tapti from Burhanpur, Maharashtra was reached, and through it Andhra where the coastline included the European factory at Masulipattanam. On the other side, Rajasthan—and eventually, Delhi, Agra—was reached through places like Mehsana in northern Gujarat which in turn was accessed via Baroda and Ahmedabad. The details of these routes frequently occur in the travellers' records, more notably in the account of the travels of Peter Mundy (Temple 1914) between 1628 and 1634. The map showing the details of his routes between Surat and Burhanpur, between Burhanpur and Agra and between Agra and Surat brings this out clearly (map facing p. 39 in Temple 1914). In the case of the stretch between Agra and Surat, Mundy adopted a circuitous route, passing mostly through western Rajasthan. A little earlier, in September 1611, John Jourdain set out from Burhanpur for Agra and then came back to Surat from Agra. His stopping places are not always the ones selected by Mundy, but a comparison between their maps (for Jourdain's map, Foster 1905: 131) clearly show that the basic orientation of their journeys was the same and preferred by all contemporary travellers. The other noteworthy accounts of the travels between Surat and Agra via Burhanpur have been left behind by De Laet (Hoyland and Banerjee 1928, chapter 1) and Tavernier (Ball 1925, vol. I, chapter 3). Shireen Moosvi (1992) has argued that, although the Surat-Rajasthan-Agra route was shorter than the Surat-Burhanpur-Agra route, the latter was preferred because of the presence of intractable chieftains on the Rajasthan route. Further, along the route via Burhanpur there were grazing grounds for the pack bullocks all along the way.

The Konkan coast begins from the south of Daman and continues right up to the beginning of the Malabar coast. The narrow Maharashtra coast, framed by the Western Ghats, provided the overland links between Gujarat and Malabar, but perhaps an easier option was to travel by the sea. The entire coastline between Daman and Goa and between Goa and

Cape Comorin was marked out with all its ports in the accounts of such travellers as Tome Pires (16th century) and John Freyer (17th century). There is a graphic description of the annual flotillas arriving at Goa from Cambay in Francois Pyrard's late 16th century/early 17th century account.

This traffic is such that two or three times a year there come together from 300 to 400 vessels, called *Cafiles*, of Çambaye, like the caravans of Aleppo. At Goa the whole city looks out for these Cafiles and fleets, as in Spain they await those from the Indies (Gray 1888: 245).

Malwa could also be directly approached from the side of Ahmedabad or Baroda, without taking the route via Burhanpur. Tome Pires refers to the city of Champaner on this line of communication and says that Champaner was 5 days' overland journey from Surat and Rander (Cortesao 1944: 35).

The routes within Gujarat itself were equally understood, but the routes with which the Europeans were closely familiar ran from Surat to Ahmedabad via Baroda and also to Cambay, both from Baroda and Ahmedabad. They were perfectly familiar with the products of this region. Because the Europeans invariably approached the various ports on the Gujarat coast from the sea, they had no reason to travel along the routes which were not important to them, such as the main communication line linking the Ahmedabad area with places like Diu or Somnath.

IV. HISTORY OF SURAT AND THE SURAT AREA

IV.1 Archaeology and Ancient History

Of Surat itself, the earlier records are desultory. We have previously noted the report of a Roman coin from Surat and another Roman coin from the Surat area, and considering the Roman familiarity with Broach or Barygaza, there is no reason why the Romans would have to be unfamiliar with the geographical potential of the Tapti estuary. However, there is no substantive evidence, and the fact that Stavorinus (1798, vol. III, p. 11) found "ancient Grecian and Roman copper coins" in the money-market of Surat in the late 18th century adds an extraordinary amount of complexity to the issue. Stavorinus had acquired a few of them and offered the explanation—not necessarily correctly—that they were brought to Surat, "among other coins, by the Armenian, Persian and Arabian merchants".

Among the earliest positively local data that R.N. Mehta (1973-74) could come up with, were a few specimens of Jaina sculptures of the 13th century AD, currently in worship in the Chintamani Parsvanath temple of the city. However, accidental discoveries were made of a memorial stone of marble, a fragmentary capital of marble showing a seated pot-bellied and round figure (identified by Mehta with *Kichaka*) and a broken image made of schist, all of which belong to the 13th century AD. These accidental discoveries were made in the Rani Ovara locality, a riverside locality of Surat, and one can infer, with Mehta, 'a settlement on the cliff of Surat in the 13th century AD' dating from the Solanki dynastic period of Gujarat's history. Mehta keeps 'the problem of earlier beginning open to careful observation'.

That Mehta may well be right is suggested by the archaeological finds in the general area. In the Tapti estuary itself, not long before the river meets the sea, F.R. Allchin and J.P. Joshi (1995) report three settlements, the earliest of which—Malvan—was excavated by them in 1970. Period I at Malvan has been dated by them between 1400 and 1000 BC, which is supported by a single radiocarbon date from the late context and the ceramic analogies of the earliest excavated level. On the whole, this level belongs to the late/or post-Harappan tradition of the region which was characterized by, among other things, lustrous red ware, black-and-red ware, stone blade industry, copper objects, terracotta figurines of cattle and bone tools. Structurally it yielded very little except a shallow (not more than 1.1 m deep), comparatively narrow (1.5 m-1.6 m wide at the top and about 50 cm at the bottom), and irregularly aligned ditch which has been traced for a length of about 40 m. There are also traces of mud-brick structures, potholes, hearths and pits. The excavators suggest some ceramic parallels with the chalcolithic culture found in the Chalisgaon area of Maharashtra (near Burhanpur), and geographically this makes eminent sense. They further observe that tide possibly reached within 45 m of the site and that it was possible to bring boats in high tides and beach them at this point, as the fishermen of the area do still today. There is evidence of both domestic (cattle, buffalo, sheep and goat, dog, horse) and wild (mostly deer) animals in Period I of Malvan and the stone tools were manufactured at the site.

Period II of Malvan is primarily represented by an adjacent site called Ghor which has yielded evidence of a terracotta ring-well, glass bangles and pottery belonging to the second half of the first millennium BC. A Mughal period settlement (16th–18th centuries) was also found in the area.

The evidence of a late Harappan tradition in the mouth of the Tapti need not cause any surprise. In the Kim estuary between the Tapti and the Narmada, there is a site (Bhagatrav) of the same general character, and up the Tapti in Dhulia district there is a plethora of late Harappan sites (Shinde 1998). Similarly, the presence of pottery of the late centuries BC is not a cause of surprise either, because Gujarat as a whole was within the Mauryan empire.

It is unlikely that the main phases of the political history of Gujarat and the adjacent regions in the post-Mauryan era right up to the 4th-5th century AD did not affect the Surat area, although the direct historical references to it seem to be absent. In the second half of the 5th century AD there was a dynasty called the Traikutaka dynasty based in south Gujarat and Konkan. A copperplate inscription of the period refers to three administrative subdivisions under the rubrics of *Ahara* and *Vishaya*, all of which have been located in the Surat area itself: Kapura-*ahara* (in the Mindhola valley north of the Tapti), Antarmandali-*vishaya* (the area between the Purna and the Mindhola) and Iksharaki-*ahara*, the last one having a *Purohita-pallika* or a priests'/Brahmins' settlement or village. In all likelihood, *Lata* or south Gujarat, of which the Surat area was a major component, became a well-focussed geopolitical unit by this period. We keep on getting the names of various administrative divisions of the area in the land-grants of the successive dynasties. What is particularly interesting is that sometime in the 7th-8th century AD. *Navasarika* or modern Navsari near Surat was the centre of a geopolitical unit. From the mid-9th to the late 10th centuries AD south Gujarat was under the Rashtrakuta dynasty of the Deccan. The inscriptions of the period refer to a number of places in the vicinity of Surat: for instance, *Kantara-grama-vishaya* (modern Katargam locality outside the Surat walls), *Trenna/Tena-ahara* (modern Ten near Bardoli to the east-southeast of Surat), and the villages of *Kammanija* (modern Kamrej) and *Karanjavashika* (modern Karanj) and others, all in the area of the modern Surat district. More interestingly, there is an inscriptional reference to *Variavi* or modern Variao, where the European travellers used to cross the Tapti on their way from Surat to Ahmedabad. This has been mentioned as a *Pattana* or market-town or a small port town. Whether this means that Variao, a little upstream from Surat, "served the same purpose as Surat did later in the 16th century" is debatable, but there is reason to believe that the nucleus of Surat as a settlement goes back at least to this period. A number of modern villages around Surat have been identified in some inscriptions of the 10th century AD—"all within a radius of 12 miles south and east of Surat". *Navasarika* or Navsari repeatedly figures as the capital of a *Vishaya* or a major administrative division. It has been argued that the control of the Surat area was a bone of contention between the

Chalukyas or Solankis of Anhilwadapatan in Gujarat and the contemporary rulers of Konkan and the Deccan (for the inscriptional references in this section, Palande 1962). Again, geopolitically this makes sense. The situation continued till *c.* 1298 and later when the Muslims conquered Gujarat and the Deccan.

IV.2 The Muslim Period Till the Mughal Conquest in 1573

Even before Gujarat was annexed to the Delhi Sultanate in 1298 by Alauddin Khilji, it was repeatedly invaded in 1194 by Qutb-ud-din, the general of Muhammad Shab-ud-din Ghori. Bhimdev, the king of Anhilwadapatan, was defeated and the Muslim army penetrated as far south as Rander and Surat. The Hindu chief of the area based at Kamrej retreated to Surat, and finding things hopeless, surrendered to Qutb-ud-din who restored him to his possessions. During the reign of Muhammad-bin-Tughlak (1325-1351) in Delhi, there was a rebellion in Gujarat and Tughlak himself came down to subdue the rebellion and plunder Rander and Surat. There is also a tradition of a fort being built at Surat in 1373 during the reign of Firoz Shah Tughlak (1351-1388) as a protective measure against the raids by the Bhils from Rajasthan. In 1391, Zufar Khan, chosen as the governor of Gujarat by the Delhi Sultanate, appointed his son Maste Khan as the governor of Rander and Surat. Under the independent Gujarat Sultans in the 15th century, one comes across the name of one Muzaffar Shah who was the governor of Surat and whose son, Masti Khan, joined an unsuccessful rebellion against Sultan Ahmed Shah I who came to the Gujarat throne in 1411.

Except such desultory references one really does not know much about the history of Surat (for a summing up of whatever is believed or discussed, Meghani 1988: 2-28) till in the final years of the 15th century a rich trader named Malik Gopi settled here and was appointed the governor of the place by the Gujarat Sultan Muzaffar II. He was also appointed the governor of Broach. Malik Gopi, Malik being a title conferred by the Gujarat Sultanate, subsequently incurred royal displeasure and was reputedly put to death in 1515. The name Surat came into prominence during the time of Malik Gopi.

This was also the time when the Portuguese invaded Surat (1512). A castle was possibly built in Surat between the first Portuguese invasion in 1512 and the second Portuguese invasion in 1530. In 1531 the Portuguese invaded Surat for the third time. Rander was invaded too and eventually its prosperity declined. The need of a stronger castle in Surat was then felt by the Gujarat Sultans who asked one Safi Agha, a Turk, to build it. This man, according to *Mirat-I-Ahmadi* (Lokhandwala 1965), received the title of Khudaband Khan and built a fort of great strength, despite the attempts of the Portuguese to stop construction. There were infights among the various officials of the area to control Surat and its fort, which came to an end in January 1573 when Akbar (1556-1605) the Mughal laid siege to it. The Portuguese help was sought by the besieged governor of Surat, but the Portuguese did not want to take on the might of the Mughal empire and paid court to Akbar instead. Akbar too came to an understanding with them because the Portuguese power at sea could affect both Indian maritime trade of the period and the passage of the Muslim pilgrims to Mecca.

Whatever references we have suggest that Surat emerged into limelight as a port only towards the end of the 15th century. Between the 13th and 15th centuries its role was fulfilled by Rander which lay about 3 km upstream. After the opening of the Tapti bridge in 1877, Rander became closely connected with Surat and it remains so till now.

A detailed history of Rander is not yet written, and one has not moved much beyond what Campbell's gazetteer published in 1877. Arab merchants settled here in the 13th century, taking over the control of the place from the Jains who were there before them. A Jain temple was converted to the main mosque here:

> The Rander mosque has a special interest as bearing marked traces of its former owners, the Jains. Such of the images and more ornamental stones as were not broken to pieces, serve as steps in the doorway of the mosque, or have been turned to more dishonourable uses. But the pillars in the mosque and the cistern in the court-yard are both of Jain workmanship, and the hollow places in the walls, intended for images, have been allowed to remain unaltered (Campbell 1877: 300).

Duarte Barbosa in the early 16th century gives a glowing account of the prosperity of Rander: a city full of pretty houses and squares and carrying on trade with Southeast Asia in very large and fine ships. The Portuguese looted it in 1530, heralding its passage into obscurity. In the 17th century it became a pleasant suburb of Surat. There is no special reason to infer that Rander has a high antiquity, although Al-beruni in the early 11th century has been supposed to mention it as 'Rahanhour'. In the Portuguese sources Rander has been called Raynel or Ranel. In the early 16th century neither Ranel nor Surat could be particularly important as ports, because Tome Pires is more or less silent about them, although he plots them among the ports on the west coast coast of India (Cortesao 1944: Pl. XIII). For some reason, Father Monserrate in the late

16th century prefers a Latin name—Rhaneerum—for Rander, although he says that it was called Raynel by the Portuguese (Hoyland and Banerjee 1932).

IV.3 The Mughal Period

This period lasted from 1573, the year of Akbar's conquest, to 1733 when the Mughal administration run from Delhi gave way to a phase of 'independent governors' before the complete British takeover of Surat's administration in 1800. Within this period itself, there were three phases, the last two of which were marked by a progressive decline from the palmy days of the Mughal empire during the reigns of Akbar (1556-1605), Jahangir (1605-1627) and Shahjahan (1627-1657). The empire remained vigorous under Aurangzeb (1658-1707) but the fact remains that Surat was raided twice by the Marathas under Shivaji during this period—in 1664 and 1670—and for years afterwards, till the end of Aurangzeb's reign, the Maratha pressure on Surat was never really off. Between 1707 and 1733, the Marathas extended their control to the area around the city, thus cutting it off from its revenue base, and although the Surat governor remained nominally under the jurisdiction of Delhi, he was very much left to his own devices. But, for all its weaknesses from the modern point of view, especially its lack of concern in maintaining a powerful imperial navy to protect its traders who contributed a lot to its prosperity, the Mughals ran, for about two centuries, a remarkably well-knit empire from Afghanistan to the Deccan and from Assam to Gujarat. The imperial might was always being challenged in the peripheries, and the internal rebellions of sundry princes did not help matters, but what should actually be looked at is the fact that there was a well-oiled machinery of revenue administration over this vast area linked by a complex network of routes, trading mechanisms, and imperial control in the form of a vast bureaucracy with properly assigned responsibilities. There is also no point in forgetting the fact that the whole integrated system ran on a communication system based essentially on horses, dromedaries and bullock-carts.

As far as the history of Surat is concerned, much, if not the whole of the current version of it, is based on the records left by European travellers in Mughal India and the documents of European trade with Surat and other coastal sites in miscellaneous European archives, notably English and Dutch archives. A proper internal history of this trade and the city still remains to be written. An essential part of this enterprise would, of course, be a search for non-European sources. Even if such sources are found not to exist in a significant quantity outside the story of political relationships and intrigues, that fact should be adequately highlighted with concrete documentations.

IV.3.1 Surat in the Mughal Revenue and Administrative Network

The Mughal revenue manual of the time of Akbar, *Ain-i-Akbari*, describes Surat as a first-class port or emporium, making it the primary port in relation to such subordinate ports as Gandevi, Rander and Bulsara. The fruits of the area, especially pineapple, are favourably commented on, and the annual land-revenue was fixed at 1,90,35,177 *dams* or Rs. 4,75,879 or £47,588, according to the conversion made in Campbell's gazetteer (40 *dams*=1 rupee, 10 rupees=£1). The area was supposed to have furnished 2,000 cavalry and 5,500 infantry.

The Mughal administration of Surat and the Surat area was divided between an army man, the officer-in-charge of the Surat fort and the safety along the river or *Kiledar* and a civil official—*mutasaddi*—who was in charge of the civic administration of both the city and the area and presided over the collection of the customs revenue. Although this civil officer would have been placed under the Mughal regional representative—in this case, the *diwan* based in Ahmedabad—in view of Surat's importance as a city, he reported straight to the Delhi court and received orders from there. Dependent on the royal whims or favours, the civil post frequently changed; during the 30-odd years of Shahjahan's reign there were 11 *mutasaddis* in Surat, giving each of them an average turn of about 3 years. The average time of posting of the commander of the fort and the river was about the same. The *mutasaddi* or the clerk of the crown had at his disposal a body of about 1,500 troops, comprising both infantry and cavalry. In civil matters he had the services of a *Kazi/Qazi* or a Muslim judge and a public recorder or *Waknavis/ Waqianavis*. The policing responsibility of the city was entrusted to *Kotwal* who went round the city three times each night. Peace in the Surat area outside the city was maintained by *Foujdar* whose people looked after the highways and the villages. *Shahbandar* or the chief of the port looked after the management of the customs duty collection, marking goods as they were passed.

The details of this administration are found in various European travellers' records, most of which refer to *Shahbandar* and his duties in some detail. The city governor, *Qazi*, *Waqianavis/Vacanavish*, *Harcarrah* or intelligence chief, and *Catoual* have been mentioned by Ovington (Guha 1979a: 100-101). When a case was brought to the governor, he usually deferred to the advice of his subordinate officers. To maintain the dignity of his post he maintained several elephants, and while out on the back of an elephant he was accompanied by a bearer of fly-whisk to 'd'ive away the busy flies and troublesome mosquitoes'. *Qazi* was skilled in the municipal laws, acted as a judge and was consulted in all matters related to civil customs. A vivid account of *Kotwal*'s duties is given by Frere (Crooke 1909: 246):

> For after the keys are carried to the Governor it is the *Catwals* Business with a Guard of near Two hundred Men, to scower the Streets and Brothels of Idle Companions; to take an account of all People late out, to discover Fires and Housebreakers, and to carry all lewd Persons to Prison, which is solely committed to his Charge....

A comprehensive description of the Surat administration under the Mughals may be found in *Mirat-i-Ahmadi* (Lokhandwala 1965), according to which there were 29 departments to look after the administration of the city and the Mughal revenue area or *Sarkar* in which it was located. B.G. Gokhale (1979: 61) divides these departments into the seven general categories of the military (artillery commander and the superintendent of magazines), judicial (the chief judge, assisted by the *Qazis, Darogas* and the superintendent of civil courts), religious (apparently all concerned with Islam), revenue (the chief *Bakshi*, the *Amin* of the treasury and the superintendent of rent collections), commerce (the superintendent of horses, cattle markets, mint, salt, customs provisions, jewellery and fancy markets, corn markets), general administration (the Post Master, reporter and peons) and Public Works Department (superintendents of public works, hospitals and *Langar Khanas* or places where free food was supplied to the poor).

The office of *Shahbandar* used to be farmed out. In addition to the customs duties, there was also revenue from *Toddy* or spirituous liquor (about £600 annually, according to Gokhale 1979: 63) and the mint (£1,23,750 annually, according to Gokhale 1979: 63, citing the 17th century Italian traveller N. Manucci). Although closed in 1600-15, the Surat mint was restarted in 1620-21 but it operated only for a few days in a month. The fact that Surat was a very important port of the Mughal empire is shown by Manucci's reference to the minting of a silver coin type here in 1659-60 with the legend *Surat Bandar Mubarak* (the blessed Surat port). The main silver coin minted in Surat was *Mahmudi* which had a fluctuating value in relation to a rupee. The copper coins were called *Dams*. The office of the mint master used to be farmed out too.

There is also no point in underestimating the role of *Toddy* in the life of the people—low and high—in the Mughal Surat. Most of the travellers mention it and many of them give a good and correct account of how it was manufactured. Downton (Foster 1939: 146) wrote that only the Portuguese in India used to make some 'raysin wine' from sun-dried grapes. Otherwise the country afforded 'no wine, but artificial distillations of simples, like our hot waters'. In his words, "very tastefull they are, and wholesome; but not so strong. So ful of spirit as ours". This better strength of the British spirits made 'The Morres to prize them (i.e. ours) farre above theyr owne, and to esteem them for the best present or marchandize (that) can be brought them".

Campbell (1877: 93) has cited some detailed financial statements of the revenue of Surat and its region in the early 18th century, during the final years of Aurangzeb's reign when the trade of Surat was already in decline and its wealth ravaged by Maratha attacks. By this time the percentage of *ad valorum* customs duty also varied according to religion: "Customs at the rate of 2 per cent from Muhammedans, three and a quarter from Christians, and five from the Hindus" (Campbell 1877: 93). An estimate, cited by Campbell (1877: 93, note 2) of the total annual revenue of the Surat governorship puts it at £1,23,659.

IV.3.2 The Maratha Invasions, Plague and the Last Years of Mughal Control

This revenue and the general wealth of its traders made Surat a tempting target for the Marathas who under Shivaji became inimical to the Mughal empire. The first major raid was conducted in 1664. The Mughal administration got itself locked in the castle, and the city was given over, but for some resistance put up by the English and Dutch traders, to loot which, according to one reckoning, came to about one million sterling. Shivaji came back in 1669 and once again plundered the city. Large contributions were exacted by him from this city in 1670 too, and in 1671 one of his generals—Moro Pandit—did the same. The Maratha plunder of the city took place further in 1674 and 1675, and in 1676, with the capture of the fort of Parnera south of Bulsar, they established themselves permanently in south Gujarat. The first Maratha invasion of 1664 led to the construction of a brick wall around the city perimeter, which, in fact, prevented the Marathas from getting inside the city in 1679, 1680 and 1684 when they were plundering the area outside the walls. During the last years of Aurangzeb's reign, the danger which the Marathas posed to Surat was always there, and as late as 1706 they could lay siege, although unsuccessfully, to the city.

Aurangzeb's reign was marked by two other important points in Surat's history. First, in 1660 he sanctioned a large stipend out of Surat's revenue to the chief of the Sidhis of the island of Janjira (south of Bombay) who was in charge of the fleet of the Deccanese kingdom of Bijapur but now offered the services of his navy to the Mughal emperor. The Sidhis were descendants of the Abyssinians who found themselves in search of jobs—mostly as soldiers—in Indian courts. They were Muslims and had their headquarters in Janjira. Secondly, Surat was subjected to an outbreak of plague in 1684 and the epidemic raged in varying intensities for six years. The records suggest that this was part of a serious outbreak of plague between Basrah at the head of the Gulf and Goa, affecting the whole stretch of the coastal country in between. At times the number of death per day in Surat was about three hundred. The figure of about 80,000 has been cited for the total number of death both in Basrah in the Gulf and Tatta in Sind (Campbell 1877: 91, note 4).

The period between Aurangzeb's death in 1707 and the acquisition of virtual independence by the Surat governor Teg Bakht Khan in 1733 was politically very disturbing in the history of the city. The Maratha control of south Gujarat and the dying Mughal power in Delhi made the position of the Surat governor very insecure, and he could not effectively seek help from the Mughal governor of Gujarat in Ahmedabad either. Left to his own devices, one governor of this period, Rustam Ali, who became the governor in 1723, marched against the Marathas and wrested the control of the area around Surat from them. However, he was killed in an offensive against the Marathas in 1725 and was replaced as the governor by his son Sohrab Khan. There was some tussle for the governorship at this stage, and eventually Teg Bakht Khan, who was not Delhi's favourite previously, got himself confirmed by sending valuable gifts to Delhi. He became the *de facto* political chief of Surat in 1733 and assumed the title of *Nawab*.

IV.4 1733-1800: The Years Before the Complete British Control

The Maratha control of the countryside of Surat cut into its revenue, and in his quest to restore some of it, Teg Bakht Khan came to an arrangement with them, by which, in return of a fixed annual contribution, he would not dispute the Maratha control or their right to collect revenue. Secondly, he intended to keep for himself a part of the stipend sanctioned by Aurangzeb for the Sidhi chief in return for a naval protection of the trade of Surat. By this time the Maratha fleet was more powerful than the fleet of the Sidhis and the Sidhis were unable to extend the protection which was expected of them. In this situation, the English, particularly with their growing ascendancy in Bombay, wanted to obtain the rights of offering naval protection and the stipend which went with it, from the independent governor of Surat. With the failure of negotiations on this issue, there was tension between Teg Bakht Khan and the English, and eventually, especially after an English naval blockade of the Tapti mouth, all restrictions on the English were lifted. Meanwhile, the Sidhis were not willing to give their stipendiary rights away, and Teg Bakht Khan was forced to come to terms with them as well.

The struggle for Surat's governorship after Teg Bakht Khan's death in 1746 is confused but something in which the English and the Dutch both participated. Eventually, the English forces sent from Bombay landed at the Tapti mouth and advanced on the Sidhi and other *Nawabi* forces, winning control of Surat in 1759. According to the terms of an understanding reached with the *Nawab*, the English retained control of the Surat castle while the *Nawab* retained control of the city. The arrangement did not last long, and the English took complete control in 1800. From then on Surat became a part of the Bombay Presidency.

The significance of the British occupation of the Surat castle in 1759 cannot be overlooked, as it marked the beginning of a new trading world in which the British were paramount and had the support of the indigenous trading merchants of Surat. As Lakshmi Subramanian (1996: 97) has put it,

> Not only had the Surat shroffs in 1758 assured the Company authorities of financial assistance, but the Bania community of the city, led by their leader Jagannathdas Laldas, had assured Mr Spencer in 1759 of their support and had in accordance with their promise come forward to defray expenses incurred by the Company.

She calls this 'the Castle Revolution of 1759' which, according to her, 'came as the clearest manifestation of the changes in the traditional power and trading structure of the region'. Stavorinus (1798: vol. III, p. 59) takes care to mention that by the closing years of the 18th century, the British had so firmly established themselves there that they gave laws to all others; "and neither Europeans nor Indians can do any thing without their special approbation".

V. A BRIEF HISTORY OF EUROPEAN 'FACTORIES' IN SURAT

The European powers which maintained 'factories' or trading establishments in Surat during the Mughal period were the Portuguese, the English, the Dutch, the French, and marginally, the Austrians.

V.1 The Portuguese

Although the Portuguese began to command the sea off the Indian west coast right from the time of their arrival (1498) and consolidated themselves strongly at some strategic locations of this coast from Diu to Goa and further south by the first half of the 16th century, they satisfied themselves, as far as Surat is concerned, principally with their system of issuing 'passes' to the Indian ships operating in the Indian Ocean and earning a substantive amount of revenue from this system. However, with the advantage of their friendship with Mukarab Khan, the governor of Surat, and the friendly presence of the Jesuit missionaries in the Mughal court, they established a factory in Surat in 1611. By 1629 there was an Assistant Agent, and in 1630 there were Portuguese representations to the governor of Surat to drive away other Europeans, such as the English and the Dutch, from the ports of Surat, Broach and Cambay. In 1653, the head of the Portuguese factory got the Mughal permission to hoist one flag on the factory and another to carry before him when he went out. Around this time, he began to be called Director in place of 'Factor'. By 1695, the title changed to 'Captain'. They kept on issuing 'passes' to ships as late as 1670. This was also the year when the viceroy of Goa wrote to the governor of Surat asking for a reduction of their customs duty to 2 per cent. In the 1680s the Portuguese trade in Surat was supposed to be a serious competitor of the English trade in that city. In 1693 there was a talk of starting a Portuguese trading company, but one does not know if anything came out of it. The last we hear of the Portuguese factory in Surat is from Stavorinus (1798: vol. III, pp. 70-71). He writes that, although the Portuguese were the first Europeans to have established themselves in Surat, 'they are, at present, the least in power and respect'. Their chief, a Jew, was put in his own factory under a guard at the order of the *Nawab* not long before Stavorinus' departure from Surat: this was occasioned by a quarrel between his slaves and the slaves of the *Nawab* and the *Nawab* was angry because the Portuguese chief could not offer him satisfaction in this matter. The Portuguese trade of that period was trifling. They bought up the cloth pieces generally neglected by other Europeans because of their patterns and sent them to their settlements on the coast of Africa via Goa.

V.2 The Dutch

The Dutch had acquired a footing in Surat in 1618 when they obtained a charter to conduct trade unmolested and free from special custom house exactions or compulsory conversion to Islam. According to the terms of this charter, their internal disputes were to be decided by the chief of their establishment. In all, between 1618 and 1729, the Dutch had received their charter or *Firman* no less than 29 times, paying on each occasion considerable sums either to the Mughal court or its local representative for the renewal of the privileges (for the details of all these *Firmans*, Stavorinus 1798: vol. 3, chapter 6; for a general background of the Dutch in Asian trade, Prakash 1985: 9-23). The chief centre of the Dutch trading activities in the east was Batavia, because the original Dutch trading company was instituted to trade with Sumatra and Java. The rival Dutch companies united in 1602 and fought with the Portuguese for the control of Southeast Asian islands between 1602 and 1614. Batavia was made the Dutch headquarters in 1610, and in 1658 they established control over Sri Lanka. However, Surat was their second most important eastern trading establishment, with 15 Dutch factories subordinate to it: five in Iran (Gombroon or Bandar Abbas, Lar, Shiraz and Ispahan), nine in India (Vingorla, Agra, Ahmedabad, Cambay, Broach, Baroda and Sarkhej) and one in Arabia (Mocha in the Red Sea). This explains the importance of Surat in the Dutch scheme of trade. The Iranian factories were subordinate to Surat between 1622 and 1633. Then the smaller factories began to be looked after from Gombroon which was placed under Batavia. Mocha was under the control of Surat from 1620 to 1686 and was then made subordinate to Batavia. Of the Indian factories Vingorla was handed over in 1677 to the Dutch commander in Malabar. The Dutch factories in Cambay, Sarkhej and Baroda were withdrawn before 1670. The Dutch factory was withdrawn from Agra and Ahmedabad in 1716 and 1774 respectively. Only the Dutch factory in Broach remained throughout under the control of Surat. P. van den Broeke was sent in 1817 to set up the Dutch factory in Surat. Although he was successful in his mission, he went to Batavia but was posted back to Surat in 1620.

The most important competitor of the English trading in Surat was the Dutch. They fought a war with the English in 1672-74, the main item of dispute in the East being apparently the control of spices trade in Malabar and Southeast Asia and the control of trade to the Gulf. In 1694-95 they felt powerful enough to seek from the Mughal court the monopoly of European trade with Surat and freedom from customs duties in exchange for providing security to the pilgrim traffic between Surat and Mecca. This was refused but in 1699 it was arranged that the Dutch along with the English and the French should be responsible for the suppression of the piracies in the sea-lanes of the Indian Ocean, especially in the Red Sea sector. In the opening years of 1700s the Dutch in Surat had developed a dispute with the Surat governor, temporarily closed their factory and undertook a blockade of the Tapti mouth in 1704. The blockade occurred again in 1706-1707 and the offshoot was that the Dutch obtained considerable prvileges including the lump sum of £81,000, free trade in Broach and a reduction of 1 per cent in the customs duties in Surat.

The Dutch continued to be powerful in the early years of the 18th century. In 1709 a fresh charter gave them the right to acquire a place for trading in Surat and another place for the residence of the chief of their factory. In 1712 they were asking for a particular house—the house of one Itabar Khan—for the residence of its servants, with the provision that it would not be strengthened by guns or embankments. According to the charter of 1729 they were allowed to purchase land by the riverside to erect buildings for storing their merchandise (for the contents of all these charters Stavorinus 1798: vol. 3, chapter 6). It would be wrong to minimise the importance of the Dutch traders in Mughal India in any way. In his review of the Dutch sources for Indian history between 1590 and 1650, W.H. Moreland (1922-23) wrote that to leave out the Dutch in studying India's foreign trade in the 17th century would be almost like leaving out Calcutta or Bombay in writing the economic history of modern India.

V.3 The French and the Austrians

The French attempt to have an establishment in Surat, first in 1620 and then on a larger scale in 1642 did not bear much fruit. The French factory was eventually established in 1667, with the support of a French royal declaration and the floating of a joint-stock company with a substantive capital. The French ambassador to the Court of Shahjahan was le Sire de la Boullaye who received the imperial *firman* to set up a trading post in Surat in 1666 (for the details, Haudrere 1990). The French *Compagnie des Indes Orientales* functioned as the arm of the French government in Paris and was thus affected by the politics of the French court. In September 1671 a French naval squadron arrived in Surat, and although it stayed here for three months, the presence of the French navy in the Tapti did not particularly help the French commercial interests. Abbe Carre (Fawcett 1948) has left behind a dismal picture of the French affairs at Surat during this period, contrasting it in no uncertain terms with the level of organization attained by the British.

> ... I admired with surprise the dilegence and business methods of the English, which they carried out in quite a different way from ours. They stored in their

warehouses the English goods which filled seven large ships, and they then reloaded them with a large quantity of rich Indian stuffs. This amazed me, as I had seen the amount of goods already shipped by them *en route* at all their factories. I wondered how it was possible for them to carry so much cargo, and to see fifteen days suffice to equip and lade these seven English ships and dispatch them back to England, whereas in four months we French had not been able to find a full cargo for only one ship (Fawcett 1948: vol. 3, p. 780).

In 1680-1686 the major French figure in Surat was Francois Martin (on Martin's impression of Surat, Mitra 1995: 173-175) under whom the French factory prospered, but the French began to develop their main interests in south and east India, and they left Surat, leaving behind debts. It may be added that Abbe Carre described the Dutch as unmitigatedly hostile to the French interests in Surat.

Little can be said about the Austrian presence between 1707 and 1733. In 1717 the emperor of Austria sanctioned the Ostend company. In 1719 this company sent a ship for trade to Surat. The British and the Dutch extended only unmitigated hostility to the people of this ship, but the local governor was more amenable. The result was that two more ships arrived in 1719 itself and the Austrian trade continued for some time. Opposition never died down and rose to such a height by 1727 that the Austrian emperor cancelled the charter of the Ostend company (for the Austrians, Campbell 1877).

V.4 The British

The British East India Company received its royal charter on 31 December 1600. The first British ship to arrive at the mouth of the Tapti was in August 1608 under the command of Captain Hawkins who carried a letter from the English king to the Mughal emperor Jahangir requesting trading privileges in the latter's territory. Mukarab Khan, the then Mughal governor of Surat, allowed him to bring his merchandise to Surat, mostly lead, iron and some treasure. Hawkins' ship, the *Hector*, left for Indonesia but he himself left for Agra, leaving behind in Surat a British merchant and some British servants to sell the rest of his goods. Hawkins was not successful in receiving the necessary imperial charter for East India Company's trade in India, but he was received well, given the rank of a noble and allowed to marry an Armenian Christian lady who was well connected in court. The Jesuits and the Portuguese took care to see that the British attempt to obtain trading permission was not successful.

In September 1609 a second British ship, the *Ascension*, arrived but was wrecked off the Surat coast. The crew landed at Gandevi, a port to the south of Surat, and found their way to Surat where, because of the Portuguese unwillingness to see them settled in Surat city, they were lodged in the village of Umra, near but outside the city limits of Surat. At the end of September most of them left for Agra. William Finch, the merchant left behind by Hawkins in Surat was called to Agra in January 1610, and the English presence in Surat came temporarily to an end.

In September 1611 three British ships under the general naval command of Henry Middleton anchored at the mouth of the Tapti, which they found barred by the Portuguese. They remained outside the bar of Surat and were advised by Khojah Nasar, the governor of Surat and Mukarab Khan, his brother and the governor of Cambay, to go to the port of Gogha on the opposite shore of the Gulf of Cambay. Middleton refused to do so, and taking control of some Indian crafts in the area, demanded the safe arrival of all the English from Surat and Cambay on board before he could release those crafts. He then went over to anchor in Swally at some distance to the north of the Tapti mouth. Minor skirmishes were fought with the Portuguese on shore but nothing serious happened. The Surat governor occasionally came to the shore and had small trade dealings. In December 1611 both Khojah Nasar and Mukarab Khan were deposed from their governorships of Surat and Cambay but the change in governorship did not change things for the English. Mukarab Khan, the erstwhile Cambay governor, became the *Shahbandar* or the customs chief of Surat, and he refused to have any dealings with the British. After the safe arrival of the British from Cambay Middleton sailed away from Surat in January 1612.

In September 1612 the East India Company's *Dragon* and *Osiander* under the command of Henry Best arrived at the Tapti mouth. A merchant was sent to Surat, and the governor, presumably Mukarab Khan's successor, allowed him to trade. In the same month, a number of small Portuguese vessels entered the Tapti and captured some members of the crew of a British ship. In retaliation the British seized an Indian vessel, refusing to release it till the British were given the right to trade in Surat. Meanwhile, Middleton's ships which came in the previous year began to force themselves on the Indian ships in the Red Sea. When the news arrived, the viceroy of Gujarat came from Ahmedabad to Swally to deal with Henry Best and a charter was drawn for the British to pursue trade in Surat, Ahmedabad, Cambay, Gogha and any other part of the Mughal territory. In November and December the British and the Portuguese had a desultory skirmish in sea off the coast of Surat, but eventually the British ships came back to Swally. In

January 1613 the imperial charter confirming the earlier charter between the viceroy of Gujarat and the British was formally and publicly presented in Surat. Soon after establishing their right to trade in the Mughal dominions, the British ships under Henry Best left Surat. What is more important is that the Portuguese arrived at the mouth of the Tapti towards the end of 1613 and in retaliation of the privileges granted to the British, seized and carried off a large Indian ship with about 500-700 persons on board and a merchandise of about £1,00,000. This led to a Mughal expedition against the Portuguese in Daman and Diu under the command of Mukarab Khan who was by now restored to the governorship of Surat. No British ship arrived at the Tapti mouth in September 1613.

In October 1614 four British ships under Captain Downton reached the Tapti. Khojah Nasar, the then customs chief of Surat, went to Swally to persuade him to join the Mughals against the Portuguese. When Downton refused, he forbade anybody from Surat doing trade with the British. He thought that the British might be in collusion with the Portuguese. When he found his fear unfounded, he allowed the unloading of the British ships to continue. In December 1614, *Rahimi*, a large (1,500 tons with the ability to carry 1,500 pilgrims) Indian pilgrim ship was burnt in Gogha by the Portuguese. Meanwhile, a large Portuguese fleet arrived from Goa to destroy the British. In the ensuing combat (1615) the much larger Portuguese fleet was worsted and left the scene. After securing the goods they came for, the British ships left Swally in early March 1615.

Soon afterwards the revenue of Surat was handed over by the emperor Jahangir to his favourite son Khurram who later became the emperor Shahjahan. Khurram replaced Mukarab Khan as the governor of Surat by his own man Zulfikar Khan who was about to strike a deal with the Portuguese when a British fleet carrying Thomas Roe who had the proper status of a British ambassador to the Mughal court arrived. This fleet arrived at Swally in September 1615, and Roe soon left for Ajmer where the emperor was then residing. In September 1617 another British fleet reached Swally and stayed up to March 1618. In about this time Roe obtained for the British the absolute right and privileges to trade in the Mughal dominions.

Despite ups and downs, the British factory in Surat fitted into a vast network of trade from the Red Sea and the Gulf to Indonesia, competing mostly with the Dutch for the control of, or an effective share in, spice trade. Its importance remained unimpaired throughout the first half of the 17th century. As Campbell (1877: 86) puts it,

Pl. 1. Tomb, British Cemetery, Surat

Pl. 2. Tomb, British Cemetery, Surat

Pl. 3. Tomb, British Cemetery, Surat

Pl. 4. Tomb, British Cemetery, Surat

Pl. 5. View of Dutch Cemetery, Surat

Pl. 6. Tomb, Dutch Cemetery, Surat

Pl. 7. Interior of the Preceding Tomb

Pl. 8. Surat Castle

Pl. 9. Portuguese Factory, Surat
(Late Building?)

Pl. 10. Dutch Factory, Surat (Late Building?)

Pl. 11. Dutch Tombs, Bharuch

Pl. 12. Sundial inside the Dutch Factory, Bharuch

Pl. 13. View of the Dutch Cemetery, Ahmedabad

Pl. 14. Tomb, Dutch Cemetery, Ahmedabad

Pl. 15. Tomb, Dutch Cemetery, Ahmedabad

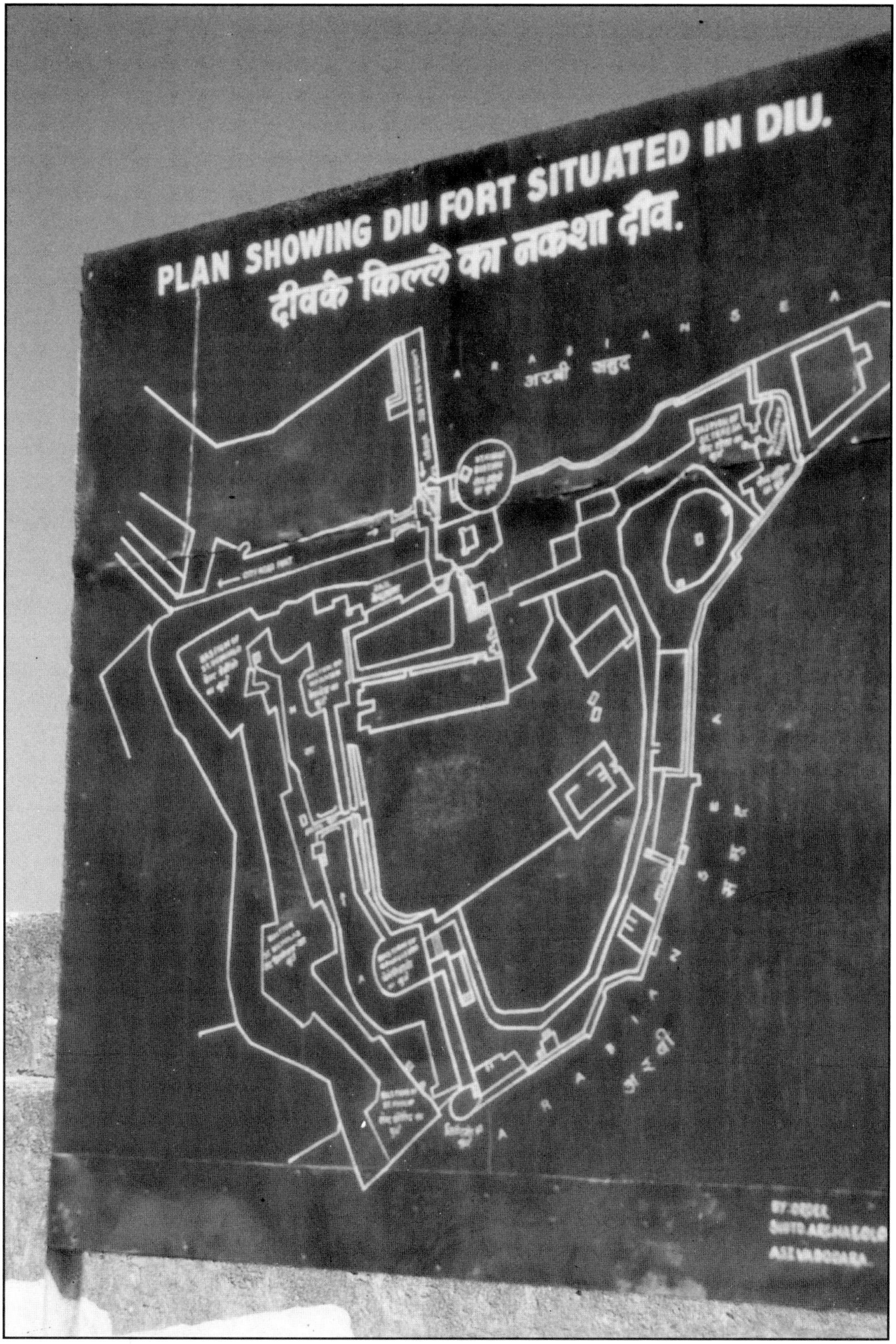

Pl. 16. Plan of Diu Fort

Pl. 17. Fortification in the Outskirts of Una, near Diu

Pl. 18. View of Daman

In 1614 (October) there were only two men in the English factory at Surat. In 1618 the company were allowed to build a house. In 1630 the president was dignified with the title of 'Chief of the Honourable Company of English Merchants trading to the East' and with the increase of trade additions were made to the strength of the Surat factory. In 1638 there were at Surat from 20 to 24 merchants and officers, and once a year the agents of eight subordinate factories came to render an account to the president at Surat. In 1642 the factory was fortified; in 1646 its quick stock was valued at £83,600; and in 1664 it is said, for space and furniture, to have excelled all houses in Surat except the Dutch factory. As early as 1623 the president of the English factory had begun to adopt considerable show. When he went out a banner and a saddle-horse were carried before him, and with him went a company of native servants armed with swords, shields, bows and arrows.

The British factories which were subordinate to the one in Surat were four in Gujarat: Ahmedabad (1 agent, 6 other persons) and Cambay, Baroda and Broach (1 agent and 4 other persons in each). The other factories were in Agra (1 agent and 6 other persons), Maslipattam (15 persons in all), Dabul (the Konkan coast, 2 persons) and Ispahan (1 agent and 8 other persons). In 1638, on the occasion of the president Methwold's departure from India, 50 British merchants met in Surat—3 chaplains and 2 doctors among them.

The British factory in Surat was on an even keel till the end of Shahjahan's reign. It was still the chief British factory in India in the first part of Aurangzeb's reign, but once the island of Bombay was transferred from the British crown to the East India Company in 1668, leading to the growth and increasing importance of Bombay, the importance of Surat to the British was slowly on the wane. As a reward of the British defence of their factory against Shivaji in 1664 (for the details of this invasion, Ovington provides a good source) the Mughal emperor remitted their customs duties for a year and ordered afterwards an abatement of 1 per cent in these duties. The years 1665-67 were marked by Anglo-Dutch war in Europe, with repercussions in the East as well. However, the British survived the Dutch onslaught, and Surat continued to retain its importance. In 1669 a council of eight members, five of whom were to be based in Surat, was selected to help the President who, although made the governor of Bombay, kept on staying in Surat. In the early 1680s the customs duties were raised by the emperor to 3½ per cent. Throughout the 1670s there was increasing competition from the British factories in east India and southern coasts. In 1701 an Act in Britain put an embargo on the import of silk and cotton cloth from India. The Maratha raids were making Surat an insecure place to do business in, although on each occasion Surat was attacked by the Marathas, the British defended themselves well. For instance, in 1670 Streynsham Master (Temple: vol. 1, pp. 190-192) defended the British factory house against Shivaji with the help of only 30 men and was later rewarded by the Company for his efforts with a gold medal. Earlier, in 1664 the British attempt to save their factory drew praise from F. Bernier (1968: 189): "The English, especially assisted by the crews of their vessels, performed wonders". It is also Bernier who says that Shivaji spared the house of the Capuchin missionary Father Ambrose on the ground that "the Frankish Padrys are good men" (Bernier 1968: 188). However, the increasing importance of Bombay and the Company's determination to carve out an independent and fortified base in Bombay could no longer be put aside. In 1687 the chief seat of the Company's trade was shifted from Surat to Bombay which was to become the capital of the Company's Indian possessions and the residence of the governor-general. Surat still had an agent and a factory, but the principal port of call for the British ships was now Bombay, the trade with Surat being the charge of the Bombay coasting vessels. Meanwhile, John Child, the then president, suffered a reverse in his struggle with the Sidhis, with the Mughal emperor taking the side of the Sidhis. The Company's fortunes in Surat were further impaired by the formation of a new British company whose chief representative Nicholas Waite arrived in Surat in 1700. At one point the new company got the upper hand and persuaded the Mughal administration to imprison the old company's Surat representatives—about 107 of them. Although the imprisonment was within the confines of their own factory and although the number of the imprisoned was slowly reduced, it was only in 1707 that the dispute was set to rest and all 'old' factors released. The two companies merged together in Britain in 1702, but that did not have much impact on the relationship between their representatives in Surat.

The uncertain years after the death of Aurangzeb did not help matters, and at one stage the factory had to remain closed for 3 years (1712-1715). In 1716 the British returned to Surat, armed with a new charter from Delhi which more or less freed it from the arbitrary demands of the local governors, replaced customs duties on imported goods with an annual tribute of only £1,000, gave the right to establish a separate custom house and granted about 15 acres of land for building a new factory. The local governors, however, continued to be intractable, and although the Surat trade remained prosperous, the days of its importance were numbered.

Meanwhile, the overall political situation of the region had changed, with the Marathas under the Peshwa administration becoming very powerful by the middle of the 18th century. The Marathas had their eyes on Surat and combined with the British to try to bring down the local 'independent' governors and their allies, the Sidhis. The Marathas soon lost interest and the British found themselves alone in their struggle against the local governors and their allies. In 1759, a British force arrived from Bombay and fought to take possession of the Surat castle.

Till 1800, the year of the complete British takeover, the years after 1759 were a period of double administration: the British in charge of the castle and a local *Nawab* in charge of the administration of the city. The revenues of Surat during this period were shared between the *Nawab*, the British and the Marathas. The dying years of the 18th century proved to be particularly bad for Surat's fortunes.

> The famine of 1790 pressed sorely upon it, and the religious riot of 1795 would seem to have been both sufficiently fierce and long enough to continue to cause Surat serious injury. Trade, too, was deserting the city, and in the decline of his revenues the nawab was allowing great part of the city walls to tumble into pieces and moulder away (Campbell 1877: 134).

VI. SURAT'S TRADE: TRANSPORT, COMMODITIES AND NETWORK

The external network of Surat's trade in the 16th to the 18th centuries was well understood before the beginning of this period: the Red Sea ports, the Horn of Africa and the east African coast down to Mozambique, the southern Arabian coast, the Gulf with its principal focus on such places as the island of Hormuz, Bandar Abbas or Gombroon, Basrah, etc., the entire coastline of India both in the west and the east and the island world of Southeast Asia. If Surat participated in trade with China during this period, that must have been indirectly through Southeast Asia. One does not come across any direct reference specifically citing Surat. The tapestry of trade over such a large zone could never have maintained a single or uniform texture, even over a limited length of time. It would be subject to all kinds of variations dependent on the local economic, political and even climatic factors affecting production, and trade on the oceanic level. The same is broadly true of a seaport's internal network — its myriad links with the hinterland which, in the case of Surat during the Mughal period, must have encompassed virtually the whole of the subcontinent in varying proportions. Geographical common sense dictates that Rajasthan, the upper part of the Indo-Gangetic plain including Panjab, and Malwa would be important in this scheme. The claims of other areas cannot be put aside; Gujarat has had a traditional linkage with Khandesh in the upper Tapti valley and the interior Deccan. At the same time, Khandesh and Deccan have other outlets too, especially in the ports along the Konkan coast. The southern Indian coasts—both Malabar and Coromandel coasts—kept their links with Gujarat more by sea than by land, although there could be land routes for the transmission of goods between Maslipattam on the Andhra coast and Gujarat. It would not, of course, be prudent to put emphasiz on this land route. The east coast of Andhra, Orissa and Bengal was reached from Gujarat by sea, as a part of the overall network reaching the Strait of Malacca and Indonesian and nearby islands. It would also not do to forget that during this period, the traditional trade between the countries at the rim of the northern Indian Ocean was drawn into the vortex of the contemporary Atlantic trade covering both Europe and the New World. Europe's tin and copper and the New World silver, among other things, were certainly finding their way to places like Surat in Mughal India.

To determine the varying intensity with which all these regions across the Indian Ocean and the Atlantic were touched by the mercantile spider's web with Surat in its centre is essentially the business of the economic historians studying the archival records of different merchant groups operating during this period in all these areas. As our purpose here is to set the material evidence of European trading establishments in Gujarat in its historical context, we shall only draw attention to the general level of intensity of this network and the basic commodities traded.

But first, some reference should be made to the issue of transport. Large-scale transport of goods overland needed large-scale organization, and it appears from the records of European travellers that the professional carrier group of *Banjaras* played a major role in this. One reads of very long trains of *Banjara* oxen transporting foodgrains and other merchandise from place to place. For the transport of delicate, brittle stuff one hears of *Kahars* or people who carry things by tying a package at each end of a bamboo pole and by putting that pole on their shoulder. The merchants could organize their own caravans too and travel with them. J. de Thevenot, a Frenchman who reached Surat in 1666, writes that he went from Surat to Aurangabad with a French merchant who had 10 wagons and servants, etc. with him: "We were eight Franks in Company, and in all five and forty men" (Guha 1979b, vol. II). On the road he met a Bishop who was on his way to Surat for returning to France. "We continually met caravans of oxen and camels upon our road, and some

I saw that came from Agra, consisting of more than a thousand oxen loaded with cotton cloth" (Guha 1979b, vol. II, p. 125). On the whole, the inland transport of goods over long distances was a highly organized affair. Tavernier who has given a thorough description of the route from Surat to Agra via Burhanpur (Ball 1925: chapter 3) wrote that this journey of 35-40 days cost 40-45 rupees. Alexander Hamilton (Foster 1930: vol. 1, p. 89) was categorical about the efficiency of the post in the Mughal dominion. At a distance of 10 miles all along the major ways, there were caravanserais which were linked by 'runners' who carried the post. The Mughal court could receive within eight days the news from the furthest parts of its empire.

Shipbuilding was an important industry of the Gujarati ports including Surat. Mughal imperial ships could be around 1,000 tons and the ships of Indian private merchants ranged from 200 to 500 tons. These ships were meant for the high seas. For the coastal trade and riverine traffic in the estuaries, there were smaller vessels built mostly locally. Towards the end of the 17th century Abdul Gafur of Surat had about 20 ships of 300-400 tons of his own. Between 1707 and 1736 he and his family had some 34 ships, one of which was *Hussaini* of 400 tons and 25 guns. Although some Portuguese ships operating out of Goa could be even of 2,000 tons, the estimate one receives about the average British and other European ships reaching Surat broadly conformed to the range of weightage of Indian ships. M.N. Pearson (1971) points out that in the early 16th century the "Muslim ships' weighed 375-800 tons. A list of 1525 shows that the biggest Portuguese ship in India weighed 550 tons. The size increased with time. After 1550 there were Portuguese ships of 1,000 tons in India and in the early 17th century the Sultan of Bijapur owned a ship of 2,000 tons, although an average of 300-400 tons was far more common. There is a reference to ship-carpenters in Surat by J. Ovington (Guha 1979: 124):

> And the very ship-carpenters at Surat will take the model of any English vessel, in all the curiosity of its building, and the most artificial instances of workmanship about it, whether they are proper for the convenience of burthen, or of quick sailing, as exactly as if they had been the first contrivers. The wood with which they build their ships would be very proper for our men-of-war in Europe; for it has this excellence, that it never splinters by the force of a bullet, nor is injured by those violent impressions, beyond the just bore of the shot.

In the late 18th century Stavorinus (1798, vol. 2, chapter 3) comments favourably on the shipbuilding industry of Surat. The ships built here were both large and long-lasting. He mentions a ship which annually transported Haj pilgrims till 1770 and was built earlier than 1702. He also describes the basic shipbuilding technique current here and comments: "Their vessels are very lasting, and can go to sea for many years, before any repairs of the hull are at all wanted". A special word of importance was attached to the teak wood of the forests of Daman in this connection by a Portuguese authority: "... from our arrival in India to the present time all the vessels (ships, galleons, caravels, galleys, foists and all the rest), whether belonging to Muslims or Hindus, have issued from these forests, which are inexhaustible" (Moreland 1939). It was argued by Moreland (1939) that the Arab and Gujarati ships of the Indian Ocean of *c.* AD 1500 were weak because they did not use iron nails in the construction. These were good only for fair weather voyages. For the use of strings instead of nails in ship-construction, he says that the wood used could be too hard for nails (in this case, he calls this teak 'benteak') or that iron was then costly in the Indian market.

The depth or intensity of the trade network can be guessed only at a general level. One may begin by drawing attention to the diary of the Dutch P. van den Broeke. The entry for 25 February 1625 says that a caravan of 450 camels carrying 600 bales of Bayana indigo, 264 bales of refined saltpetre and 36 bales of cotton goods and drugs under the junior factor Cornelis Arentssen had arrived on that day to Surat from Agra. On the same day two British ships—*Blessing* and *William*—had sailed for Britain with a cargo of Sarkhej indigo, Malabar pepper, cotton goods and a large quantity of cotton (Moreland 1932: 10).

The caravan trade and the sea trade were naturally closely linked because the ships could be filled at the port only by the goods transported from the hinterland. Gokhale (1979: 78) argues that "the influx of large *caphilas* meant an accretion of an itinerant population of between 5,000 to 10,000 persons at a time". It has been said that every 10 or 20 days, 200 carts left Ahmedabad for Cambay laden with merchandise. It must be remembered that any estimate of the intensity of trade can be meant to convey only a general idea because this must have been subject to various economic forces of the period, mostly the question of fluctuating demands and supplies. It has been estimated that between 1658-59 and 1681-82—a span of 23 years when Surat was at the heyday of its mercantile supremacy–84 British ships arrived in Surat, an average of about 3 ships per year. In the table of ports of origin of ships passing Bab-el-Mandeb, i.e. the southwestern tip of the Arabian peninsula, in 1611, 1612 and 1616, there were 3 ships from Surat in 1611 and 1 in 1616. The Sind ports contributed a larger number: 4 in 1612 and 14 in 1616. Other Indian ports were involved too—Gogha, Dabhol,

Diu, Goa and miscellaneous ports of Malabar. Diu sent 1 ship in 1611, 3 ships in 1612 and 7 ships in 1616 (for this table, Steensgaard 1973: 90).

The general level or intensity of contact can also be guessed from the presence of Gujarati merchants in various parts of the seaborne Asia. In the context of the 15th century Pearson (1971) speaks of "the inevitable Gujaratis with their ubiquitous cloths" in the points east of Aden, as far as Hormuz, Bengal, Pegu, Sumatra and Malacca, and east Africa where they virtually monopolized trade, collecting gold, ivory and slaves in exchange for their cloths. On the basis of Tome Pires (Cortesao 1944: vol. 1, p. 45) Arasaratnam (1994) writes that by the end of the 15th century there were about 1000 Gujarati merchants domiciled in the port of Malacca and a few thousand more Gujaratis in the back-up support of these marchants. A separate *Shahbandar* was assigned to them. It is tempting to quote Tome Pires on this point.

> There used to be a thousand Gujarat merchants in Malacca, besides four or five thousand Gujarat seamen, who came and went.... The Gujaratees were better seamen and did more navigating than the other people of these parts, and so they have larger ships and more men to man them. They have great pilots and do a great deal of navigation (Cortesao 1944: vol. 1, p. 45).

Peaceful merchants moving from island to island in Southeast Asia, the Gujaratis did not previously keep armed men in their ships, and "if they were captured and (their captors) wanted to kill them all, they did not resist. By the time of Tome Pires they had many men-at-arms to defend their ships, taking cue no doubt from Pires' compatriots, the Portuguese.

On the other hand, as Godinho wrote in the context of Surat:

> There will be found at all times of the year in Surat ships from China, Malaca, Macassar, Maluca, Jacatara, Maldives, Bengal, Tenacerim, Ceylon, Cochin, Cananore, Calicut, Mecca, Eden, Suez, Magadaxo, Caxem, Mascut, Madagascar, Ormuz, Basra, Sind, England; in short from every part of the world (Moraes 1952: 127).

The extensiveness of the network and the tremendous expansion of the mental horizon in this regard may be highlighted by the case of an Armenian merchant called Hovhannes, which has been narrated by Steensgaard (1973: 23-28). His journal describes his journeys between 19 December 1682 and 6 December 1693. He left Ispahan for Surat, travelling through Bandar Abbas. From Surat he travelled to Agra, and having stayed there and travelled in its vicinity and the Deccan for some time, he left for Lhasa where he stayed for 6 years till 1692. From Lhasa he went to Calcutta via Patna and Hooghly where his journal abruptly ends. He left Ispahan with a small capital, mostly in the form of English cloths but some as a bill of exchange drawn on Shiraz. He sold the cloth in India and bought indigo with the proceeds. It took him about a year to convert 3 camel loads of cloth into approximately as many loads of indigo, and the ease with which he moved around is clear from the following summary given by Steensgaard (1973: 24) of his movements after he reached Surat in March 1683:

> He was in Surat from 23rd March to 15th May, in Aurangabad from 29th May to 15th July; he arrived in Burhanpur on 21st July and continued after some time to Sironj, where he stayed from 11th August to 24th November. He was in Agra from 2nd December to 6th January 1684. From Agra he made a detour to Khurja to buy indigo, and on 13th March he was back in Agra. Eight days later, on 21st March, he again left Agra... he was in Surat already on 12th April.

Part of the indigo was sent through an Armenian based in Surat to Ispahan and part to Basrah. He left Surat again on 29th May to repeat the preceding year's internal journey, buying this time cloth and sending that to Ispahan through his Armenian connections in Surat. With an increased capital he left for Lhasa in 1686, dealing in gold and musk and once taking 'the almost 1,250 mile long route from Lhasa to Sining on the Chinese border to buy tea and gold'.

This was not an isolated incident. Steensgaard (1973) underscores the fact that in the early 17th century, after the Portuguese lost Hormuz, the British ships were carrying many individual merchants with their bales of goods. In 1626-27 the British ship *Blessing* on her journey from Surat to Gombrroon or Bandar Abbas carried 6 merchants with altogether 65 bales and chests. On the same route the *Royal James* carried 100 passengers with a total of 689 bales and carried, on her return journey to Surat, 70 passengers with a total of 70 bales of goods.

Such trade can in no way be described as primitive. There was a system of maintaining meticulous accounts, handing over part of the transport to others and transfering money by bill of exchange. This was certainly no peddler's trade. Ina B. McCabe (1999) has strongly contested the notion that the Armenian traders of the period were peddlers: "It is difficult to speak of the Armenians as peddlers once one realizes that they were the bankers to the Safavids and had brought their organization with them" (McCabe 1999: 349).

The two most important commodities exported from Surat were cloth and indigo. There were different varieties of textiles, each suitable for a specific purpose. Their centres of production were spread throughout Gujarat and there were important production centres in Burhanpur, Sironj and Gwalior in Madhya Pradesh, Agra and Banaras in Uttar Pradesh and Patna in Bihar. Some varieties came from Panjab, Sind, Andhra, Karnataka and Tamil Nadu as well. Their market was organized in Surat, with traders and their agents procuring goods from different parts. Particular varieties of cloth were manufactured at particular places and the varieties were oriented towards export in particular foreign markets. Trade in silk cloth which was acquired from as far as China and Bengal was a part of this general trade in textiles. Cotton yarn was in great demand too. Large quantities of cotton yarn were bought in various areas of Gujarat, with Broach alone selling 10 to 12 maunds of cotton yarn to the British every day. Also included in the textiles trade were a large number of ancillary craft industries such as embroidery, the manufacture of gold and silver threads, tailoring, printing of fabrics, etc. The European companies sometimes tried to organize textile production according to their own specifications but the weavers were seldom obliging. Gokhale (1979: 101-102) finds a figure of 75,000-1,00,000 pieces of cloth sold annually to the Dutch and the British. When one adds to this the number of pieces required for internal consumption and the markets in Southeast Asia and elsewhere, an annual production of about a quarter of a million cloth pieces implying a turnover of many millions of rupees every year becomes a distinct possibility.

The second most important commodity traded in Surat was indigo. Indigo was produced in some areas of Gujarat—notably Jambusar near Broach and Sarkhej near Ahmedabad—the Agra area where Bayana in Rajasthan supposedly produced the best indigo in India, Lahore and the Deccan. Care was taken to avoid the adulteration of the bales of indigo, and the European companies had their agents and factors at the relevant places to acquire the stuff for export from Surat.

Surat was a redistributive centre of spices which came both from Southeast Asia and south India and Sri Lanka. Pepper, clove, mace, nutmeg, cinnamon and cardamom–each had its own main production areas and there were struggles among merchants to control them. Pepper was double its price in Bantam in Indonesia in Surat, the profit margin thus being quite impressive. In 1669-1686 the British bought 15.26 million pounds of black pepper in Surat for export to England.

Other agricultural products figure too in the list of export commodities from Surat—butter, wheat, rice and sugar, among them. The main sources of butter were Broach, Ankaleshwar and Baroda and single orders of 400-500 maunds are known. Wheat came from north India and there were orders of 2,000 maunds at a time. Rice and sugar came from the same area and elsewhere. Sugar went principally to the Gulf and rice principally to Southeast Asia. In 1629 the British sent 10,000 maunds of rice to Batavia. Among the other agricultural and forest products, mention should be made of shellac and tobacco, the latter product in cultivation in Gujarat and Andhra by the early part of the 17th century.

Except iron and steel which were exported from India, metals, mineral products, coral and ivory came to Surat from outside. A lot of copper and tin from the British mines went to Surat. The Chinese and Japanese copper came through the Dutch company, although the British too brought Chinese and Japanese copper for the Surat market. According to the estimates obtained for 1661-62 thousands of maunds of imported copper were sold in the Surat market. The main competitor of the British tin in the Surat market was the tin from Southeast Asia. Derbyshire lead had a ready market in Surat, and there was a steady influx of gold from various points of origin including Abyssinia, Arabia and the Guinea Coast. Silver came in great quantities as ingots and currency, the most important item of the latter being Spanish dollars.

In Surat there was an important market for precious and semi-precious stones, the carnelian from Cambay and coral from the Gulf, the Red Sea and the Mediterranean being among them. Diamonds and rubies were included too, a traditional source of diamonds being the mines of Golconda in the Deccan. Quicksilver was imported from China, Japan and Europe whereas saltpetre was produced in India and exported. Turtle shells, ivory, rhinoceros horn and hide came to Surat from various sources, principally Africa and Southeast Asia. A British estimate of 1619 lays down that about 2,000 maunds of ivory could be annually sold in Surat. There is also no need to forget the import of a great deal of wine from Iran and Europe.

Perhaps the best summing up of the commodities traded in Surat was offered, among the European travellers, by Thevenot (Guha 1979b: 30-31).

> At Surat, are sold all sorts of stuffs and cotton cloths that are made in the Indies, all the commodities of Europe, nay and of China also, as purceline, cabinets and coffers adorned with torqueses, agats, cornelians, ivory, and other sorts of embellishments. There are diamonds, rubies, pearls, and all the other precious stones which are found in the east to be sold there also: musk, amber, myrrh, incense, manna, salarmoniac, quick-silver, lac, indigo, the root roenas for dyeing red, and all sorts of spices and fruits which are got in the Indies and other countries of the Levant, go off here in plenty; and in general all the drogues that foreign merchants buy up to transport into all parts of the world.

The foregoing list of commodities based principally on Gokhale (1979) and contemporary European travellers' records does not discuss the fluctuating markets in these commodities and the various factors influencing their price mechanism, but on the whole this list underscores the importance of Surat as a very rich hub of commerce in the Indian Ocean trade of Mughal India and the strands of its spider's web of contacts. We use the description 'spider's web of contacts' deliberately because that is what the tradings contacts were like. They were not always straight point-to-point affairs, taking European cargoes to Mughal India and returning to Europe with Indian cargoes. In many cases, the merchants picked up, in the course of their Asian travels, goods which would be in demand in some sections of the Asian market itself and travel to those areas to sell them. The European merchants cut into all the sectors of Gujarat's indigenous trade—the ones to the Red Sea and the Gulf, the African coast, the coastal trade with Konkan, Goa and Malabar, the spice trade with Southeast Asia.

In our chapter on Gujarat's maritime trade we discussed the chronological depth of this basic pattern of the maritime links of the region and there we also pointed out how some of it lingered on even in the 19th century. By the late 18th and early 19th centuries Surat was no longer the principal port of the west coast, having been replaced long back by Bombay. What is interesting is that even in the context of the late 18th century Parson's testimony clearly lays down the fact that Surat was not yet dead, nor had she lost her old network.

> ... there are more than 30 ships, from five hundred to one thousand tons burthen each, which load here communibus annis, with cotton-wool for China and Bengal; besides several ships of smaller burthen, which trade to the different ports in the gulph of Persia and the Red Sea, with piece goods of various sorts, made of silk, silk and cotton, and all cotton: all these ships belong to the natives of Surat, but have English captains, officers, and colours (Parsons 1808: 261).

He then goes on to describe the imported and exported commodities. His list is also corroborated by the lists available in Milburn's account a little later (Milburn 1813: 160-161).

VI.1 Comments on the Historical Character of Surat's Trade

One cannot move away from this trading world rooted, as we have observed, in deep antiquity without raising some issues about its specific historical character. Giorgio Borsa (1990) has tried to apply the three defining traits of F. Braudel's 'economy–world' (*economie monde*) to Surat during this period. First, this world is defined as a space which changes slowly. There is no doubt about the validity of the Indian Ocean trade of this period as a single economic space defined along the Aden-Malacca axis. The second feature of Braudel's 'economy-world', i.e. it has to have a dominant urban pole, is difficult to apply in this case, because instead of a single dominant urban pole there were a number of urban foci all along the ocean rim, corresponding to all its trading areas. However, if an element of dominance has to be sought among these cities, especially in such areas as navigation, trade, industry and credit, perhaps some dominant role can be envisaged for Surat which had a large fleet, merchant capital, large multi-ethnic and multilingual population and a superbly organized mercantile structure. The third Braudelian element in this case is that his 'economy-world' implies a number of economic areas, each with its own characteristics but shaped at the same time to serve the interests of the dominant town. What is envisaged is an area ordered in three concentric circles: a highly developed and diversified centre with a middle region and beyond it, a periphery. Borsa's delineation of Surat as the dominant centre fully understands the compulsions of both economy and geography:

> The centre of the Indian Ocean *Economie Monde* could be visualized as a quadrilateral dominated by Surat, the perimeter of which was formed by the Coromandel and Malabar coasts and by the two arterial roads that connected Delhi to Surat and to the Ganges Delta. This centre was surrounded by a number of economic areas—the Red Sea, the Hadramut coast, the Persian Gulf, the Bay of Bengal, the Malacca Straits, North Sumatra and Java—connected with the centre by a system of oceanic and feeder routes and participating in a varying degree to its economic development. In the third girdle, we could place the African coast seaports where ships from Gujarat, Aden and the Hadramut coast came to exchange textiles with gold, ebony, ivory and slaves; the Maldive Islands, the main source of cowrie; and some territories in the Java Sea like Flores, Timor, the Banda islands and Borneo that were visited intermittently by Indian merchants (Borsa 1990: 7)

This 'economy-world' came to an end, not because of the presence of the European merchants who linked it to the contemporary global system, but because the Safavid empire of Persia, the Ottoman empire in the Red Sea and the Mughal empire of India fell or declined almost simultaneously. This disarticulated the economic system by bringing about insecurity in all areas of economic activities. Two more factors signalled the defeat of the Asian merchants in competition with the European ones: their unwillingness to accept the joint stock company system of the Europeans, which enabled them to raise more capital beyond the means of the wealthiest Asian *mahajan* or money-investor, and the absence of support from their ruling states, which again the European merchants received in plenty from their own governments.

Ashin Dasgupta (1979) in his masterly study of the decline of Surat between 1700 and 1750 does not find any of the three general explanations particularly acceptable: the silting of the Tapti, the growth of Bombay and the menace of piracy in the sea-lanes. In 1701 Surat was not a crippled city, having at least 112 sea-going vessels at that time. As we have argued above on the basis of the testimony of Parsons and Milburn, Surat was far from being totally crippled even by 1800. Dasgupta (1979: 8) writes,

> The real explanation for the eclipse of Surat lay in the simultaneous weakening and collapse of the three great Muslim empires which had in the first place brought the city to her eminence two hundred years ealier.

As early as 1798 Stavorinus (1798: vol. 3, pp. 116-117) pointed out that the first cause of the decline of Surat was the fall of the Mughal empire. Secondly, he mentions the growth of Bombay which, apart from the British peace, had also the advantage of the trade of the Deccan being diverted to that place. Thirdly, in Surat itself, the rise of the British power then made the capitalists "afraid of putting out their money to interest, or of risking it in the operation of commerce". The third observation of Stavorinus is in contrast with Subramanian's observation that the British ascendancy in Surat was possible only with the help of the indigenous trading community and that this period witnessed the emergence of an Anglo-Bania order. It is possible that Stavorinus, while writing this, had only the Dutch capitalists in mind.

It is also worth pointing out that Dasgupta's observations on the causes of the decline of Surat were echoed long back by Milburn (1813: 161): 'subversion of the Mughal empire' and 'the decrease of the lucrative trade to the Gulfs of Persia and Arabia, owing to the anarchy in which Persia is involved, and into which the Turkish dominions have long been sinking'. By the Gulf of Arabia Milburn meant the Red Sea.

VII. SURAT AS A CITY: THE GENERAL PICTURE

There are abundant references to various features of the Mughal city of Surat in the records of many European travellers, and there is no difficulty about understanding its general features and the categories of its inhabitants. Before discussing some of its important features in detail, it might be useful to collate a general picture of the city.

As far as the different stages of its growth from the 13th-14th century to the early 18th century is concerned, we are on an insecure ground, although some hints are available both in travellers' records and R.N. Mehta's sketches of the successive urban occupational areas of Surat on the basis of 'archaeology, topography and toponymy'. Initially, in the 13th century, if not before, the high ground along the river bank was used for settlement and the low-lying areas to the east were transformed in places into tanks known as *Rani Talav* and *Bhaga Talav*. The high ground, according to Mehta, is a stretch of about 0.75 km long and 300 m broad, lying between *Mulla Khadaki* in the north and *Makai Pul* in the south and covering the present area of the fort and Mughal Sarai. To its east one encounters slopes and low-lying areas interspersed with some high grounds. In his map of the 13th-14th century riverside Mehta shows the locality of *Raja Ovara* which, according to him, denotes an entrance or *ovara* from the river into the city. In his map for the 15th century two more *ovaras—Lati Ovara* and *Mirbahar Ovara*—are added to the side of *Raja Ovara* and apparently there were significant additions in the southeastern direction in the form of markets, a locality called Gopipura and *Gopi Talav* or the tank of Gopi. This tank, although copiously described by various travellers, is now silted up and analysed by Mehta in the following terms: a circular earthwork of about 2 km, which is 50 m broad at the base, 5 m high and *c.* 10 m broad at the top. The earthwork was first protected by a brick wall and then further strengthened by a 16-sided stone pavement. Mehta infers that in the low-lying area to its east, there was a sluice area with a silting chamber attached. Thus there was a mechanism to regulate the flow of floodwater into the tank and de-silt the coming water. The earthwork, now used as a Muslim burial ground, has an opening near Navsari bazaar, with a cruciform limestone-built step-well nearby. According to Mehta, 'The construction of this tank is ... in a style very well known in mediaeval Gujarat'. It was originally a local tank of the neighbourhood and was taken up in the 15th century by Malik Gopi who reputedly established Surat as a part of a development programme in this direction.

Thevenot in 1666 already noticed the lack of repair of *Gopi Talav* but was otherwise full of great praise for it—"It is certainly a work worthy of a king, and it may be compared to the fairest that the Romans ever made for public benefit" (Guha 1979b: chapter 14). To Peter Mundy it was simply 'the Great Tancke' of Surat, "admirable for its workemannshipp and bignes", and he describes it in detail:

> Suratt Tanck is neere half a mile about, made into 16 squares, built of great hard hewen stone, having from the upper Superficies stepps descending downewards about 20 in number, which goe round about. Betwene every 5 or

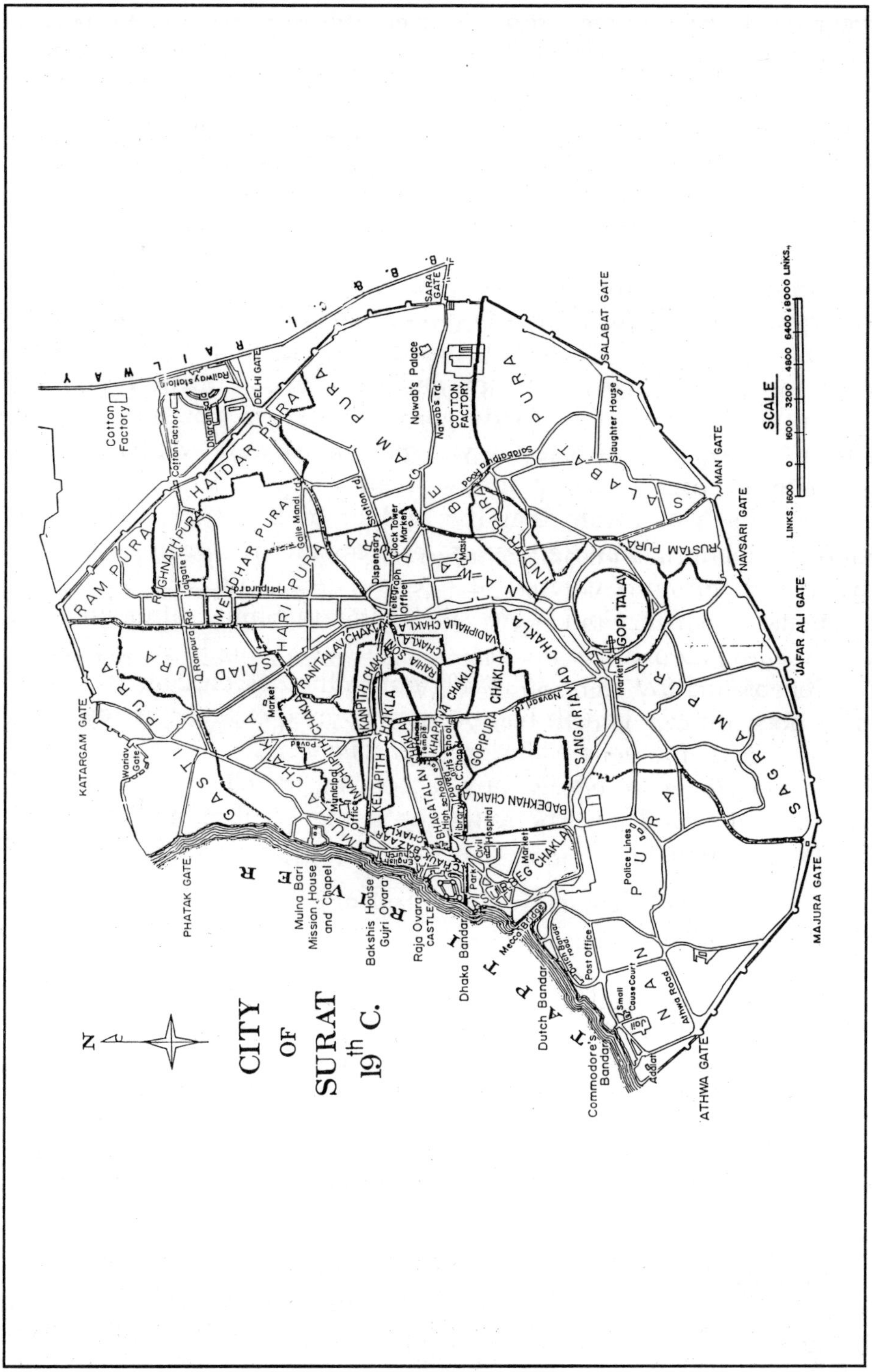

Fig. 6. Surat (after Campbell 1877; courtesy M.B. Meghani)

6 is one much wider than the rest to walke on. It hath 8 entrances for people and Cattle, which goe downe wards; with walls, turretts and very faire pavement of great Stones. In the midle of all stands a house. The passage where the water cometh in deserves also notice, walled on each side, vaulted and supported with pillars. In the Midle of this Entry lyes a very prettie small Tanck, hard by the greater. This I conceive is that the troubled water might settle there before it runne into th' other, beinge that the litle one must be first filled... (Temple 1914: 31-32).

Watermelons and musks used to be grown in the bed of this tank in the dry months. There were 'many faire Tombes, gardens and trees' around the tank which, when full during the rains, offered a pleasant prospect and was visited by Mundy and his friends "manie tymes for recreation'. In the rains, the 'Toddy gardens' (i.e. gardens full of palm trees from the sap of which toddy was produced) were 'very faire and green, yeilding forth a most fragrant smell'.

Della Valle was aware that the builder of this tank, Gopi, was mentioned, about a hundred years earlier, in the writings of the Portuguese historian Giovanni di Barros. According to him, the descendants of Malik Gopi were still living in Surat, although in a penniless state ('hath scarce bread to eat') and he thought it very mean of the citizens of Surat to be so indifferent to the descendants of a man 'who for their publick benefit had been at so great expense' (Grey 1892, vol. I, pp. 32-34, for della Valle on *Gopi Talav*)

In fact, there is hardly any European traveller who has not commented on *Gopi Talav*. The following reference in Hamilton (Foster 1930: 91) is evocative:

I was one day walking by the side of a great tank or pond near Surat in company with an English lady.

This was in the late 17th or early 18th century. Considerably earlier, towards the end of 1579, Father Monserrate commented,

... the eye is delighted by the flights of marble steps which surround this lake in a broad sweep. These steps are two hundred feet wide, and are divided into several sections. In the centre rises a finely built tower which is reached by boat whenever the citizens resort thither to amuse themselves (Hoyland and Banerjee 1932: 10).

The additional urban features of the 16th century included the fort built by Khudaband Khan between 1540 and 1546 which was an irregularly shaped square of about 200 m with round towers and curtain walls and a 20 m wide ditch encircling it on all sides except the side of the river (for an original description of the castle, Stavorinus 1798: vol. 2, pp. 473-474). The ditch is now filled up. Although built in the mid-16th century, this castle is somewhat unlike the typical Mughal period forts that one comes across northern India: rather crisply defined enclosures with running parapets offering great scope for musketry. The Surat castle was a stolid affair with possibly a limited number of cannon placements to dominate the river. Its main purpose was not so much to defend Surat as to protect it from any danger coming up the river. Freyer (Crook 1909: 248-249) speaks of '30 or 40 stout Pieces of Ordnance' and '300 *Luscarries* or Soldiers armed with Gun, Sword and Buckler'. In 1751 the castle fell to the Sidhi admiral of the Mughal fleet—by that time the Mughal administrative organization was in its final days–and in 1759 it was captured by the British who held it jointly with the post-Mughal *Nawabs* of Surat till 1842 when the last *Nawab* died. Between 1759 and 1859 two flags used to fly from its bastions: the British flag from the southwest bastion and the *Nawab*'s flag from the southeastern one. There was a small body of European and Indian troops in the castle till 1862. In his book *The Empire of the Great Mogol* published in Latin in 1631 (Hoyland and Banerjee 1928) J. De Laet, one of the directors of the Dutch East India Company found this fort defended by 'a number of warlike engines', some of which were of exceptional size. Its only gate opened on what De Laet referred to as 'Medon' or *Maidan* and described as 'a most beautiful plain'. References to this *Maidan* are frequent in the European travellers' records.

About 200 paces to the southwest of the castle was the court or the palace where the *Nawab* of Surat held his court in Stavorinus' time. He did not find it impressive. The entry gate was protected by a guard of Abyssinians and a couple of old cannons, and the complex reminded him of a 'ruinous hovel, than the entrance to the residence of a prince'.

The mint was apparently located in the same area. Stavorinus found it "a large pile, surrounded by a high wall", with work-sheds along the walls, an elevated apartment for the supervisory staff on the right hand and an adjacent walled square enclosure for the melting of the metals used for the currency.

The other major feature is a mosque known as the mosque of Marjan Sami, located near the tomb of Khudaband Khan in the Nanavat locality of modern Surat. The burial grounds outside the city limits in the northeast also developed during this period. There was also an expansion of settlement in the eastern direction. In the mid-17th century a *Sarai* or inn was built in the Nanavat area near the tomb of Khudaband Khan by Hakikat Khan who was the deputy of the Mughal princess Jahanara,

Shahjahan's daughter, to whom the revenues of Surat were gifted by the emperor in AD 1643. To the east of this inn, which still stands in its entirety and presently houses the Surat municipal administration, there is a Jain temple full of marvellous wooden and stone tracery work, whose image was consecrated in 1645. This temple is known as the temple of Chintamani Parsvanath.

Before Shivaji's raid in 1664, the city was not, as Godinho (Moraes 1952: 126) very clearly emphasized, walled but had a low enclosure (possibly of mud) pierced by four gateways. According to Godinho, the defence of the city as a whole rested with the Surat castle. Shivaji's raid in 1664 led to the construction of a burnt-brick fortification wall around the civic localities which then existed. This fortification is now mostly destroyed. But on the basis of his fieldwork Mehta argues that its east-west alignment was from the riverside to the locality of Burhanpuri Bhagol and the north-south limits were from the tomb of Adrus to the Makkai bridge. He further points out that the possibilities of the watercourses in the north and south were used while planning this wall, around which a moat also was dug. Four gates—Badshahi gate, Makkai gate, Majura gate and Navasari gate—are marked along the wall in Mehta's plan. The fortification was given the name of *Shaharpanah* or 'the protection of the city'.

> This monument is practically destroyed. Only parts of the brick fort are seen in Dhastipura, Rampura and Saiyadapura and in Ruderpura, Nanpura area, but the moat and the fort line along with its gates is completely ruined in other parts and it is replaced by a ring road which runs partly on the fort-wall and partly on the moat and within the wall line (Mehta 1973-74: 87).

By this time the burial grounds of the British, Dutch, the Armenians and the Portuguese came up beyond the city limits.

J. Ovington who was the chaplain of the British factory for some time in the 1690s found the city fortified "with a wall, which is flanked at certain distances with towers and battlements, occasioned by the frequent incursions of the enemies.... The entrance into the city is by six or seven gates, where are sentinels fixed continually, requiring an account, upon the least suspicion, of all that enter in, or pass out of the city" (Guha 1979: 95). The gates apparently numbered more than four.

When Thevenot arrived in Surat in 1666, only 2 years after Shivaji's first invasion, he found only an earthen wall, 'almost all ruinous'. But he adds that a new wall of brick, 'a fathom and a half thick', was being built because of the necessity of making it strong after Shivaji's invasion.

The new wall made Surat smaller, because, according to Thevenot, "a great many houses made of canes that formerly were within its precinct are now left out" (Guha 1979: chapter 7). The earlier mud-wall has been mentioned by various early travellers including Mundy (Temple 1914: 29) who described the city of Surat as being 'neere 2 miles in Compasse, environ'd with a badd ditch, excepting towards the River side'. According to him there were seven gates along this periphery. However, De Laet who found it, except on the riverside, 'fenced by a dry ditch and an earthen rampart' noticed only three gates—the Variao, Burhanpur and Navsari gates.

According to Campbell's gazetteer in 1880, the masonry of the inner wall or *Shaharpanah* had been 'almost entirely removed'. It describes the condition as reported in 1817: the height varying between 20 and 28 feet and the width between 8.5 and 12 feet; 12 gates—Wariavi on the north, Syedpuri and Burhanpuri on the east, Navsari and Majura on the south, Mecca and Badshahi on the west, Dacca, Raja Ovara (or Custom-house water-gate), Mir Ber, and Mulla Khadki (or Lati) on the riverside. The gates were flanked by towers.

By the early 18th century Surat expanded further, and the new localities were taken inside the city limits by erecting another wall around them. It was built in 1715 and called *Alampanah* or 'the protection of the whole world' (of Surat). It covered an area much larger than the ground covered by *Shaharpanah*. It may be observed that *Shaharpanah* covered less than a half of the city now within the second wall or *Alampanah*. If we assume that the former covered all the civic localities which then existed, we have to assume further that the city expanded more than double during the 50-odd years that elapsed between the constructions of these two walls. We find it a bit unlikely that the first wall covered the whole of the city area. In any case, *Alampanah* had about 12 gates: Fatak in the northwest, Variavi and Katargam on the north, Lal and Delhi on the east, Sara in the southeast, Salabatpura and Mana on the south, Navasari, Jafarali and Majura on the south and Athava in the southwest. Campbell's gazetteer adds some more detail. When Surat towards the close of Aurangzeb's reign began to be frequently attacked by the Marathas, the people built small defences and set cannon on them. No attempt was made for the first 10 years to link these defences and convert them into a wall. Haidar Kuli Khan who was the governor of Surat between 1717 and 1719 collected stones from *Gopi Talav* and began to construct an outer wall which could be completed only during the succeeding governorship of Tahawar Khan who also gave it the name *Alampanah*. The circuit was about 5.5 miles (*c.* 9 km). Its height was between 14 and 20 feet and the width 7 and 8 feet. Each gate had a roofed-over platform with guns. These platforms were 25 to 30 feet high.

Some interesting insight into the configuration of different localities within the city has been provided by Mehta's study of the current names of these localities. First, they suggest the existence of four approaches to the city from the riverside: *Mulla Khadaki* or *Lati*, *Gujari* or *Mirbahar*, *Raja Ovara* and *Furja*. The first two terms are indicative of markets while the last one indicates a toll station. *Raja Ovara* means royal entrance. The markets in this case could mean the international market-places of the city where one also finds two suggestive names in use—*Nanavat* (banking locality) and *Mughal Sarai* (Mughal inn). Banking places and inns are most likely parts of an international market scene. It appears that the old market extended from Marjan Sami's tomb in the north to the castle in the south. It is interesting that the locations of the former British factory and the Portuguese house are easily visible in this area. The Dutch house lay in the area of *Furja*, south of the castle. The location of the French establishment is not yet clear. Even at that point of time there was a suburb called Shahpur (*pur* being indicative of such a locality) to the east of the old bazaar area. There were also minor bazaars as adjuncts to the main market and Mehta groups them into two—the earlier group with names ending in *pith* and a later group with names ending in bazaar. By the end of the 15th century, the eastern limits of Surat were marked by the tanks such as *Rani Talav* and *Gopi Talav* and the different neighbourhoods up to these limits were peopled by different Hindu, Muslim and Parsi groups. The area up to the *Alampanah* walls was peopled mostly by minor professional and artisanal groups catering to the various needs of the city. The names in these localities which recalls potters, blacksmiths and miscellaneous caste-groups clearly suggest this fact.

A straightforward account of the general houses and city-planning of Surat has been given by Ovington (Guha 1979a: 95-96). Many houses were 'fair and stately', built of brick and stone, flat-roofed and with open windows and tiled floors. The poor mud-and-reed houses were thatched by palm-leaves. Some streets were too narrow but some of normal breadth. The market roads were very crowded, especially in the evenings when the traders hawked their wares in the streets. "For here they stand with their silks and stuffs in their hands, or upon their heads, to invite such as pass by to come and buy them". The open ground—'the spacious vacant place, called castle-green—'in front of the castle was used for laying goods in open air—'both day and night, excepting the mussoun time'—before they were loaded for ships. Here 'the English, French and Dutch, with the natives, placed their bales, and prepare them as loadings for their ships'. His reference to *Mughal Sarai* is clear: 'In the middle of the city is built a noble spacious caravanserai, or inn … for here are no public houses for the entertainment of guests or travellers…' (Guha 1979a: 139).

The Italian traveller Pietro della Valle came to Surat in 1623 and found the city to be of 'handsome greatness, and for these countries, of sufficiently good building' (Grey 1892: 30). Peter Mundy arrived in Surat in 1628 and found it a city "neere 2 miles in Compasse, environ'd with a badd ditch, excepting towards the River side'. There were 7 gates, the Broach, Burhanpur and Navsari gates among them.

> Here are some reasonable long straight streetes, as that goeing to Nunsaree gate etts., some faire buildings scattered heere and there, a strong Castle furnished with good ordinance. By it is a very faire spacious greene, called Castle Greene, alsoe the Bunder (*bandar*) or wharffe, where Goods are emarqued to be transported unto shipps or Juncks rideinge att Swally or the River's mouth (Temple 1914, vol. 2, pp 29-30).

Della Valle's estimate of the size of the city of Surat in Jahangir's time has also been borne out by the Dutch traveller Francisco Pelsaert (Moreland and Geyl 1925: 39): fairly well built and 2 (Holland) miles in circumference. There was no city wall but there was a ditch and there were 4 city gates on the land side. The German traveller J.A. de Mandelslo, a guest in the British Factory in 1638 does not mention any ditch but refers to three gates—the ones leading to Broach, Ahmedabad and Cambay, and to Burhanpur and Navsari.

The general habit of piling up dirt in front of one's houses has also been commented on, and the outburst of plague between 1684 and 1690 has been related to this habit.

Comments were not always complimentary. T. Herbert (1638: 36), who identified—wrongly, of course—that Surat was Ptolemy's Muziris, found no worthy monument or mosque in the city except *Gopi Talav* and 'the English garden without the town' with 'pretty walks, sweet flowers and a water-worke'. Tavernier (Ball 1925: 6) found 'a city of moderate size' without any decent house with the exception of 9 or 10 well-built ones. F. Martin (Mitra 1995: 173-175) found the city "very badly built, dirty and infectious in several places, filthy and full of water during the time of rains".

By the late 18th century things were perhaps a little more disagreeable.

> The place cannot be said to be an elegant city, as there are few good streets, and the narrow lanes and alleys are so dirty and stinking, that a man must take great care how he walks. None of the streets being paved, in the wet season it is a quagmire, and in the dry a small breeze of wind raises the dust in such clouds, as to make either walking or riding very disagreeable. The European gentlemen all keep palanquins and chariots, but even these are uncomfortable in the dry season, as it is too hot nine months in the year to bear the blinds or glasses shut (Parsons 1808: 253).

Stavorinus wrote of an 'intolerable stench in the city'. It was both difficult and noisome to pass through several parts of the town before sunrise 'on account of the horrid stench arising from carrion, human ordure, and other impurities'. As the sun's heat increased, the situation became somewhat more bearable. Freyer called the city "very nasty by their want of privies, and their making every door a dunghill". Godinho contrasts the poor exterior of the rich Muslim houses with the splendidly rich furnishings of their interior. However, there was no doubt about the grandeur of its wealth. Francois Martin himself thought that "it was a small Babylon because of the coming of all nations of the world". In the same vein Godinho wrote:

> You will find there Spaniards, Frenchmen, Germans, Englishmen, Hollanders, Flemings, men from Dunkirk, Italians, Hungarians, Poles, Swedes, Turks, Arabs, Persians, Tartars, Georgians, Scythians, Chinese, Malabarians, Bengalis, Ceylonese, Armenians, with other infinite variety of barbaric and strange nationalities (Moraes 1952: 125).

Hamilton describes the wealth of Abdul Gafur, a merchant, with some awe. According to him (Foster 1930: 89), Gafur

> drove a trade equal to the English East India Company, for I have known him fit out in a year, above 20 sail of ships, between 300 and 400 tons, and none of them had less of his stock than 10,000 pounds, and some of them had 25000; and after that foreign stock was sent away, he behoved to have as much more of an inland stock for the following year's market.

Not all the descriptions of the Mughal Surat dwell on its wealth which was no doubt accompanied by an equal measure of dirt and dust. Perhaps the following description by Niccolao Manucci catches the essential image of this city more than any other European traveller of the period:

> It is a great delight to take a seat on the bank of the river and behold the numerous boats which shot to and fro like arrows. It is the largest port in India and the best river (Irvine 1907, vol. 1, p. 61).

The records of European travellers infuse a glow—all too uncommon in the usual Indian historical records—into the ordinary sphere of life in Mughal Surat: the generally prevalent feeling of amity between the Moors (Muslims), Banians (used in the general sense of Hindu traders including the Jains), Christians (Surat had a Capuchin missionary establishment as well) and Parsis; the lack of violent incidents; the Banians' emphasis on vegetarianism and non-violence; fermented palm juice or *toddy* as a popular drink; the attraction of the 'dancing wenches' (Ovington uses an Indian term for them—*Kinchnees* or *Kanchanees*); the myriad groups of mendicants—in fact, a whole, vibrant panorama of Indian life that has been observed in close quarters with an air of simple curiosity about it. Thevenot commented that the town was so full of people that lodgings could hardly be had in January to March and even in April, the months which marked the peak of the maritime season.

VIII. THE DETAILS OF SOME IMPORTANT LOCALITIES AND FEATURES IN EUROPEAN RECORDS

VIII.1 Swally, Swally Road, Swally Hole, Swally Marine

The Indian name is *Suali* which lies in the vicinity of the villages of Koliwara in the south, Rajgiri in the north and Mora in the east. The modern name is easily recognizable in Swally and its variations in the early European records. By all accounts this is the place where the English, the Dutch and possibly other European ships berthed, avoiding the bar at the mouth of the Tapti which provided the usual anchorage for the Indian vessels. Initially at least the Portuguese vessels too used to anchor in the Surat Road or the Tapti bar. Considering that goods have been unloaded and loaded at this place for about two centuries, and considering that there were structures of different kinds in and around the place, Swally deserves a more than careful consideration among the areas in Surat and its vicinity where archaeological excavations can be fruitfully undertaken in future.

Basically it was a sheltered anchorage protected from the open ocean by a sandbank which could easily be got over by ships in high tide. It lies to the south of the Tena or Tanna creek and at some distance to the north of the Tapti mouth. The total length of the area seems to be several kilometres from the Suwali Point or the promontory created by the inward turn of the Tapti to the Tanna creek.

A claim has been made by some later writers that Swally was added to, or 'discovered' in the map of India by the first British sailors. In view of the sources discussed here, it is difficult to maintain this position.

The high point of the initial Portuguese-British conflict at the river mouth of Surat was in 1614 when the Portuguese fleet riding at the bar of Surat could not destroy the English fleet under the command of Nicholas Downton. The Downton report (Foster 1939) contains a wealth of detail about this conflict, and although it mentions *Swallie*, he is silent about its specific description or the circumstances of its discovery by the British. These details are best discussed in *The Journal of John Jourdain, 1608-1617* (Foster 1905). The Portuguese-British conflict began in 1611 when a British fleet under Henry Middleton found, on his arrival in September 1611, the mouth of the Tapti barred by a Portuguese navy from Daman and Diu, which prevented him from sending his boats up the river and anchoring his ships near the land. Previous to this, the British ships used to anchor at the Bar of Surat. For instance, the *Hector* under John Hawkins anchored at the Bar of Surat on 24 August, 1608.

John Jourdain was present in Surat during the Middleton incident, having been in India since September 1609. According to him (Foster 1905: 177), the commander of the Surat castle and the governor of the area (the latter named by him as Hoghenazam or Khwaja Nizam) were both interested in helping the British, provided they were interested in setting up a factory and trade. If so,

> he would shewe us a place where the shipp might ride within muskett shotte of the shoare, in eight fathome water, and might land their goods att there pleasure without danger.

When the governor received assurance that trade indeed was the only British motive behind their presence in Surat, he told Jourdain that 'the place was called Swallye' and about a league north of the Tapti mouth and that Middleton could easily find it by sending small ships. He also said that he would have Jourdain guided by the master of one of his own ships but to avoid the Portuguese interest, Jourdain would have to be dressed like a Mughal.

> We departed by night and the next morning wee came to Swalley, wheare the Portugalls weare washinge of their cloathes. We lay in the towne till the eveninge, that they ewent aboard. They knewe mee not because of my apparrell. After they were gone aboard wee went by night and got neere the waters side ... (Foster 1905: 177-178).

The rest of Jourdain's experience here does not concern us but what is clear is that both the Mughals and the Portuguese were aware of the existence of Swally. None of them needed it for themselves because their ships could always ride at the Bar of Surat. It is only the hostile circumstances of the period which forced the British to go to Swally and eventually they found that the place afforded easy shelter, some protection and even the advantage of finding the Tapti mouth within the distance of cannon shots from here.

The most evocative description of the general atmosphere of Swally comes from Peter Mundy who was there in February 1633 (Temple 1914, vol. 2, pp. 311-312).

> The Mareene of Swally is a place on the strand or sand, close to the waterside where the ships ride in the port (or hole), where for the tyme there is great doeings, as landing and ladeing of goods. There being a Factor Appoynted with an assistant to discharge the place; Also a purser of the Marecue, for matter of provision, shippes, stpores, etts, whoe have their severall Tents, besides the presidents great tent set upp to receive him when he commeth downe about the companies affaires, which this year was solely let to us (though not so much for our ease). Before it is erected the English coullours or Red Crosse on a Waste (field), etts. Here are also 50 or 60 Soldiers with a Captaine of the Guarde, livetennant, corporalls, etts to secure the place for Portugalls etts. Enemies. Theis have also Tents, vizt. The Captaine of the Guarde by himselfe and the court of guarde ... for all the rest. Here are also the coopers, Sailemakers, etts. With several Temts belonging to each shipp, where they trimme (put in order) their caske, mend sailes, drye powder etts shipps business. Here is a great Bazaare, made by Banianes, of Bambooes, Reed, etts, where all manner of Necessaries and Commodities are to be had, Also provision, especially Toddy, which findes currant and quick dispatch. The said Bazaare (as soone as the shipps make way to be gon) is sett on fire.
>
> When they (the ships) are enordered for Persia, Then come downe the Moores (Muhammedans) goods and their owners, whoe have each their severall Tent according to his quallitie, where they remaine untill their goods are shipped off, soe that it resembles a good Campe for Souldiers, munition (provision) tents, people, etts, And great Mart for the aboundance of Rich goods all over the Mareene. It is a place of great Trouble, care and vexation for the while, as I my selffe proved by experience, and could demonstrate, having soe many shipps to unlade, relade, to receive from one and Consigne to another, all in hast, one upon the neck of an other.

It is clear that within a period of a little more than two decades of its being given over, so to speak, to the British, Swally was a thriving commercial place. It is not clear from Mundy's description if the Dutch too had begun to use the facilities of Swally by this time. He does not refer to the Dutch presence. His reference to the Muslim traders coming down with their goods to Swally and staying in their own tents means that they booked themselves and their goods in the British ships ordered to sail to Persia. From the records of the French Abbe Carre (Fawcett 1948: 768-769) who was in Surat in about 1673, it appears that the French too used Swally. There is no doubt that the French then had a warehouse at Swally (Fawcett 1948: 781). In the context of 1690 Ovington wrote that only the European ships were permitted to ride at Swally, "but no Indian vessel is allowed that freedom, they are either all of them to enter the river of Suratt, or to anchor at the mouth of it"(Guha 1979a: 72). It is apparent that the Mughals thought it better to keep the European ships together for an effective monitoring of their movements. The place of the Portuguese in this set-up is not clear. According to J. de Thevenot (Guha 1979b: chapter 15), all vessels could come here to anchor but none except the British and the Dutch after 1640. They had some warehouses in that place. The prohibition was imposed because there were thefts of goods, which affected the realization of customs dues. The British and the Dutch had even gardens at Swally by the seaside and each had a small harbour where they put their boats or barks.

Mundy made a second visit to Swally in the 1660s and noted major changes there (Temple 1936: 70).

> Here on Swally sands I found some alteration since my last beeing in this place, which was in February anno 1633, the Presidentts tentt beeing removed a greatt deal further up and pitched upon a rising ground, a spacious place enclosed, wherein are courts, yards, warehouses, chowtrees, ballaconnas (upper storey, *balakhana*), etts, (that is) to say elevated roomes fairely built of bricke, timber, etts. To sit, eat, drincke, discourse and take the aire, covered with tiles; a plattforme allsoe with ordnance. The bazaare likewise completely built with a handsome streete of shoppes, covered with bricke tiles allso.

As the term 'tentt' has been used on both occasions and as the term certainly stands for brick and timber houses in his second visit, it is possible to suggest that 'tentt' on the former occasion too did not always mean something of canvas or cloth, as it means today. Houses of semi-permanent materials seem to have been there even in 1633. It is clear, however, from Mundy's sketch of 'Swally Marine 1656' that orthodox canvas tents were also there.

Compared to the other notices about the distance of Swally from the mouth of the Tapti, Mundy's estimate is precise: "From Swally Hole to the mouth of the River Tapia (Tapti)–9 miles" (Temple 1936: 69). Among the other miscellaneous references to Swally, one may mention Abbe Carre's reference to a British factory at Swally: "Afterwards I went to the English factory at Swally where I found all the captains of the fleet in a conference with Mr (Matthew) Gray" (Fawcett 1948: 773), Mr Gray being the person in charge of the Surat factory then. The following record of Ovington is noteworthy: "Within less than half a mile from the sea are three Choultries or convenient lodgings made of timber, for the English, French and Dutch factors, at a bow-shoot distance each from other; and made fit for their reception by a variety of apartments" (Guha 1979a: 72). A little before this period John Freyer was welcomed by Matthew Grey (mentioned also by Abbe Carre) who took care of his 'entertainment',

> Which here was but rude, the place admitting of little better Tenements than Booths, stiled by the name of *Choultries*: Before President Andrew's time (*c.* 1663) they always lodged in Tents; but since, Wooden Houses tiled with Pan-Tiles have been raised in an inclosure allotted by the Governor. In which Compound are included Warehouses, Stables, and other Out-houses, with as good a Garden as this Sandy Soil will allow; in which ours exceeds the other two (i.e. the Dutch and the French), being far pleasanter seated (Crooke 1909, vol. 2, p. 211).

The distance between the shore and the above facilities is not always clear, but one gets an idea from the report of Pietro della Valle's arrival at Swally in 1623: "The Captain went on foot to a Town a mile off, called Sohali ... Franks, who have houses there for repositing the goods" (Grey 1892: 21). Later on, della Valle himself was entertained there by the song and dance of "certain Indian Women of the Town, publick dancers".

At Swally, John Freyer, M.D. (Cambridge: Pembroke), FRS did not take kindly either to the *Banyans* (in this case, Indian brokers) whose persistence in trying to attach themselves to European traders as their brokers made him compare them to vermins or the notoriety of the two nearby villages, Damkin (modern Damka) and Mora (modern Mora). One source refers to the village of Batty, 'famous for good Toddy' and from a letter of 1623 we learn that on a particular day "there were no less than eighty Englishmen straggling drunck in Swally, Dampkine, and the like places" (for the references, Crooke 1909, vol. 2, pp. 212-213).

Freyer puts the distance of the journey by land from Swally to the river crossing at Surat (now spanned by a bridge called the Makkai bridge) opposite the custom house at 10 miles, which is the case in all accounts. According to Ovington goods were transported from Swally to Surat by boats and other vessels. It is probable, land and river routes were both used. There is a description of the road from Swally to Surat in della Valle (Grey 1892: 23):

> The high-way from the Sea side to the City ... is all very even; the soil green all the year round, and about the town Sohali grow abundance of Trees and Indian Nuts, Tamarinds, and other fruits. Beyond the Town the trees are not so plentiful, unless near certain houses; but the fields are every where either ploughed, or full of living creatures feeding in them.

VIII.1.1 The Problem of Thomas Coryat's Tomb in Swally

Freyer (Crooke 1909, vol. 2, p. 212) clearly records that, before departing for Surat from Swally, he "viewed the Tombs by the Sea-side, and some more conspicuous at the end of the Plain belonging to the English; others seated behind the Dutch Choultry, partly English, partly Dutch". Apparently there were three clear clusters of British and Dutch burials at Swally.

At this point it is important to take note of the controversy surrounding the only currently standing burial monument now at Swally. The monument lies a little north to the present village of Suwali and overlooks an undulating sandy surface strewn with some straggling agricultural fields. It is generally claimed that this monument was erected over the burial of Tom Coryat who died in December 1617 at Swally. The monument does not carry any inscription and is in no way different from the burial monuments of the British cemetery outside the walled limit of Surat. A.F. Bellasis (1862) who wrote on the Surat British cemetery also discussed the issue of Tom Coryat's grave. As far as the claim of its location at Swally is concerned, Bellasis cited Edward Terry (Purchas 1905, vol. 9, for an abridged version of Terry's Indian record) who arrived in Surat a few months after the death of Coryat.

> At the East Indian shore at Swally, on the banks thereof, amongst many more English that lie there interred, is laid up the body of Thomas Coryat. He overtook death in December 1617, and was buried (as aforesaid) under a little monument, like one of those that are usually made in our churchyards (Terry cited by Bellasis 1862: 154).

Both Terry and Freyer speak of a substantive number of other European burials at Swally, the burials which cannot now be traced here except the standing one traditionally associated with Coryat. Terry says that the monument which marked Coryat's grave was a little British churchyard monument. The typological dissimilarity with the Swally monument is obvious because the latter is a large monument bearing an onion Mughal dome. Coryat's burial may well lie at Swally but there is no proof whatsoever that the monument which is currently pointed out as his burial belongs to him. On the other hand, T. Herbert who came to Surat about 1627 reports the death of the Persian ambassador Nogdi-Ally Beg whose body was conveyed to Surat by his son Ebrahim Khan and buried "not a stones cast from Tom Coryat's grave, knowne but by two poore stones" (Herbert 1638: 35). Herbert's evidence cannot be brushed aside, as Bellasis has done. The death of the Persian ambassador was an important event, more so when the cause of death was opium-poisoning. He mentioned Coryat's tomb only in relation to the burial of the Persian ambassador, in which he was interested. Further, he describes Coryat's burial marked only by two stones and not by any proper monument.

Some years later John Freyer reports the same. Going out of Surat by the gate which led in the direction of Broach, he found the way "all strewed wth Moor-men's tombs", among which he mentions "one of especial note of a Persian ambassador" (Crooke 1909: 252-253).

> Not far from whence, on a small hill on the left of the road, lies Tom Coriat, our English Fakier (as they name him), together with an Armenian Christian.

The confusion seems to be worse confounded by the note added to this statement of Freyer by his editor W. Crooke (1909: 253, note 1). Crooke cites, without any reference, one Mr Bonus who wrote:

> A tomb still exists at Rajgari, which tradition declares to be that of Coryat; but there is no other evidence. This tomb is kept in repair by the Public Works Department. It is said that there was once a row of seven, of which this one alone remains.

The village Rajgari lies immediately to the north of Swally and the tomb there denotes undoubtedly the tomb traditionally associated with Coryat in Swally. However, the question here is the allegedly former existence of a row of seven tombs.

The issue of Coryat's tomb has to remain unsettled till some conclusive evidence emerges. Born in a Somersetshire parsonage in 1577, he spent three years in Oxford but did not take a degree, preferring to be a kind of jester in the court of James I and, later on, a traveller in Europe. He reached India by travelling from Ispahan to Lahore, and earned a reward of a hundred rupees from the Mughal emperor Jahangir by giving an oration in Persian before him in Ajmer (on Coryat, Prasad 1980, chapter 6).

No such controversy attaches to the tomb of John Vaux which is now only a pile of ruins in the compound of a lighthouse near the Tapti mouth. A former judge and Deputy-governor of Bombay, he died, while having a sail in the Tapti. The tomb supposedly rose 30 feet high and acted as a landmark for vessels sailing up the Tapti. The tomb was raised by his widow and his diary is supposed to be kept in the British Museum. Vaux was a controversial character (cf. Wright 1918). Apparently, the site of his tomb used to be visited by the Europeans from Surat for recreational purposes till 1777. On December 19, 1777 Parsons went on a shooting party with the chief of the Surat British factory and four other gentlemen to Swally by water and from there to Vaux's tomb in 'shooting carts', light carts drawn by oxen.

VIII.2 The Surat Wharf and the Custom-House

What Della Valle called the *Dogana*—or custom-house, the seat of *Shahbandar*, was in all accounts one of the most important places in the city. The thoroughness and the occasional rapacity of the people in its charge have frequently been commented upon—mostly adversely. Della Valle strikes a balanced note:

> … they observe very narrowly all goods that are brought in, (although they be but Clothes for change) to see whether there be anything coming to the Customes; nor will they suffer strangers to enter till they be first known, and have license, as 'tis also practis'd in Venice. In all things they proceed with … great wariness, and good order … in lawful things, there is no difficulty, either through diversity of Religion, or upon any other account (Grey 1892: 24).

Thevenot wrote that the boat by which he came up the Tapti and approached the custom house 'put in to land as near as it could' and he was carried ashore upon men's backs—a situation which should be familiar to travellers along even the modern Indian waterways. However, steps must have led to the custom-house from the wharf where boats from the Tapti bar and Swally were unloaded. The local knowledge of the location of the custom-house is still there in Surat. Part of the original place is now occupied by a motor-repairing compound, but the whole complex needs a close scrutiny, accompanied, if possible, by clearance work. We do not expect a regular, well-defined wharf-area, but some careful probing should lead to the pinpointing of the centre of the riverside area where goods were unloaded and came up for customs inspection. The custom-house itself has been described by Thevenot: a large court and then a hall where the customs people searched those who were coming in. There was a wicket-gate for going out in the street after the inspection was over.

VIII.3 The European Factories

VIII.3.1 The British Factory

VIII.3.1.1 Some Observations on the Life in the Factory

There are many descriptions of the life in the British factory (especially in Ovington): a proper hierarchy from the President or the chief factor to the juniormost writer (writers > factors > senior factors > merchants

> chiefs of factories > members of the Council in Surat > President), a chaplain to look after the needs of the soul, a British and an Indian doctor to take care of illness, the main meal of the day at lunch with copious provision of alcoholic beverages, the bustling atmosphere throughout the day, the business premises and the residential accommodation both in the factory compound, and the general standard of pomp and ceremony maintained by the president, especially when out on a visit. Traveller after traveller have thought it fit to record these details, and if anything, the sense of pomp and ceremony considerably increased by the late 18th century when the British were the *de facto* ruling power in Surat.

When the English chief goes out or comes in at the gates, the drums beat, and the guard is turned out; which ceremony is observed when he passes the mauin guard, which is on the esplanade near the castle: besides two union flags borne before his carriage, it is preceded by a serjeant and 20 seapoys, with swords drawn, who run before it from the gate to his house, where the guard is turned out on his arrival, and the drums beat. A lieutenant's guard, which has good barracks, is always mounted between the outer and inner gates leading to his house: there are ten centinels always on duty at the gates, and in different parts about the garden (Parsons 1808: 252).

The tradition of pomp, although not on this scale, goes back to the early days of the Company. About a hundred years before the time of Parsons (1777), Freyer wrote of the president travelling in a palanquin, preceded by guards, 'a noise of trumpet' and a pennant carried by a flag-man. There was also an ostrich feather fan to keep him cool and undisturbed by insects. In fact, the style was very much like that of a nobleman of Mughal India. It appears that the late 18th century style described by Parsons took on the basic character of the British ceremonial pomp.

The general atmosphere, in Freyer's language, was that of 'a continual hurly-burly'—'a mere Billingsgate; for if you make not a noise, they hardly think you intent on what you are doing'. The Banians or Indian brokers played a major role in the Company's mercantile affairs, mostly in the procurement of goods both in the market and in the countryside where money was advanced to the producers for finished products and the next year's crops. The Banians certainly picked up some English, as the Indian errand-boys did. Although the Company encouraged the British young men to write and speak the official courtly language of Farsi and employed a teacher for this, offering an extra remuneration to those who acquired the requisite proficiency, Freyer complains that there was not much progress in this direction.

However, life was easy-moving. Of all the descriptions that one comes across in this regard, one likes most Downton's gentle observation that in their leisure hours they spent time

...visiting this garden; now that orchard. Today fresh rivers; tomorrow open fields and faire monuments (whereof there there are store). But alwaies (after the countries custome) in coach or on horse, to prevent disgrace. Our recreation, for the most part, bow and arrowes. And free from all molestation of the inhabitants: a mixt people, quiet, peaceable, very subtill; civill, and universallie governed under one king, but diversly law'd and customed (Foster 1939: 143).

Peter Mundy (Temple 1914, vol. 2, pp. 26-27) provides a good description and a sketch of the Company's garden in Surat, set inside the factory compound with a tank in front. Downton was a quiet and observant man, and the monkeys of Surat and the parrots and parakeets afforded him good material for observation. His description of the *Bandarlog* on rampage is, according to us, one of the treasures of the English literature on India (Foster 1939: 151)

Downton wrote in the context of 1614-15, but by the late 17th century the need for 'pious behaviour' came to be loudly emphasized, and nowhere more so in a letter written by Streynsham Master (Yule 1888, vol. 2, pp. cciv-ccxviii). It is learnt that in 1668 the Company circulated a set of printed rules which they also put up in the factory for the information of all persons.

By these he that omitts Prayer on a weeke day pays 2s:6d; on a Sunday 5s; If any be Drunke or abuse the Natives they are to be sett at the gate in Irons all the day time; and all the Night be tyed to a Post in the house; If any lye out of the House, without leave of the President, he pays 40s: and these Penaltys are some of them, almost as often inflicted, as the offences are Committed... (Yule 1888, vol.2, p. ccvi).

VIII.3.1.2 The Factory Building

Although an inordinate amount of detail on the life inside the British factory is available, there is really not much on the actual location and description of the factory building. To begin with, according to the terms of the imperial *firman* received by Thomas Roe, the British factors were to be permitted, under certain restrictions, to *hire* (italics ours) any house they pleased for a factory. They were, in fact, specifically denied the liberty to buy or build any permanent dwelling (Foster 1899: p. xlii-xliii). Ovington clearly mentions that the building of the factory, located in the northwestern part of the city and endowed with the provisions for the accommodation of about 40 people including separate apartments

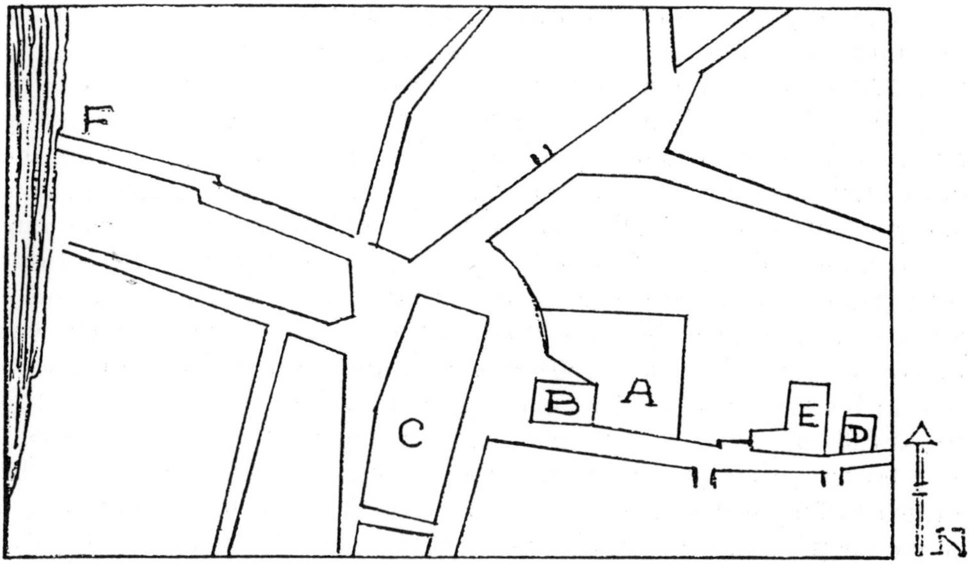

Fig. 7. Position of Old British Factory (after Foster, *English Factories*, 1661-64: courtesy Y.M. Chitalwala). A: British; E: French; D: Armenian Church; F: British Extension.

for the President, several cellars, warehouses, a tank and a *hammam*, belonged to the Mughal. The annual rent was £60 but hardly demanded by the landlord, most of it being spent by the Company itself on keeping the building in good order. Freyer echoes this by saying that it was partly the king's gift and partly hired. It was built of stone and wood, the latter excellently carved with non-representational designs. Each floor was half-a-yard thick and made of cement. The plan was that of a Muslim building, with upper and lower galleries and a central courtyard. There was an 'oratory', a convenient open place for meals. Peter Mundy's description is equally vivid:

> Suratt howse is of the best sort in Towne, very faire and stronglie built, the Rooffs in general flatt and tarrassed alofte to walke on, very substantiallie done with lyme, etts., soe that noe rayne can peirce it, and belowe a faire hall, Chambers and roomes for the President and Councell etts. Marchants with compleat warehouses, Walkes (etts.) belowe (Temple 1914, vol. 2, p. 25).

Mundy's description dates from *c.* 1630 whereas Ovington is considerably later, *c.* 1689. John Freyer is only a little earlier than Ovington. The location of this particular building is undecided. Campbell's gazetteer puts both this and the later factory site in the same *Mulla Chaklo* area. Without further investigations one cannot be sure.

The original factory is unlikely to be the site which passes for the 'old English factory' now. Foster (1899: 310, note 1) is categorical about this: "At some later period a move was made to the building on the river bank in the *Mulla chaklo* (Mulla's ward), which is still standing and is today pointed out as the English factory". According to him, the old factory was "once the city mint, and was close to the Kaji masjid, and not far from the castle". Foster is no doubt right, because, among other things, the late 18th century English factory that Stavorinus describes—besides the castle, in the inner town with a garden and a wharf—is very unlikely to be the site of the old factory which was defended against Shivaji in 1664 and 1670. Interestingly, Stavorinus adds that in his time most of the members of the British Surat Council used to "dwell dispersed in different partts of the inner and outer town".

Foster (1911: the frontispiece) gives an illustration showing the British factory in Surat, as it stood in 1638. This is clearly reminiscent of the description we have in Mundy, Freyere and Ovington. Foster also offers a plan showing the location of both old and new British factories. According to this plan, the old factory lay, not far, to the west of the Armenian church, with the site of the old French factory in between. What is now called Cooper House and pointed out as the site of the British factory is obviously the site of the new factory. More work is obviously needed on this issue.

VIII.3.2 The Dutch Factory

The Dutch had two clear structural complexes in Surat: the original Dutch factory which possibly changed place at least once, and the warehouse-cum-wharf complex which they built much later. The first clear reference to the Dutch factory may be found in the entry for January 6, 1623, in the diary of van den Broeke: "I moved into the new house, hired for four years for 1,250 Mahmudis a year from Pahlawan Safid" (Moreland 1932: 1). The location of the second complex was clearly known locally when the gazetteer was being compiled in the 1870s. Campbell, the editor of the gazetteer identified it with "the Walanda Bandar, or Dutch wharf, immediately above the present commodore's bangalo". The Dutch did not enjoy this as an exclusive privilege. Stavorinus (1798, vol. 2, p. 476) clearly mentions that the Portuguese, French, English and Dutch had wharves of their own in the suburbs, in addition to the factories in the inner town. Stavorinus clearly mentions that the Dutch built up this complex under the terms of a charter sanctioned in 1729. A previous chapter—that of 1712—laid down that the house of Itabar Khan should be given over to the residents of the Dutch factory, although they would not be allowed to fortify it. Stavorinus (1798, vol. 2, p. 476), writing in the context of 1774-75, had the following to say about the Dutch factory:

The factory of our Company is an old building, situated nearly in the centre of the town; there is nothing worthy of observation about it, and it is in an extremely ruinous condition: it is at present only made use of for *bazaaring* the piece-goods, that is, for examining them when they come from the manufacturers, and comparing them with the patterns. The Company still pay a yearly rent for the use of the building, to one of the natives, to whom it came by inheritance; besides which, it must be kept in repair at the expense of the Company.

One cannot be sure if this is Itabar Khan's building mentioned in the charter of 1712 or the first Dutch factory. However, Itabar Khan's building seems to be more of a residence than a factory, and if so, Stavorinus was referring to the site of the old factory. The gazetteer's observation is that the English and the Dutch had both their factories in the *Mulla Chaklo* part of the inner town. The low-tiled building which is now pointed out as representing the site of the Dutch factory is perhaps the site of Itabar Khan's building, because the site of the Dutch wharf is close by.

A general idea of life in the original Dutch factory is available in the account of Pietro della Valle who came to Surat in *c.* 1623. As he was accompanied by a young lady, he was put up in the Dutch factory which had the wife of the Dutch president or 'commendator', as he was called, and other ladies living there. The particular lady della Valle entrusted his young lady friend to, was called Donna Lucia. About P. Van den Broeke who was the Commendator then, he wrote:

He lives in a goodly palace, which hath many distinct apartments, with several entrances into a Court, like so many different houses, only included within the same wall, which is entered into by one great gate: Here the Commendator holds the best, and largest, apartment, to himself; in the rest lodge some of their gravest merchants, which are of the council for management of affairs, in order to their better conveniency, and union, besides many others of inferior condition, which live out of this great inclosure, dispersed elsewhere in the city, and when occasion requires, they all repair to the Palace of the Commendator. Amongst those whose habitation was in the Palace of the Commendator Donna Lucia's husband has one of the principal, where he lives with his family and wife, whom, according to the custom of India, he maintains with much splendour and gallantry (Grey 1892: 25-26).

In Stavorinus' time the pomp and spendour were by and large missing from the Dutch factory. The ornaments of gold and silver and the service of silver plate, etc. were shipped to Batavia, but the fact that formerly the Dutch here lived in great pomp, in accordance with the Indian norms of the period has been mentioned by him. In addition to the services of gold and silver and various ornaments acquired at the Company's expense, a few horses, "one or two elephants, chariots of ceremony, and palankeens, with trappings of gold and silver, were kept at the charge of the Company, to furnish a splendid appearance whenever the director went out in state" (Stavorinus 1798, vol 3, p. 149).

VIII.3.3 The Portuguese Factory

The gazetteer pinpoints the location of the Portuguese factory: behind the Capuchin chapel. In the 1870s the factory was in ruins, and only a few rooms were used as a dwelling. One is not sure if this position tallies with that of a large and mostly intact complex which is currently pointed out as the Portuguese factory. This building which is set in a large and walled compound with a single entrance is double-storeyed, access to the upper storey being gained by a steep and long set of stairs. The rooms are high-ceilinged with a wide, connecting verandah in front. The roof is tiled and slopes on either side of the central ridge. Architecturally this complex is most unlikely to date from the Mughal period; it is unlikely to be earlier than the late 18th century. Like the old Dutch factory, the Portuguese factory too still remains to be conclusively identified.

VIII.3.4 The French Factory

The French factory was located to the east of the Armenian church, according to a plan published in Om Prakash Singh's book on Surat. The site remains to be investigated on the ground. The factory must have been a 'handsome' one, because this is exactly the term used by Manucci (Irvine 1907: 63) to describe the French factory. He does not add any detail. Stavorinus (1798, vol. 3, p. 70) writes that in his time, i.e., in *c.* 1775-78, the French had a lodge or factory in the inner town and also a garden out of the Mocha or Attua gate, which they called *Bel Air*. The French establishment used to have a 'chief' before the abolition of their company, but when Stavorinus was there, he was called the French consul and appointed as such by the king of France. In the 1670s Abbe Carre stayed in the French factory and was, in fact, very disparaging about the lack of discipline and organization there: "As for order, discipline, or obedience, I have never seen any among the servants of our French Company" (Fawcett 1948: 782). In the case of a French junior clerk behaving impudently with his 'chief', the president of the British factory told Abbe Carre that "among themselves it was quite an unheard of thing for a mere clerk, or any other junior officer, to speak or appear before his chief, except hat in hand and in a most respectful manner" (Fawcett 1948: 783). However, Abbe Carre does not describe the factory.

VIII.4 The British and Dutch Burials

These are not the only European or generally non-Indian burials in Surat. The British cemetery lies a little outside the modern Katargam gate at the northern periphery of Surat whereas the Dutch burial lies not far from it, but within the city wall near the Katargam gate itself. There is an Armenian burial ground adjacent to the Dutch cemetery and the location of the old Portuguese burial ground seems to lie in the general direction of the Katargam gate.

Apart from Ovington who basically praised the monumental character of the British and Dutch tombs, some specific details about the location of these and Portuguese and Armenian burials are found in Freyer, Stavorinus and Parsons.

After mentioning the tomb of Coryat Frere mentioned "the Dutch tombs, many and handsome, most of them Pargetted" (Crooke 1909, vol. 1, p. 253). He also mentions that there was an Armenian cemetery adjoining the Dutch one. He gives the measurement of the Armenian burial yard: 40 yards long and about 5 yards wide. From there he passed on to the British tombs which he did not find as crowded as the Dutch ground. The important thing is that he mentions a Portuguese burial-place before he reached the British one ("the English tombs, dort of which the Portugals have a bural-place").

In the context of the late 18th century Parsons (1808: 249) wrote that the Portuguese and the Dutch grounds were "within the walls, the English without". Stavorinus (1798, vol.3, p. 47) also mentions the Dutch and Portuguese grounds together. He describes the Dutch ground by saying that there was scarcely any grave that had not a tomb with lofty spires on it, "the meanest have a gravestone with a sculptured epitaph". He specifically comments on the monument over the grave of Van Rheede, "commissary-general of the East India Company over the western factories" which excelled "all the others in largeness of dimension, elegance of architecture, magnificence of ornament and richness of material". This particular tomb was kept in repair by the Dutch factory which spent nine thousand Dutch guilders or six thousand Indian rupees for the purpose not long before Stavorinus' time.

The locations of the British, Dutch and Armenian tombs are easily identifiable. All three of them are currently under the protection of the Archaeological Survey of India. The location of the Portuguese ground would need some local investigation.

These burials formed the topic of an article by A.F. Bellasis (1861?/ 1862) in *The Journal of the Bombay Branch of the Royal Asiatic Society*. In the British ground emphasiz has been laid on the tomb of the Oxinden brothers—Christopher and George who died in 1659 and 1669 respectively. Christopher was placed in a domed structure with four pinnacles at the corners. There was a Latin epigraph (dated 18 April, 1659) put up in his honour by his brother George. Bellasis has given an English translation of this epigraph which simply contains personal feelings. After his death George was put in a structure which enclosed the earlier tomb and rose to *c.* 13m, with a diameter of *c.* 8 m. There are two cupolas supported by strong round pillars and there are galleries in the interior, to be reached by flights of stairs. There is a Latin epigraph (dated 15 July, 1669) in his memory in the upper compartment of this building. Again, a translation has been provided by Bellasis but this is of no special historical value. Almost straight to the north of the Oxinden tomb is an uninscribed monument traditionally associated with Gerald Aungier. The general range of inscribed tombs belongs to Bernard Wyche (1736), Samuel Annesley (early 18th century), Francis Breton (1649), Henricus Gary (1658) and Bartholomew Harris (1686). Apart from the armorial bearings on the tombs of Wyche and Annesley, there is nothing specifically European about these early tombs. Bellasis calls their general architecture semi-Saracenic, although the pinnacles which go up at the four corners of the dome over the Oxinden monument are not certainly Mughal minarets; they are modelled on them but retain a non-Islamic identity. The small circle of painting at the inner centre of the dome and occasionally at the top of the arches supporting the dome is reminiscent as a type of the exuberance of the Mughal period painted scrolls.

Among the monuments in the Dutch ground Bellasis mentions the monuments erected over the remains of Hendrick Adriaan Baron Van Reede (death dated 15 December, 1691—Dutch epigraph and its Engish translation provided by Bellasis), Magdalena Haijers (1642, wife of the Director Paulius Croocq), Bastina Theodora D. LeBoucq (1743, wife of the Director John Schreuder), Carolus Pelgrom (1655), Jacob, the little son of Heer Jan Schreuder (1741), Christiana Hendrietta (1787) and

Gertrude Cornelia (1789), child and infant daughters of A.L. Bratiaare, and others.

Architecturally the early Dutch tombs too conform to the style adopted by the early British ones.

The details, as we have observed in the case of the British cemetery, now located on what is called Kadagaon Main Road (?), are the following.

The complex lies in a walled compound to which the main entrance is from the west. It is an irregularly shaped piece of land (*c.* 70 m from the west to the east, *c.* 85m from the north to the south; the eastern edge is shorter, *c.* 35m). The present eastern boundary wall is arbitrary and reputedly contains on the other side a part of the original cemetery. We did not have access to that sector as its ownership now rests with a private individual. The graves now bear numbers which, we believe, are latter additions. The highest such number that we observed is 558 in the centre of the enclosure. Of all the graves that bear inscribed tablets with a date, the most belonged to the 19th century. The 18th century graves are infrequent and cover the following names:

Grave 213—30th June, 1736—Mrs Elizabeth Wyche, widow of Bernard, 'Chief for Affairs of the Honourable United British Company in Surat'. She died in her 54th year and was born in Bombay.

Grave 124—June 1772—Mrs C. McMillan, widow of A. McMillan of 'the Honourable Company of Marines'.

Grave 265/275—6 July 1747(1714?)—James Hope, 'Chief of Affairs of the British Nations in Surat.

Grave 261—November 1751—Anne (aged 30), wife of Samuel Court, a 'servant to the Honourable East India Company'.

Grave 129—1795—M.C. Macalister (aged 53).

Grave 131—13 September 1775—Geraldinesh James (24 years 7 months)—wife of William James of the Surat Council.

Grave 282—1761—Mary Price—wife of W. Price, 'Chief for Affairs of the British Nation and Governor of the Mogul's Castle and Fleet of Surat'.

Grave 283—1774—W. Price.

Grave 294—1788—Lt. Watkinson.

Grave 304—1767—G. White (38 years), 'Captain and Command of the Surat Castle'.

Grave 307—1790—G.O. Goddard.

Grave 318—1797—burial of a child.

Grave 326—1781—Captain West.

Grave 328—1767—S. Arnot (a girl).

Grave 378—1780—Captain A. Forbes of the Bengal Army.

Grave 193—1790—Annesley Brownvicc.

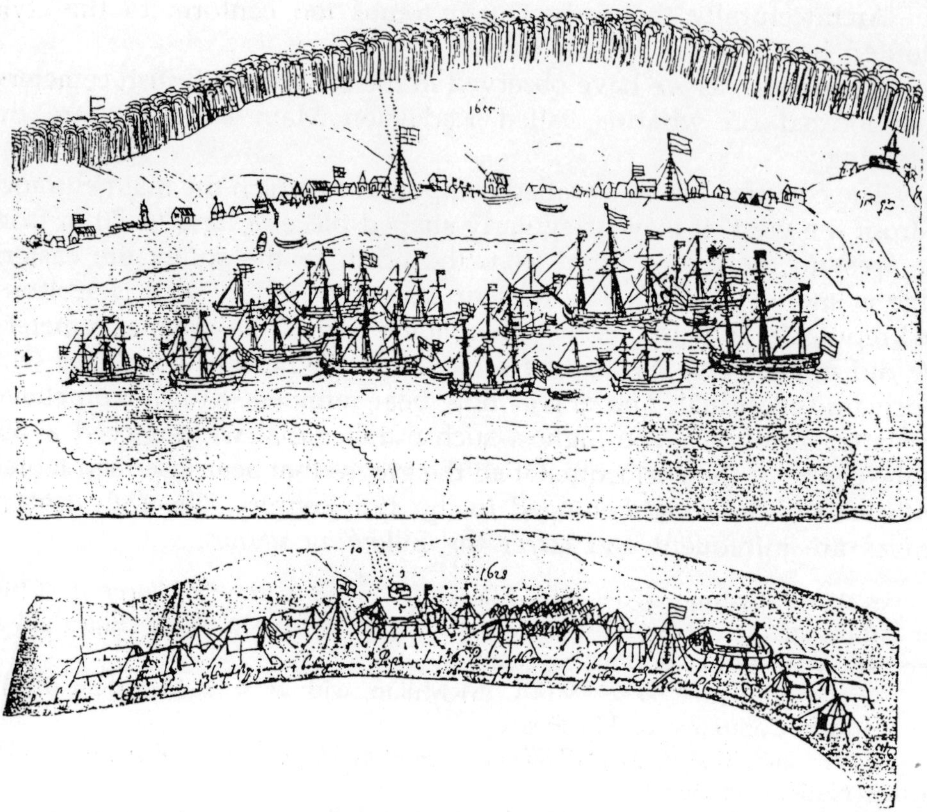

Fig. 8. Sketch of Swally by Peter Mundy (after Temple 1914, 1936)

Grave 195—1698—S.E. Annesley.
Grave 347—1790—Matilda, daughter of Col. G. Burgess
Grave 366—1694—Harris Armiger, 'Surat President'.
Unnumbered mausoleum—1649.
By the side of Aungier's tomb—Ben Gary—obelisk—19 August, 1658.
Grave 214—President Oxinden's tomb.

It is apparent that the 17th century tombs are very rare; even the early 18th century ones are rare. We, however, admit that some early inscribed slabs could have gone missing, and this is the reason that it has not been possible to satisfactorily identify all the 17th century tombs mentioned by Bellasis. Architecturally our attention is dominated by the

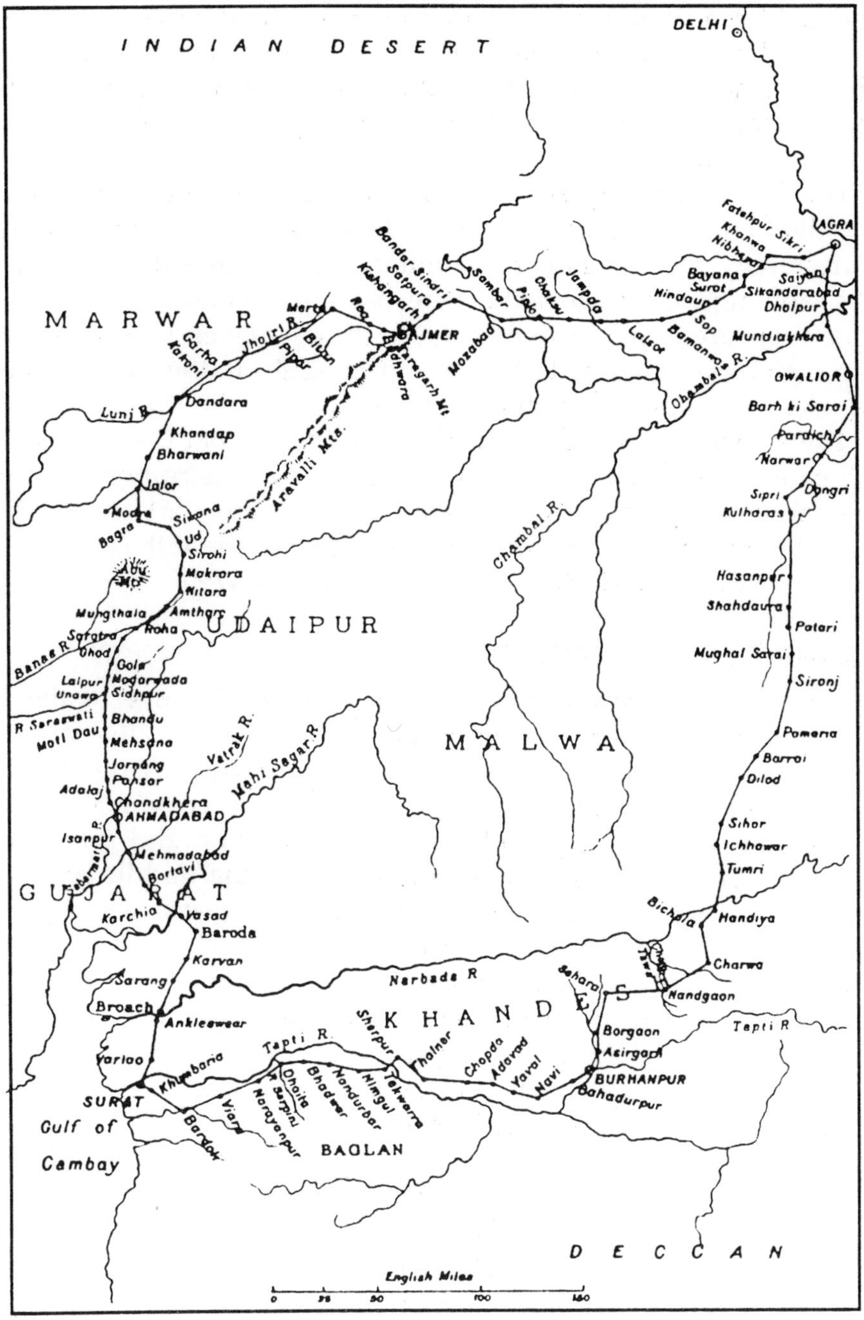

Fig. 9. Routes of Peter Mundy in North India (after Temple 1914, 1936)

round, solid pillars standing at four corners and continuing in an attenuated form as minarets at four corners of the domed roof. Both the upper and lower chambers have verandahs round them and are fronted by high, generally closed (except for doors) arches. None of them, however, looks exactly identical. In some cases the arched galleries are open all around.

The Dutch cemetery is located in the modern Anuchhara Mahalla. The walled enclosure is roughly 65 m (north-south) x 60 m (east-west). Architecturally there is not much difference with the British cemetery tombs, although the main tomb here has an octagonal base with two offsets. There are 24 pillars in this case at the base level. The round pillars are on high rectangular pedestals. About 12 tombs in the Dutch cemetery show clear Muslim architectural influence.

The Armenian cemetery close by is on a somewhat L-shaped ground (*c.* 65 m east-west; *c.* 20-25 m north-south). The inscriptions are all in Armenian language, and two of them bear the dates 1661 and 1681. The other dates which we could recognize belonged to the 18th century: 1709, 1731 (?), 1733, 1776, 1778, 1785, 1788, 1791 and 1795.

IX. SOME GENERAL OBSERVATIONS

If one takes in a broad sweep the entire historical frame of the 16th-18th century Surat that we have briefly outlined in the preceding sections, one should realize that Surat is perhaps the only place in India where the European traders began by functioning directly in a throbbing, cosmopolitan and rich city under the administration and protection of the Mughal empire in its heyday and where by the middle of the 18th century one of their groups—the British—took the decisive step towards territorial acquisition on a grand scale. In Calcutta, Madras and Bombay, the British virtually carved out new places; these were certainly the places where their thrust for power in the Ganga plain, southern India and the Deccan including the Konkan coast was consolidated. It was only in Surat that they began as a trading group in a powerful Mughal metropolis and after about 150 years became its ruler. The battle of Plassey in 1757 and the occupation of the Surat castle in 1759 are among the most important signal posts of the rise of the British empire in India, but it is only in Surat that the whole earlier process can be traced, certainly on the basis of the historical documents which throw light on their close interaction with the indigenous merchant class—bania order, if one prefers—and hopefully on the basis of archaeology as well—on the basis of their material remains, as evidenced in the emergence of a new town plan of Surat by 1817 when the European, especially the British, features had become important in an erstwhile Indian landscape, with Swally marking the first phase of the beginning of this process. From this point of view Surat occupies a place of crucial importance in the archaeology of European expansion in India.

4

Broach, Ahmedabad, Cambay, Diu, Daman

I. BROACH (BHARUCH)

In our chapter on Gujarat's maritime trade till *c.* AD 1600, we have already noted how as the ancient Indian *Bhrigukachchha* or the classical Barygaza, Broach or modern Bharuch occupies a major place in the history of the Indian Ocean trade. The place lies on the northern bank of the Narmada, about 30 km from the mouth of its estuary. In the winter of 2000-2001 the Narmada at Broach was completely dry, the flow being stopped at one of the dams under construction upstream. One cannot say that the Narmada, one of the holiest rivers of Hinduism with a string of pilgrim places on her banks from the source at Amarkantak in the Vindhyas downwards, has fared well under the modern Hindus, and it is with some pathos that one cites here what the compiler of the first Broach district gazetteer (Campbell 1877) wrote in this context more than hundred years ago: "An oath on the water of the Narbada has a special sanction. Few Hindus would dare to swear falsely standing in the river with a garland of red flowers round the neck, and holding in the right hand the water of the sacred stream". The same gazetteer refers to the ordinarily year-long custom of *Narmada Parikrama* where one begins at a point downstream and walks around the river, first by going up to the source and then following her along the other bank till one reaches the point opposite where one started.

At Broach the river bed is about a mile (1.6 km) wide, flanked by high, precipitous banks. At the point where the estuary becomes the sea, the width is more than 13 miles (*c.* 21 km) with the large island of *Alia Bet*. The estuarine land is a strip of sand backed by a salt waste. Proper cultivation begins in the Black Soil country further inland but even here, with the annual rainfall being about 30 inches (*c.* 76 cm) and the level of the Narmada water being unsuitable for lift irrigation, agriculture is always a little precarious. The influence of the tides which reaches as far as about 40 km upstream from Broach is quite strong; at the river mouth the tidal wave can be up to 8 m high in the season of spring-tides. Navigability of the river up to Broach was always possible, provided one knew one's way around the shoals and depended to a large extent on the tides, but even then it was difficult for the vessels of more than 70 tons. This was in the context of the late 19th century when the first gazetteer was written, but even in the late 17th century when John Freyer crossed the river at Broach, the situation was perhaps broadly similar. In Freyer's time a journey from Surat to Broach could also be made by sea up to the river—mouth and then up the river, but Freyer chose to travel overland and found the road "pestered with Caphalaes of Oxen, Camels, and Buffaloes, with heavy waggons drawn by Teams of Oxen" (Crooke 1912: 156). While crossing the Narmada at Broach he found it 'broad, swift and deep' but clogged with sands, calling for good pilots under whose directions 'good lusty vessels' could be brought up to the city walls to be laden with salt and corn. It is implied that the vessels, although 'good' and 'lusty', could be used only for coastal trade in salt and corn.

One cannot, however, be certain because J. Mandelslo (Commissariat 1931), some years earlier (1638), offers a different picture. Broach then used to trade with Arabia, sending vessels carrying cotton, cloth, indigo, camphor, tobacco, alum, benzoin (a type of gum), pepper and other spices, myrobalan and preserved fruits in March and getting them back laden with gold, silver, coral, amber, a red dye, coffee and opium in September. The vessels left for the Gulf in January-February and came back in late-April/early May carrying brocades and silk, pearls and dried fruits and plenty of rosewater. There were also vessels up to 300 tons going in May to Sumatra to bring spices, benzoin, camphor and porcelain, among others, in October. Similarly there was trade with Malabar, with the Malabari boats reaching Gujarat in December and leaving in April. Before Surat came up, the European trade was conducted through Goa, and there was some amount of trade, possibly via Goa, with China and Japan too. It appears that till Mandelslo's time Broach was a significant maritime entrepot, whatever might the navigability of the Narmada in detail. Mandelslo does not mention African trade but it was likely to be there. A statement of the first gazetteer is interesting: 'a vessel occasionally sails to Zanzibar and brings back white dates; but this rarely happens'. By the early 19th century, Broach's trade was reduced entirely to coastal trade, mostly with Bombay, Kutch and Karachi.

In the 16th century Tome Pires (Cortesao 1944: 38)) clearly mentions Baruez or Broach as an important point of sea trade between Cambay and Surat. It is important to note that in the late 18th century Stavorinus (1798) noted at the entrance to the Gulf of Cambay "an open road for ships in seven fathoms, mostly sandy bottom". We think that this reflects the true situation. As in Surat, the goods were unloaded at the roadstead and brought over in smaller boats. In the second half of the 17th century Abbe Carre (Fawcett 1948) who came by ship from Gogha in six hours to the Narmada mouth had to wait there for the high tide to move further into the river. It took him two days to reach the Broach custom-house. Carre's testimony has also been borne out by one of his early contemporaries, Philip Baldaeus, a Dutch "Minister of the Word of God in Ceylon", whose *A True and Exact Description of the Most Celebrated East Indian Coasts of Malabar and Coromandel as also of the Isle of Ceylon* was published in Dutch in 1672 and in an English translation in 1704 (Churchill 1704, vol. 3). According to Baldaeus, the Narmada below Brochia (Broach) afforded a good passage for ships but only "about half way from the sea towards Brochia, the passage being stopped there by a sandbank, which has not above 9 or 10 feet water" (Churchill 1704: 574). He was aware that the British and the Dutch had factories here 'a considerable time ago'. The two suburbs of the city were inhabited principally by calico-weavers and merchants. Formerly 9 or 10 vessels used to come to Broach every year from the Malabar coast. He also noted that the Vindhyan mountain ('the mountains of Vindat') began about 5 or 6 leagues to the southeast of Broach and that the Narmada came down by the Deccan and Mandu.

Despite its significance in the early historic period, there has been very little archaeological research at Broach (for a summary, Chakrabarti 1997: 227). The modern town stands on what looks like a hillock from a distance but in reality this seems to be largely composed of the ancient mound where an excavation in 1959-60 established a *c.* 8 m thick cultural deposit going back to a level marked by the proto-historic Black-and-Red Ware. The date of the succeeding Northern Black Polished Pottery phase of the site has been put in the 3rd century BC, although we feel that there is no reason why the date of this pottery in Gujarat has to be 300-odd years later than its date in the Ganga plain and Malwa. The excavations isolated a mud rampart with a moat outside in this phase which also seems to have possessed a rich stone bead industry. Red Polished Ware, the hallmark of Gujarati sites of the early centuries AD, also occurs at the site, along with the evidence of burnt brick revetments added to the defence wall in this phase.

More recent explorers of Broach (Howell and Sinha 1994) feel that the several watercourses and tanks at the base of the city mound may be the remnant of the old moat. There could be a number of entries into the city from the riverside, but there were only two entrances by land—one at the west end of the north wall and the other in the centre of the eastern wall. Our observations suggest that select and careful excavations in different areas of the modern city (excavation space is certainly available) will lead to a proper understanding of the ancient town plan of Broach.

In 1966-67 F.R. Allchin and J.P. Joshi (unpublished but reported by Howell and Sinha 1994) reputedly found a chain of early historic sites downstream from Broach, of which two—Chavaneswar and Bharbut, especially Chavaneswar—were important. Chavaneswar showed over a large area a variety of early pottery including Black-and-Red Ware and Red Polished Ware. An early historic site was also found at Ankaleswar, on the south bank of the Narmada, almost opposite Broach. This find at Ankaleswar and the find of early historic pottery at Variao, the traditional Tapti crossing near Surat (Howell and Sinha 1994), proves that the Surat-Broach alignment marked, in fact, an early historic route. James Howell and A.K. Sinha (1994) established Kamrej, upstream from Surat, as a major early historic site with a moat around it and thought that it could mark the site of the inland port of Akabaru mentioned by the Periplus. They also examined exposed sections at Rander, and although the river-bank section is about 8 m thick, no early historic material could be identified. Sunil Gupta (1993) has identified Kamrej with Kammoni of the Periplus. These diverse identifications only substantiate the general significance of the Narmada-Tapti estuarine regions as an important centre of trade and commerce in the early historic period.

The basic political history of the Broach area is basically that of south Gujarat as a whole, and that includes Surat too. An interesting aspect of its ancient history is that a number of land grants date here from the period of the Gurjara dynasty and a number of villages mentioned in these grants have been identified with some villages near Broach. Broach also denoted an administrative division—*Bharukachchha Vishaya*. Broach was important enough to be mentioned in Hsuan Tsang's itinerary in the 7th century AD. For the next two centuries south Gujarat was under the domination of the southern Chalukyas and the Rashtrakutas, both of which had their centres of power in the Deccan. However, from about the 10th century onwards the area was included in the domain of the Chalukyan dynasty with its capital at Anhilwada

Patan. The Islamic phase is divided into three phases: the rule of the Delhi Sultanate (1297-1391), the independent Sultans of Gujarat (1391-1572) and the rule of the Mughals. In the 10th century Al-Masudi, while describing the coasts of the Persian Gulf and the Indian Ocean suggested that the iron lance-shafts imported from *Barus* (Broach) were famous. In AD 1100 Al-Idrisi mentioned *Baruh* as a large town built of bricks and plaster, where the inhabitants were traders and businessmen, receiving vessels from China and Sindh. The Mughal rule was followed in Broach by the rule of a family of semi-independent chiefs (1736-1772). The British took over in 1772, although the Maratha power of the Deccan continued to exert influences over the area. The ruling chief put up resistance and in 1772 a battle had to be fought by the British for Broach.

The fortification wall which one can now observe only on the riverside and only in fragments elsewhere was put up possibly by the kings ruling from Anhilwada Patan but tradition affirms that it was strengthened and rebuilt by Bahadur Shah (1526-1536), an independent Gujarat Sultan. It was partly pulled down at the order of Aurangzeb in 1660 but rebuilt after some years to handle the problem of the Maratha raids. At the southeastern edge of the fortification on the riverside, a ruined structural complex is still pointed out as the place where the boats landed and the customs duties were collected. From here a road goes up the mound, and at some point one detects the traces of a gateway. At the northwestern corner of the fortification, somewhat away from the bastion in this part, the British commanding officer David Wedderburn died in the battle for Broach in July 1772. The inscribed tomb which was erected over the spot and which has been described in the gazetteer could not be located by us.

In the 16th century there were two Portuguese raids (1535 and 1546) on Broach, and one more in 1614. These raids testify to its trading wealth during that period. The British factory here was set up in 1616 under the jurisdiction of the Surat factory and in 1616 the Dutch set up their establishment. In Mandelslo's time the factor of the British factory in Broach also looked after their factory in Baroda. Mandelslo, as summarised by Commissariat (1931), found Broach a strongly fortified place on the top of 'a pretty high mountain'. It had two large gates on the land side and two small ones towards the river. A great quantity of timber used to come by the river. This suggests that timber was floated down the Narmada from the forests on her banks upstream and collected at a riverside gate in Broach. A Mughal garrison was stationed in the fort and collected 2 per cent duties on all commodities coming to the place. Many of its inhabitants were weavers producing the *bafta* cloth for which

Broach was famous. The countryside was fertile and yielded rice, wheat, barley and cotton in abundance. Indigo of Jambusar was well-known. Much later, Stavorinus (1798) also gives a more or less similar description: a large and square fort standing upon a hill which is the only eminence for miles around; the production of a good quality of *bafta*; a peculiar quality of the water of the Narmada here, which made possible bleaching of cloth to a perfect whiteness, and agate imported from Burhanpur as an article of trade. Freyer (Crooke 1912) found nine gates in the fort within which he noted a "heathen temple, now converted into a mosque", referring thereby to the Jumma mosque of Broach which was built entirely by pulling down pillars from a Hindu temple.

According to Thevenot (Sen 1949), the walls of Baroche were three fathoms high and flanked by large round towers set at a regular distance of 30 or 35 paces. It was a manufacturing centre of *Baftas* and the Narmada water was excellent for the whitening of cloths. He found little signs of trade except a traffic in agate. He mentions the Dutch factory in Broach, which, according to him, was set up for the quick despatch and custom-house clearance of the goods passing through the place. Thevenot's silence regarding Broach's maritime trade contrasts sharply with what has been mentioned by Manucci (Irvine 1907) and Abbe Carre (Fawcett 1948). Manucci inludes Broach in his list of seaports supplying good revenue to the Mughals, whereas Abbe Carre thought that the place was 'very rich, with a great trade and very convenient for carrying on business between Cambay and Surat'.

According to him, the upper Broach, i.e. the portion located on the top of the old mound, was more ancient than the lower town which was newly developed and extended from the riverside to about a cannon-shot inland. "Here are the bazaars, the customs house, foreign merchants and Hindus who hold the principal trade in this place".

We could not identify the ruins of the British factory in Broach but there is a local tradition about the location of the Dutch factory which now is a partly dilapidated privately owned building in one of the main residential areas inside the fort. The only major signs of its former occupation by the Dutch factors are the base of a fountain and a sun-dial in the courtyard. The major surviving European remains in Broach are the burial tombs of the Dutch outside the city limits, about a mile to the west of Vejalpur in the suburbs. The earliest inscribed tomb dates from 1654, but the majority belong to the 18th century. Architecturally the tombs are identical with the general style displayed in the Dutch cemetery of Surat.

II. AHMEDABAD

Both as the capital of the independent Sultans of Gujarat and as a provincial capital of the Mughals, Ahmedabad's urban prosperity lasted uninterrupted for almost three centuries—from its establishment by Ahmed Shah in 1411 to the death of Aurangzeb in 1707. In the later part of the 18th century it went into a precipitate decline. In the 1770s James Forbes (1834) witnessed that many families were forced to sell cheaply their old jewellery merely 'to procure the necessities of life' and that marble corridors were 'filled up with *choolas*, or cooking places, composed of mud, cowdung, and unburnt bricks' (Forbes 1834: 193-194). But even in the context of this great degeneration he wrote that he had no conception of the extent of 'oriental magnificence' until he had visited Ahmedabad, after which 'the palaces and splendid chambers described in the Arabian Nights' Entertainments' appeared 'no longer overcharged or fabulous' to him. Even now, beyond the overcrowding and filth which have been allowed to creep over the lyrically designed and filigreed monuments of the walled city and the neighbouring village of Sarkhej, one can sense its former beauty and the love and care which went into its making. One is not surprised that Ahmedabad as a city received encomiums from every European traveller who passed through it.

One may pick up at random T. Herbert's description in the early 17th century. He was scholarly enough to find in Ahmedabad echoes of Ptolemy's 'Amacastis' or of Arrian's 'Amadavastis' but he was also sensible enough to know that it was made large and beautiful by Ahmed Shah ('king Hamet').

> ... circled by a beautiful strong stone wall of six miles compass, well and orderly advanced with many pretty towers and a dozen posterns: out of which few pass or repass without a pass.... The streets are many, pretty large and comely; most shops redundant with aromatic gumms, perfumes and spices, silks, cotton, calicoes, and choice of Indian and China rarities, owned and sold by the abstemious, fai spoken, crafty Banians, who here surpass for number the other inhabitants: of most note is the bazaar, rich and uniform; the castle is strong, large and moated ... (Herbert 1638: 62-63).

More or less the same was observed by J. De Laet (Hoyland and Banerjee 1928: 19-20) who added that the city was as large as London. Every 10 or 20 days 200 carts used to leave for Cambay laden with merchandise. The city gates were strictly guarded and nobody could come in or go out without proper permission. The houses were equal in magnificence to any in Asia and Africa. The governor, the *Qazi* and the *Kotwal* formed the three principal points of the local and district

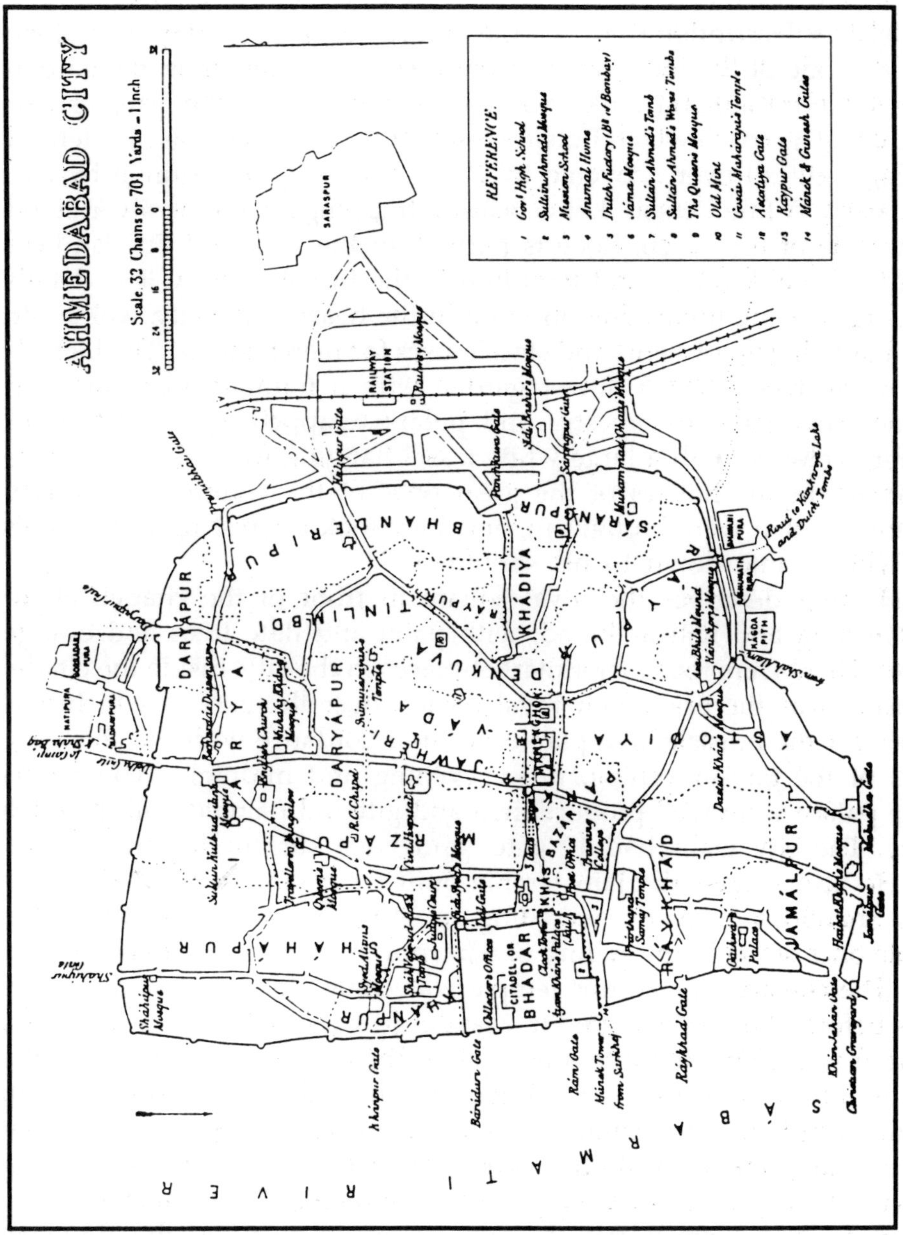

Fig. 10. Ahmedabad (after Campbell 1879)

administration. In the district around Ahmedabad indigo, although inferior to that of Bayana, was produced.

Of all the early European descriptions of Ahmedabad, J.A. Mandelslo's description based on the experience of a few days stay there in 1638 is one of the most detailed ones. He was received in the garden of the modern Kankaria Tank area by Benjamin Roberts, the British factor in the city. The coach which Roberts brought for his guest was 'a splendid equipage, gilt all over', covered by Persian tapestry and drawn by two white oxen. A fine Persian horse bearing trappings made of silver stood by the side of the coach. Roberts partook of the sack and English beer that Mandelslo brought and took him to the British factory. The details of this factory are interesting: location in the heart of the city, well-built, with many fine apartments and storehouses for merchandise. The factor's own room overlooked a flower garden with a fountain in it and had its floor covered with tapestry and pillars wrapped by 'silk stuffs of different colours' with a large white tassel hanging from above, 'as was customary in the houses of the great ones of the country'. Six pretty dancing women were brought in, and they took interest in Mandelslo's hair which came down to his shoulders.

He first describes the royal square in front of the citadel: about 1,000 m long and half as broad, with palm and date trees and orange groves. There were four major market-places in the city. Inside the citadel enclosure was the brick-built royal palace, over the gate of which was a place for the musicians to play tunes in accordance with the changing hours of the day—morning, noon, evening and midnight. The rooms of the palace were well proportioned and gilt and painted with pictures inside. The city walls had 12 gates and were surrounded by a moat.

He also visited the Jain temple built by a famous jeweller of his time, Shantidas Zhaveri. According to M.S. Commissariat (1987) this temple once stood in the suburb of Saraspur but no trace of that survives now. The construction of this temple was complete in 1625, only a few years before Mandelslo visited it. Mandelslo's visit was also a few years before it was converted into a mosque at the order of Aurangzeb as the viceroy of Gujarat in 1645. However, Shantidas was successful in procuring in 1648, after Aurangzeb's departure as the viceroy, an imperial *Firman* asking the Mughal officers in Ahmedabad to restore the building to Shantidas and make him complete restitution for all the damages done. According to Commissariat 'he was in many respects the foremost personality in Gujarat during the first half of the 17th century outside the ranks of Mughal hierarchy' (Commissariat 1987: 76). The temple episode also underlines the influence of the rich merchants in the life of the 17th century Ahmedabad.

The importance of trade in Ahmedabad in his time is amply reflected in the following comment by him:

> There is not in a manner any nation, nor any merchandise in all Asia, which may not be had at Ahmedabad, where particularly there are made abundance of silks and cotton stuffs (Commissariat 1931: 26).

Indigo of Sarkhej was another major commodity but there were also other commodities including musk and ambergis. According to Commissariat (1931) ambergis came from Pegu and Bengal or from Mozambique and Cape Verde islands off the west coast of Africa. According to Mandelslo, the bills of exchange issued by Ahmedabad's traders could be drawn upon 'in all parts of Asia as also at Constantinople'. There was no customs duty to be paid in Ahmedabad but the *Kotwal* and his people expected 15 pence per wagon of goods. Foreigners could trade free in all except the prohibited goods such as gunpowder, lead and saltpetre. Mandelslo was full of praise for the gardens of the city: 'The whole city is so full of trees, that a man may say it makes all but one garden'. The trees also attracted monkeys, and Mandelslo counted 150 of them in the British factory house in Ahmedabad. He was introduced to the Mughal viceroy by the British factor and invited to dine with him on two occasions. On the second day he went wearing the courtly Indian dress of the time.

Thevenot's description too is as detailed as that by Mandelslo. Thevenot was there in 1666. First he went to lodge in a caravansarai but later on stayed with the factors of the Dutch factory which was located 'in the fairest and longest street of the town'. This was wider than the average streets of Ahmedabad, which are considered wide by themselves. There were three large arches at the west end of this street. These high arches led to the royal square or *Maidan Shah*—400 paces in breadth and 700 in length with trees planted on all sides. The gate of the palace was on its west side and that of the caravansarai on the south. The castle was as spacious as a little town and was entered by a high gate between two large and high round towers. The British factory was in the middle of the town: good building and fair courts. Their warehouses were full of cloths from Delhi and Lahore, with which they drove a good trade. In Thevenot's words,

> The Commodities that are most traded in at Amedabad, are Satins, Velvets, Taffeta's, and Tapistries with Gold, Silk and Woollen Grounds: Cotton-Cloaths are sold there also; but they come from Lahores and Dehly: They export from thence great quantities of Indigo, dried and preserved Ginger, Sugar, Cumin,

Lac, Mirobalans, Tamarins, Opium, Saltpetre and Honey. The chief trade of the Dutch at Amedabad consists in schites (chintze), which are painted Cloaths; but they are nothing near so fine as those of Masulipatan and St. Thomas (Sen 1949: 17).

Thevenot also describes the major monuments of the city, including the temple built by Shantidas. He also describes the monuments of Sarkhej or 'Serquech which is a small town about a league and a half from the city', adding that indigo came from Sarkhej.

Pietro della Valle (Grey 1892), on his arrival in Ahmedabad, 'went directly to alight at the house of the English merchants'. Although the streets were large, fair and straight, they were not paved and in consequence very dusty, dusty enough for the foot to sink deep 'with great defilement'. He stayed in *Darzi* caravansarai which was in the street where the British factory was also located.

The Ahmedabad gazetteer (Campbell 1879) records that the building or the site of the building of the British factory in Ahmedabad has not been identified. The Dutch factory has been clearly identified in this publication. Across the main road from the tombs of Sultan Ahmed Shah's wives—Moghalai Bibi and Murki Bibi—is a large, heavy upper-roomed building. In the 1870s this building housed Bombay Bank. According to Stavorinus (1798, vol. 3, p. 107-108) the Dutch factory in Ahmedabad was established in 1618 and closed in 1744. The Dutch had a factory also in Sarkhej which was established in 1620 but by 1670 it was closed down. The Dutch and the British both had for a short period factories in Baroda but they did not last long.

When Mandelslo stopped at Kankaria Bagh in the outskirts of old Ahmedabad and was received by Benjamin Roberts, the British factor of Ahmedabad, he did not notice any European, especially Dutch, burial ground there. What is interesting is that Thevenot who stayed with the Dutch in Ahmedabad in 1666 does not mention it. It appears that the present Dutch burial tombs overlooking the Kankaria lake came up later, in the late 17th century. However, the Archaeological Survey of India volume on Ahmedabad (Soundara Rajan 1980) mentions—without citing any source—that the tombs range in date between 1615 and 1700 and that one of the tombs belonged to the British factor Aldworth who died here in 1615. However, the earliest burial inscription the gazetteer (Campbell 1879: 285)) can cite is 1664, which makes sense in view of Mandelslo's and Thevenot's silence about the burial ground. The idea that some burials may go back to the early 17th century is based, as the gazetteer points out, on a casual reference by James Forbes (1834, vol. 2, p. 202) that 'some of the inscriptions are dated at the commencement of the 17th century when the Dutch had a factory in Ahmedabad'. Assuming that Forbes was right, the writer of this section of the gazetteer speculates that, if Forbes is right, one of the early tombs could belong to Aldworth who died in Ahmedabad in 1615. The gazetteer mentions an inscription dating from 1641 but does not cite that. The inscriptions which are cited belong to 1664, 1669, 1679 and 1699. Architecturally the tombs are of the same type as the Surat tombs, although on a lesser scale. This is understandable because the Ahmedabad factory was under the control of the Surat factory. Some Armenian tombs have also been reported by the gazetteer in this tomb. The inscribed 'Armenian' slabs of the type one can still observe in the Armenian burial ground of Surat are missing in the Kankaria burial ground and thus we could not identify any tomb as specifically belonging to an Armenian. The earliest inscriptions that we noted in this burial ground are dated 1654, 1668, 1669. There was also one dating from 1767. It is apparent that some inscribed slabs have been removed from this burial ground which lies to the east of the modern Kankaria lake.

Baldaeus (Churchill 1704) wrote that 'Amadabath', the capital city of the province of Gujarat and located on the bank of very fine river, was 'both strong and populous, being fortified with a goodly wall with round turrets and 12 gates'. The fortification and turrets are clearly visible in Baldaeus' 17th century painting of Ahmedabad, with the suggestion of an undulating vast plain dotted with a few palm trees beyond it. The fortification with its series of regularly spaced bastions is shown rising up from the river bank. There are indications of multi-storeyed houses, minarets and obelisk-type towers inside the city. The foreground is dominated by the wide expanse of the Sabarmati. Obviously it shows the river in the dry months because the water flows only through the middle and two persons are, in fact, shown wading across it. The space between the water and the fortification wall is dotted with grazing cattle, a few human figures and even a dilapidated building. In the right-hand corner a man is shown trying to dry something hung over a beam which joined two apparently wooden or bamboo pillars. A small laden boat has reached the far bank of the river and a human figure seems to be trying to dock it. A boat with a boatman is moving on the river. The immediate foreground of the painting, which shows the river bank on this side is dominated by three palm-trees (one fruit-bearing) in the left and a leafy, unspecified tree in the right. There is also the suggestion of two unpaved and worn-out roads here. Men carrying loads or driving bullocks move along one of them, with a seated or half-reclined human figure by its side. A camel and its rider rest in the shade of a palm tree and two camels, one of which is being led by a driver and the other one has a man with an umbrella on its back. On the riverside two human figures are shown beating something with a stick. *Dhobis* or washermen beating cloth with a stick in the river water has always been a part of the Indian riverbank scenario.

III. CAMBAY

The Arab references to Cambay date from the 10th century onwards (Quin 1896: 514-515), which suggests that Cambay was an established port by the 10th century. In the 12th century it was one of the major Indian ports which imported horses from the Gulf area. The area itself has a proto-historic and early historic antiquity, as the excavated early historic site of Nagara, located 3 km to its north, indicates. Cambay lies on the northern side of the Mahi near its estuary. There is a few kilometre long mud-flat between the port and the city, although at high tide ships could be brought close to the city wall. The city is located on a high ground overlooking the mud-flat. The earliest evidence of human occupation at the site is placed in the 6th-7th century AD by Mehta (1975), although one is doubtful if the site was a port then. Mehta further argues that the site was a pilgrim place for both the Hindus and the Jains. His study of toponyms of the modern Cambay town leads him to believe that the focus of pre-Muslim Cambay was on the southeast section, whereas the Muslims and Parsis occupied the western side. Under the Mughals Cambay was an important port, although not as important as Surat. Initially in the Mughal administration it was placed under the *Mutasaddi* of Surat but later on Cambay and the ports of Gogo and Gander/Gandhar were placed under a different *Mutasaddi* who was based in Cambay and acted as its peace-keeper and mint-master as well. Generally he used to be appointed by the Mughal viceroy of Ahmedabad and he himself could appoint his *Shahbandar* or the chief of the custom-house (for the details, Ray 1992; for an authoritative discussion of the administrative machinery of the Mughal period port towns, Singh 1985).

Before the rise of Surat, Cambay was the chief port of Gujarat and had apparently a wide and far-reaching hinterland. In the 17th century its hinterland was perhaps reduced to the cotton-growing areas in that sector of Gujarat (Ray 1992: 137). It is difficult to be clear on this issue because De Laet's evidence that every 10 or 20 days 200 carts laden with merchandise for Cambay used to depart from Ahmedabad. In our second chapter we have drawn attention to the importance of Cambay in the

European accounts of the 14th-15th century and later, and in the local epigraphic records before that. In 1292-93 Marco Polo (Ross 1931: 334-335) found much trade here—in cotton, many other commodities and tanned and dressed hides. There were no pirates and the people were good, living by trade and handicrafts. The Portuguese advent in the Gujarat seas in the early 16th century had its negative reprcussions on the sea-trade of Cambay, but even then, as drawn out by the gazetteer (Campbell 1880: 189-192) from the various sources, it was very impressive.

Inland, it was linked to Ahmedabad, Anhilwadapatan, Champaner, Delhi and Lahore, which means that its major inland trade axis was along the traditional Delhi-Gujarat axis via Rajasthan and Malwa. The seaports with which it had links were Gogha and Diu in Gujarat, Diul in Sindh, Calicut and Cochin on the Malabar coast, Ormuz in the Gulf, Sheher, Aden and Jedda in Arabia, Mogadishu, Mombasa and Melindi in east Africa, Sri Lanka in the south, and Chittagong, Martaban, Tennaserim and Malacca to the East. The Cambay exports then comprised the following: agates, carnelians and crystals including their finished products to Malabar, Arabia, the Red Sea and east Africa; rice to Konkan, Malabar, Arabia and Africa; pulse and sesame to Malabar; cotton to Malabar and Arabia; ginger and pepper to Persia; *turbith* to Malabar; opium to Aden, Persia, Malabar, Pegu and Malacca; indigo (one of the chief exports) to the Gulf and the Red Sea and east Africa, and also to the Portuguese ports of Konkan; horses to Konkan and Malabar; and finally,—to all the areas where Cambay merchants traded—cotton thread, cotton cloth, coarse camlets, thick carpets, inlaid work-boxes and bedsteads, lac and lacquered ware, silk and articles of ivory.

The land imports were the following: diamonds from the Deccan, wheat and barley from Malwa, spices from Sindh (the chief Sind spice: 'costus'), indigo and spices from Lahore and silk, horses, myrobalans and spices from Kabul. The imports by sea were the following: copper, lead, quicksilver, vermillion and alum from Aden, Goa and Chaul, 'uncoined' gold from east Africa inclusive of Ethiopia or Abyssinia; both coined and uncoined gold from Mecca and Ormuz; silver from the Red Sea and the Gulf; iron from Malabar; tin from Thailand/Malayasia (Siam); salt and sulphur from the Gulf; rubies from Pegu and Sri Lanka; topaz and cat's eye from Sri Lanka; turquoise, emerald and lapis lazuli from Persia; rice, cardamoms, betel leaves, areca nuts and coconuts from Malabar; opium, madder, ginger and galls from Arabia; raisins, dates, dyes, musk and rhubarb from Persia; clove, nutmeg and mace from Pegu and Banda; clove from the Moluccas; white sandalwood from Timor;

camphor from Borneo and Sumatra; benzoin from Thailand/Malayasia, Malacca and Sumatra; cassia from Malabar; cinnamon from Sri Lanka and Java; ginger from Quilon; horses from Persia and Arabia; elephants from Sri Lanka and Malabar; coral from the Red Sea; pears from the Gulf and Sri Lanka; ivory from east Africa; tortoiseshell and cowries from the Maldives; pigeon's dung as a dye from east Africa; lac from Pegu and Martaban; musk from Ava (Myanmar); ambergris from east Africa, Socotra and the Maldives; velvets, brocades and woollen cloth from the Red Sea; muslins from Bengal and Konkan; and porcelain from Martaban and China.

That was Cambay in the 16th century, with resident Cambay merchants settled or having branches all along the network. And, there were many foreign merchants in Cambay. The preceding enumeration of the imported and exported commodities of Cambay in the 16th century (Campbell 1880, based mainly on the accounts of European travellers), before it lost its importance to Surat, brings to us almost a complete panorama of the trading world of this part of Gujarat's coast.

The gazetteer (Campbell 1880: 195, note 2) also argues that "the chief local cause of the transfer of trade from Cambay to Surat was the silting of the head of the gulf". It has been claimed that in the beginning of the 16th century large ships could come up to Cambay. One cannot be sure how one can examine the idea that the present shoreline beyond the mud-flat below the city-cliff of Cambay is significantly different from the 16th century line. Here we cite the account of how James Forbes landed in Cambay after a sea-journey from Surat in the late 19th century and argue on this basis that the situation in the previous two or three centuries was unlikely to be much different.

> The voyage from Surat to Cambay was uninteresting. We anchored that evening with the ebb tide near Gongwa, a village.... When the tide had ebbed a few hours we were left aground; and before the flood made, the gulf was perfectly dry for many leagues around us. The tides flow there with amazing rapidity, and occasion fatal accidents; when the south-west monsoon blows strong, they are said to rush faster than the swiftest horse can gallop, and sometimes rise to the height of forty feet. The flood carried us on with wonderful velocity; but with fair wind, fine weather and skilful pilots, we were not apprehensive of danger.... We anchored on the 17th in Cambay road, about a mile and a half from the city' (Forbes 1834, vol. 1, pp. 313-314).

Forbes was a part of an important British delegation to the *Nawab* of Cambay, and his vessel was a part of a convoy of vessels carrying British soldiers. It is unlikely to have been a small craft. The point is that Forbes' description of the tide flowing in is remarkably like the one given by Thevenot in the 1660s, more than a hundred years before him.

> The sea is half a league distant from it, tyhough heretofore it came up to the town; and that has lessened the trade of the place, because great ships can come no nearer than three or four leagues. The tides are so swift to the north of the gulf that a man on horse-back at full speed, cannot keep pace with the first waves; and this violence of the sea is one reason also why great ships go but seldom thither (Sen 1949: 18).

Earlier in the 17th century Mandelslo went from Ahmedabad to Cambay and commented on how the Hindu merchants of the place 'carried on an extensive business with Achin, Div, Goa, Mecca and Persia', without any suggestion that the trade had declined greatly from the earlier times, especially because of the recession of the sea (Commissariat 1931: 41).

In the 1620s De Laet devoted a small section to the description of Cambay which found to be surrounded by a triple wall of brick and 'twice as big as Suratte'. The houses were lofty and magnificent, 'its streets straight and well-paved, each one of them being closed by a separate gate at night'. The well-paved streets seem to be too good to be true, but De Laet's description of the port merits attention:

> The port is so crowded that not infrequently 200 vessels may be seen here at one and the same time (Hoyland and Banerjee 1928: 19).

According to Baldaeus, the city was reckoned as big as Surat, being well-built and fortified with a triple wall. Its circuit was about 6 or 7 miles and outside the walls were four large tanks and "fifteen gardens, for the diversion of such of the inhabitants as are pleased to divert themselves there with walking in the cool of the evening".

The time-gap between De Laet's and Thevenot's descriptions is less than 50 years. On the whole, it is difficult to concur with the premise that Cambay as a port declined because the sea receded. Of one thing the European writers are unanimous about: the sea off the Cambay coast was infested by pirates, their common name being *Malabars*. Mandelslo in Cambay visited Mirza Beg, a leading merchant of the place who was recommended to him by the British factor. Soon after Thevenot, Hamilton (Foster 1930) found Cambay 'still a place of good trade, though not half inhabited'. He was full of admiration for the embroidery work done here—'best of any people in India, and perhaps in the world'. He adds that their fine quilts were formerly carried to Europe.

The Dutch had established a factory in Cambay in 1617, although to close it before 1670. By 1616 the British factory was in full swing. The British maintained their factory throughout the declining years of the Mughals and the unsettled years of the independent governors/ *Nawabs* and the Marathas till the area came into their area of influence. In name, the family of the Cambay *Nawabs* continued to rule the area in the form of a princely state. In 1818, the British Resident in Cambay was withdrawn and the duty was given to the District chief of the newly constituted district of Kaira. In British India, the *Nawab* who had the power of life and death over the people of his state was entitled to receive from the British the salute of 11 guns and had continued to keep a small army of his own.

Modern Cambay is a dusty little town, and its only present interest, apart from its ruined monuments and the city wall which on the cliff-side is mostly unbroken, is the number of workers in agate, carnelian and similar other stones.

The chief monuments of Cambay are the surviving portions of the city wall and the 14th century Jama mosque. The site of the British factory is known locally and not far from the mosque area. The site is now occupied by a private building which may, in fact, be a part of the original complex. Before the building went into private hands, it was reputedly used as a sanatorium for European officers. Outside the city wall, at the northern edge of the mud-flat creeping up to it, there is a dilapidated burial ground. The still standing but damaged lone tomb of the Surat style seems to belong, according to an inscribed tablet, to Robert Lambert, "president of the British nation" and is dated 1754. He died at the age of 28. The other burials belong mostly to the 19th century: Margaret Adriana, wife of Captain Harvey, 1815 (age 23), Catherine, wife of T. Wilson (the rest illegible), T.J. Young, Civil Surgeon, Kaira, 1856, and Rev. John Rawlinson of Bombay Establishment 1817. These are the ones whose memorial tablets survive.

IV. DIU

An island measuring about 11 km by 3 km on the southern coast of Kathiawar, Diu remained exclusively under Portuguese occupation except a short phase of its early history when it was possessed by the independent Sultans of Gujarat who under Mahmud Begara defeated a local Hindu dynasty in 1472 and took possession of Diu, possibly for its strategic position on the sea-lanes to the Gulf of Cambay, Konkan coast and Malabar. No remains of the Hindu period have been reported from the Diu area. Mahmud Begara appointed Malik Ayaz as the

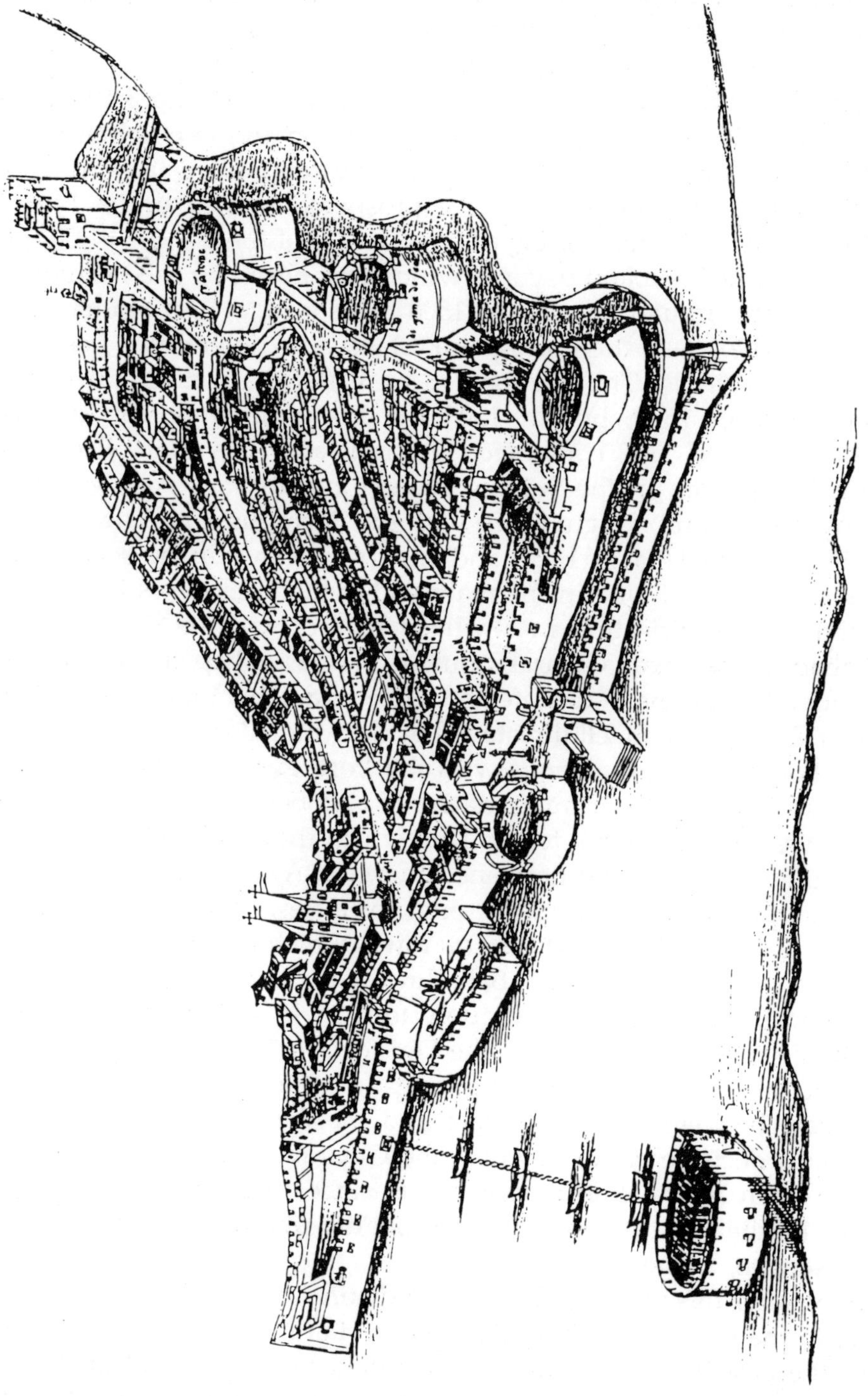

Fig. 11. Diu Fort (after *Lendus Da India* by G. Correa)

governor of that region and it was Ayaz who decided to have his headquarters in Diu and constructed a fort and a tower on the rock at the sea, joining the two by a chain. He also built a bridge linking the island with the mainland. Ayaz also built a navy consisting of 100 *fustas*, each *fusta* with 25 pairs of oars, one heavy cannon and two lighter pieces of artillery. He also had a few large war vessels and a large number of armed merchant ships. Commerce prospered in Diu under him.

The Mameluk Sultans of Egypt were aware of the danger to Egypt's trade with the Red Sea and beyond, which was posed by the Portuguese presence in the Indian Ocean. In 1508 they sent a fleet under Amir Hussain to drive away the Portuguese. Malik Ayaz joined this fleet with 40 of his own *fustas*. The Portuguese were defeated at Chaul off the Konkan coast in 1508, but in 1509 the Portuguese viceroy of Goa, Almeida, defeated the combined Gujarati and Egyptian fleet. Diu continued to remain in the Sultans' hands, and in 1522 Aga Mahmud, Malik Ayaz's admiral, fought again with the Portuguese and drove them away. He died in Una in 1522, and his grave can still be seen in the busy market town of Una in the mainland, which possesses in addition a Mughal-type fortification in a village in the outskirts.

Bahadur Shah was Gujarat's Sultan in 1531 when the Portuguese fleet under Da Cunha was defeated once again by the Gujarati fleet. However, Bahadur Shah felt threatened by the Mughal emperor Humayun, and he thought that an alliance with the Portuguese would strengthen his hands. According to a treaty dated 25 October 1535, the Portuguese were allowed to construct a fort in Diu, which they completed by March 1536. It is not known what happened to Malik Ayaz's fort. It is possible that it was pulled down to make room for a new fort with Portuguese planning. Or, the wall around the Diu town, which partly survives today, belongs to the period of Ayaz. Bahadur Shah partly contributed to the cost of construction of the Portuguese fort. In 1537, Bahadur Shah was accidentally drowned in front of the Diu fort. In 1538, an Egyptian fleet came but sailed away without fighting a battle. In 1539, there was a fresh treaty between the Portuguese and the Gujarati Sultans. In 1546, there was a decisive battle in which the Gujarati Sultans were defeated. Diu had been in the Portuguese hands since then. In 1670, Diu was attacked by the Muscat Arabs and thoroughly plundered (for the details of this section, Gune 1979).

Soon after this sacking, there was a distinct decline in the prosperity of Diu. In the late 17th century Alexander Hamilton wrote that Diu was one of the best built cities and best fortified by nature and art that he ever saw in India. According to him it was a fairly large city with walls around it and with a fort of high stone walls, bastions, cannons and deep moats hewn out of rock. Above 100 large cannons could be brought to bear on the mouth of the harbour from the fort. There were five or six fine churches. However, he noted that not above one-fourth of the city was inhabited.

Diu was visited a few years earlier by Abbe Carre (October 1672). The fort was situated in the south of the island on a steep rock, and about half-a-cannon shot distant from the city. There was a smaller fort on a rock in the sea in front of the main fort, making two channels to enter the harbour. The channel by the side of the major fort could be used only by small craft whereas the second channel on the other side of the sea-fort was used by large ships which could pass at high tide by keeping very near the coast. The moat around the fort was 20 feet wide and 30 feet deep and dug into solid rock. It was filled at each tide but could be emptied by opening well-made locks. The bastions were faced with cut-stones and were about 30 feet apart. There were two bridges, about 15 feet wide, leading to double gates which were separated by a guardroom and a chapel. The interior of this fort was as large as a small town where the three thousand persons belonging to the garrison could stay in the large two-or-three-storeyed buildings. There were two churches—one a Parish church and the other dedicated to St. Thomas. The Convent of the Carmelites was at the highest point of the town. Abbe Carre found it in a bad state of repair. The Convent of St. Francis had a cistern full of freshwater. The royal monastery of St. Dominic was a very important establishment and at the Church of St. Dominic there was music every evening.

The best period of Diu's prosperity was the 16th century. Ralph Fitch arrived here in 1583:

> It is but little, but well stored with Merchandize; for here they lade many great ships with divers commodities for the straights of Mecca, for Ormus, and other places, and these bee ships of the Moores and of Christians. But the Moores cannot passe, except they have a Pasport from the Portugals (Purchas 1905, vol. 10, p. 169).

In 1553 Master Caesar Frederike (Purchas 1905, vol. 10, p. 89) thought that Diu was the greatest strength the Portuguese had in all the Indies, and although small, it had great trade, 'because there they lade very many great ships for the straights of Mecca and Ormus with merchandise'.

In the late 16th/early 17th century Francois Pyrard wrote in the same vein, although with more elaboration:

It is of great renown, and brings in good revenues to the Portuguese in consequence of its good port and haven, wherein vessels ride in complete safety, by reason of the protecting fortresses. It is the mart and staple for all the vessels coming from Cambaye, Surat, the Red Sea, the Persian Sea, Ormus and other places in the Indies. The merchants land there willingly enough, as well for the good haven as for the cheapness of commodities; also because they fear to enter the Gulf, where contrary winds often prevent them from coming out; but the chief cause is that the Portuguese constrain them to touch there, so as to reap the dues and customs, and thus to make the place more prosperous.... The people there carry merchandise to and from Cambaye in great barques of 15 to 20 tons burthen each, with a full cargo each way (Gray 1888: 255)

These small vessels operating between Diu and Cambay were an easy prey to the pirates operating off the coast. On one occasion when Pyrard was there they seized 40 or 50 of them in one swoop. After Goa that was the richest Portuguese possession in India, and if there was too much of Christianity in Goa, there was more 'liberty of conscience' in Diu: "Nowhere in all the Indies is there greater freedom with women than there". Things being so, 'even the soldiers in the Indies' went 'to spend the winter there with great pleasure'—a remarkable throwback to the modern situation when the thirsty citizenry from the 'dry' Gujarat make a beeline for the bars of the 'wet' Diu.

Early in the 16th century, before Diu fell to the Portuguese, Tome Pires wrote that the best town on this coast from the point of view of buildings and of garrison was Diu (Cortesao 1944: 41).

In the 16th century again, but after it was annexed by the Portuguese, Linschoten visited Diu and was equally enthusiastic about it.

This Towne hath a very great Haven, and great traffique, although it hath verye kittle or nothing (at all) of it sefe, more than the situation of the place, for that it lyeth between Sinde and Cambaia, which Countries are abundant in all kinds of things, whereby Diu is alwaies ful of strange nations, as Turks, Persians, Arabians, Armenians, and other countrie people: and it is the best and the most profitable revenue the King hath throughout all India, for that the Banianen, Gusaratten, Rumos (Turks) and Persians, which traffique in Cambaia, and (from thence) to Mecca, or the Red Sea, doe commonly discharge their wares, and take in their lading in Diu, by reason of the situation (thereof), for that it lyeth in the entrance of Cambaia, and from Diu it is shipped (and sent) to Cambaia, and so brought backe againe to Diu (Burnell 1885: 58).

Reading between the lines, one would think that the Portuguese coercion to redirect the Cambay merchandise through Diu had a lot to do with its prosperity under the Portuguese rule.

By the early 19th century Diu had lost all its significance. Milburn's *Oriental Commerce* gives it a mention, possibly because it could be considered the best station for trade on the western side of India. He dwells primarily on the cheap price of the fish and fowls in the local market.

V. DAMAN

It marked a kind of demarcating line between Gujarat and what would be called the Konkan coast proper. Located on both the banks of the Damanganga at its junction with the sea, Daman drew the attention of the Portuguese in 1523 when it was under the control of an Abyssinian chief owing allegiance to the Gujarat Sultans. It was attacked by the Portuguese in 1529 and such attacks were repeated till 1556 when Daman was ceded by the Gujarat Sultans to the Portuguese. The Mughals laid siege to Daman in 1581 and 1683, mainly to put pressure on the Portuguese for their brigandage in the high sea. On no occasion was the siege carried to its logical conclusion. The area in which Daman is located came under the Maratha occupation in 1739 and according to a treaty in 1740 with the Marathas, the Portuguese retained the fort of Daman and 22 surrounding villages. Geographically the Damanganga valley provided access to the interior of the Deccan and it marked an important coastal staging post between the ports like Diu, Cambay and Surat on the one hand and the ports on the Konkan coast beginning with Sinjan and Bassein/Vasai on the other. The Portuguese fort lies on the northern bank of the Damanganga overlooking the harbour and dominating it. This side is known as *Nani Daman*. The town, which is much larger in size than the fort and is also protected by a high wall with bastions, lies on the southern bank. This area is known as *Moti Daman*.

The Portuguese fort and the town were built soon after the take-over of the place in 1556. There is a fair number of religious buildings in the fortified Portuguese city with at least two major gateways, one each on the north and the south. The ruins of the Convent of St. Dominicus date possibly from 1567. There are also ruins of the Convent of St. Augustine. The old Convent of St. John of God dates from 1693. On the whole, the major Portuguese churches are still standing and in living worship. They are beautiful monuments in their own right.

In 1672 Abbe Carre saw general signs of neglect all around Daman but he found the fort 'the moost symmetrical one' that the Portuguese possessed in India. It was surrounded by strong walls with several fine ramparts, each protecting one another. All this was encompassed by a large moat which used to be filled up at high tide before his time but was then nearly 'blocked up on the land-side from the prevailing neglect and misery'. Daman is mentioned by Linschoten as one of the strong forts the Portuguese possessed on the west coast of India. According to Pyrard, Daman furnished much rice to Goa. Daman was known to Tome Pires as well, although that was before the Portuguese had owned it.

The comment by Ralph Fitch in the 1580s brings out the relative insignificance of Daman in the contemporary trading scheme:

> Going from Diu wee come to Daman, the second Towne of the Portugals in the Countrey of Cambaia, which is distant from Diu fortie leagues. Here is no trade but Corne and Rice. They have many Villages under them which they quietly possesse in time of Peace, but in time of Warre the enemie is master of them (Purchas 1905, vol. 10, p. 169).

Hamilton (Foster 1930: 104) found Daman 'reduced to poverty', although he is aware that it was formerly a place of great trade. Its large cathedral was 'conspicuous a long way at sea'. The fort on the opposite side of the river was christened by the name of St. Salvadore.

5

Conclusions

What has been attempted in this volume is to offer a historical frame of the European presence in Gujarat between the 16th and the 18th centuries and put our understanding of the possible dimensions of the archaeology of that presence within this frame.

By rounding the Cape of Good Hope and sailing with the help of an Indian pilot from the east coast of Africa to Calicut on the Malabar coast of south India on 20 May, 1498, the Portuguese broke the control of the Italian city-states like Genoa and Venice over the import of spices to Europe. They also cut into the millennia-long traditional seasonal rhythm of trade of the Indian Ocean, which was mainly between the areas on its rim and along the landward arc of the Bay of Bengal. The world beyond the Strait of Malacca was certainly a participant in this trade but its active role was, at least initially, intermittent and did not always extend up to the fullest extent of the axis from Malacca to Aden or Mozambique. The rapidity with which the Portuguese carved out for themselves defensive and trading bases at the geopolitically crucial points all along this axis must, in retrospect, be considered an amazing tribute to the sense of geopolitics of these early sailors and warriors. One wonders which pool of geographical knowledge did they draw on. The issue does not seem to have bothered the historians at all. Pending detailed research, all that one would like to opine is that the earlier extensive geographical literature in Arabic followed by such travel documents of people like Marco Polo towards the end of the 13th century probably served as the basic geographical guide to the Indian Ocean trade for the Portuguese.

Their persistence in this matter is amazing too. None of the two places where they acquired a foothold in Gujarat—Diu and Daman—was made easily available to them, but they persisted and eventually gained their control, and were successful, on that basis, to dictate terms to the traders who had so long been operating off the Gujarat coast.

Cambay was the major Gujarat port in the 15th century when the Portuguese armed ships were a force to reckon with in the Indian Ocean. They did not try to take possession of Cambay, which would have been very difficult to retain, because it was too close to Ahmedabad, the centre of political power in Gujarat, but they ensured that Diu became the transhipment centre of the goods both imported to and exported from Cambay. Further, their system of *Cartaz* or 'pass' for the Indian ships operating in the Indian Ocean and their ability to enforce this patently unacceptable 'protection racket' in the high seas are a telling commentary on the inability of the Indian powers including the Mughals to understand that the new sea powers had risen in the Atlantic, setting new economic forces in motion.

The Portuguese castles of Diu and Daman look toward the sea. Strongly defensible, and in both cases dominating the harbour, these castles were a far cry from the Mughal period fort of India in its general architecture and defensive planning. The way the ramparts are arranged—the way they can offer protection to one another—seem to be a novel innovation in the range of military architecture in India. Besides, these seem to have been built with heavy artillery barrage in mind, both to withstand and to pour. These were, as Geoffrey Parker (2000) has shown, 'artillery fortresses' which developed in Europe and were taken by the Portuguese as an arm of their domination overseas. Parker has shown that from the 1540s onwards such forts became common in the Portuguese dominions, and it is important to note that both Diu and Daman, although with earlier pre-Portuguese fortifications, had new forts erected after this period. The point is that the sense of geopolitics combined with changes in military fort-building technology acted as a fundamental pivot of the Portuguese power in the Gujarat coast and elsewhere in Asia. What is also important to note is that such forts were almost exclusively defensive in their orientation; merchants and their shores were protected inside their walls and the enemy ships trying to enter the harbour could be bombarded at will. As Parker (2000: 396) argues, "Construction of isolated fortifications overseas … tended to make sense where the Westerners sought to trade, rather than where they sought to settle". The way the Portuguese settlements at Diu and Daman look toward the sea immediately suggests this.

The Fort was not the only arm of these two settlements. In the case of Diu there was a walled city to its west. No specific history of this walled city exists but it is likely to be pre-Portuguese and date from the time when Malik Ayaz had his headquarters here. This was the place for ordinary inhabitants of Diu including the merchants to live in. The artillery fortress was meant for the residence of the Portuguese garrison which numbered at one point about 3,000 people. The churches were built to cater to their spiritual needs and also perhaps to take Christianity to the locals. In the case of Daman there was no old city; at least nothing survives. *Moti Daman,* the walled complex which houses ordinary residential buildings and the churches and other religious places, were an integral, although separated by the Damanganga, part of the St. Salvadore or *Nani Daman* fort. Although some modern authors have written that one of the factors behind the Portuguese decline in India was that they began to interbreed with the natives, the settlements they built up at Diu and Daman do not suggest that they tried to become parts of the local landscape.

A detailed study of the plans and the general architecture of the Portuguese buildings including their forts and churches and the details of their links to the contemporary European architectural practices seem to be a logical initial field of archaeological studies in this context. Parker (2000) points out that an Italian architect, Giovanni Batista Cairati, supervised the construction of artillery fortresses at Bassein and Daman in India. We would also think that excavations can be planned inside the Diu fortress and the general Portuguese complex at Daman to find out about the general life led inside them. The harbour areas also would need some work, mainly to identify the actual wharf areas.

In this volume we have put the historical frame of the European presence in Gujarat in the 16th-18th centuries in its proper context, i.e. the context of the traditional harbours, trade and trade-links of Gujarat, around which there is a richly documented historical tradition going back to the period of the Indus civilization. We have consciously tried to visualize the presence of Europeans in this tract as a part of a long historical continuum. In enumerating the possible aspects of the archaeology of European expansion in India, it is important not to lose sight of this simple fact. In the case of the Europeans who came in the 17th century after the Portuguese—the British, Dutch, French, Danes and others—it is doubly important to be aware of this dimension of continuum, because for more than 150 years in the beginning they remained as properly accredited traders who were as much parts of the human landscape of Mughal India as its any other trading group. First, they had no residential area specifically set apart for them. Even the buildings they lived in were taken on rent and not built by them. If the Swally Hole in Surat was reserved mainly for the British, Dutch and possibly French ships (when the French ships were there), that was mainly because the Mughal administration was anxious about getting its exact revenue from them and to have a clear idea of what was being imported from and exported to Europe. Even in Swally, the indigenous business people—the 'banians'—arrived in strength and put up their shops during the shipping season. The Europeans were not isolated from the rest of the population even at Swally. Secondly, they had their own 'banians' or brokers. However insistent and vociferous they were in offering their services to the newly arrived European merchants, it is doubtful if the latter could at all operate in India without them. Goods had to be bought in the country bazaars and advance had to be given to the cultivators and weavers for the next year's crops and products. It is through the large banian houses with their branches scattered in India and elsewhere along the Mozambique-Aden-Malacca axis that the European merchants could transfer their money from place to place. Trading life in Mughal India was not possible without taking recourse to the time-honoured Indian system of *hundi*, basically bills of exchange. Moreover, it is extremely doubtful if the private trading of the European merchants, which was endemic and generally covered the goods which were not on the primary agenda of the concerned Company, would have been possible without closely interacting with the local merchants. Thirdly, there was considerable social interaction as well. The records of the contemporary European travellers are full of clear references to this element of interaction which ranged widely in scope. If the finer points of the Indian dancing girls and their song and dance, or of *Tari* and *Bhang* were understood, so were the thousand and one intricacies of the other aspects of Indian life including life as lived at the ordinary peoples' level.

One is not sure if the full potential of this vast European literature on India of the 16th-18th centuries has been realized. The observations which were made there on the India that these travellers saw were honest observations, bearing marks of genuinely curious minds. The upper stratum of the European mercantile community behaved and lived like their Indian counterparts, acquiring in their topmost echelon the behaviour of the Mughal nobility. The engraving of Surat in Baldaeus' book which was first published in 1672 is very suggestive in this regard. The city is neatly spread along the river bank on the far side. The castle is shown perhaps by the complex at the extreme right and there is a suggestion of a moat filled up by river water at its far side on the right. A large undulating plain stretches indefinitely beyond the city. The central section of the painting is dominated by the Tapti with a few boats shown on it. The small boat on the right is interesting in the sense that it carries a flag which may be somebody's insignia. In the foreground, on this

Fig. 12. Surat (after Philip Baldaeus 1672)

side of the river bank, there is a mixed scene in which the palm trees on the left, the grazing and restful cattle in the foreground and a few scattered human figures engaged in different tasks bring about a sense of panorama. An indeterminate figure seated on the ground near a grazing buffalo seems to be smoking a clay pipe and has a gun kept on one side. He is being addressed by a standing, equally illegible, figure. Towards the right of the foreground is a road which leads to the ferry, suggested by a moored large boat with its sail hung up. Two persons in conversation are shown wearing distinctly European dress including breeches, cloaks and hats on this road and they seem to have an escort of three local persons, all of whom are shown with bare torsos. Two of them carry long lances, while the third one holds a parasol. Apparently these two Europeans were important enough to move around in a certain style, according to the custom of the local nobility. Although this aspect of the European presence in Mughal India is well understood from the European records, the physical disposition of the European factories in the cities and above all, the tombs of the important Europeans, the Surat engraving has a special importance for bringing this clearly to the fore. There are other contemporary engravings but they deal almost invariably with Indian themes. Peter Mundy's sketch of Swally, of course, belongs to a class of its own.

The potential of future archaeological investigations of the 16th-18th century European remains in Surat, Cambay, Ahmedabad and Broach seems to be immense. Some idea of the overall city plan of this period is already available in all these cases. Further work is, of course, necessary. The Surat custom-house and mint, and perhaps one of the bazaar areas should have their proper plans drawn up with the help of some clearance work. The sites of the European factories merit close investigations on the ground, with some excavations thrown in to have an idea of their material day-to-day life. At this point we have to point out that the available documentary records are unlikely to throw any significant light on this matter. Even the archival records are unlikely to be helpful. For instance, we have come across references to some tobacco being grown in Gujarat during this period, but nowhere is there a reference to the fact that clay pipes used to come from Europe and were used for smoking by the expatriate European community. And yet, Baldaeus' engraving clearly shows its presence. We suspect that the Portuguese burial ground in Surat which was located in the general direction of the British cemetery has been mostly destroyed, but still its location remains to be precisely pinpointed. One also fondly hopes that some explorations in the river bank aided by a close examination of the

Fig. 13. Ahmedabad (after Philip Baldaeus 1672)

local tradition should lead to the identification of the ferry places on the Tapti at Surat and also of the wharf area with a stair going up to the custom house. Swally remains an important focus of enquiry in its own right. The shipping and commercial area of Swally should not be too difficult to discover and proper excavations of that area are bound to lead to unsuspected facets of knowledge regarding the trade of the Europeans. The tradition of multiple burial grounds at Swally is an important point of enquiry too.

In Ahmedabad, Cambay and Broach, the task is relatively simpler and may merely be one of identification, supplemented by the preparation of proper plans, of the European factories at these places. Both in Ahmedabad and Broach the locations of the Dutch factory are known. The locations of the British factories at these places will need a careful search of the local traditions, especially in the localities concerned. What is interesting is that the Dutch factories of both Ahmedabad and Broach were located, as in Surat, within the general residential area. In Cambay there is a tradition about the location of the British factory and that needs careful placing in the context of the general town-plan of the Mughal and pre-Mughal Cambay. In the Ahmedabad area attempts may be made to identify the prominent villages associated with cotton manufacture and some manufacturing traces associated with both cotton and indigo—large dyeing vats in the case of cotton and the brick-built reservoirs where indigo plants were processed. This may not be directly concerned with the archaeology of European expansion in Gujarat but will lend a touch of reality to it. Proper town-plans of the 16th-18th century Broach and Cambay do not seem to be available. It would be important to mark the locations of the European factories in those plans. There has never been an investigation of the location of the Cambay dock area, i.e. an area beyond the present mud-flats where the ships were actually anchored and loaded/unloaded. Considering that Cambay was one of the most important ports of pre-Mughal India, it is a little surprising that its port area is still totally uninvestigated.

In our chapter on Surat we have argued that the silting of the Tapti was unlikely to be the cause of the decline of Surat. The almost simultaneous decline of the three empires which politically sustained the Indian Ocean trade on an even keel—the Mughal, Safavid and Ottoman empires—destabilised the flow of commerce at Surat, among other places. Surat, if one looks carefully into the records, had a problem of silting even at the peak of her life as the principal port of Mughal India. In 1609 William Finch (Purchas 1905, vol. 4, p. 27) writes that the Surat bar, i.e. the bar at the mouth of the Tapti where the ships loaded and unloaded was 'some 3 miles from the mouth of the river'. At spring-tide there were three fathoms of water over this. He then adds, "over this the channel is faire to the citie side, able to beare vessels of fifty tunnes laden". It is not that large ships used to sail up to the shadow of the Surat castle at any point of history.

As far as Cambay is concerned, we have cited in the previous chapter Forbes' report that his boat had to wait for the arrival of tide to get near the city wall. That was in the late 18th century. The earlier records too do not paint a different picture. Pending further investigations, we would claim that the main cause of Cambay's decline was the Portuguese attempt to draw some of its revenues to Diu by forcing its ships to use Diu not merely as the place where they had to take their *Cartaz* but also as the transhipment centre of their goods. We believe that Abbe Carre's evidence which is valid for the 1670s is fairly conclusive in this regard.

Within the geographical frame of her traditional harbours, the relative significance of the major ports of Gujarat has no doubt changed over the centuries: Lothal and a few others distributed on the shores of both the Gulf of Kutch and the Gulf of Cambay during the period of the Indus civilization, Broach at the mouth of the Narmada in the early historic period, Cambay in the later but pre-Mughal period, and finally, Surat, the *Bandar Mubarak* or the 'blessed port' of the Mughals. In understanding the locations of the Indus civilization and early historic ports of Gujarat a simple geographical point is almost invariably ignored. The Ahmedabad gazetteer of 1879 (Campbell 1879: 16) mentions that the Nal depression of southeast Kathiawar and the lower course of the Bhogavo river represented possibly an arm of the sea 'at no very distant date' and that this arm of the sea 'possibly at a still earlier time combined with the Rann of Cutch to isolate Kathiawar from the mainland'. This premise gets added strength if we remember that the combined flow of the Indus and the Ghaggar-Hakra used to flow once into the Rann of Kutch area, which must have made the Rann and Gulf of Kutch a much more significant marine expanse than what they are now. If Kathiawar were an island separated from the mainland by an arm of the sea, many Indus sites at the edge of the modern Gulf of Cambay would have been easily accessible by the sea, and that should make a vast difference to the accessibility of Broach too in the early historic period. However, the whole issue of the changing configuration of the major ports of Gujarat need specific investigation. We have only tried to show that the problem could be more complex than what is generally adduced.

Finally, in the general theoretical background of the archaeology of the colonial periods in the Americas, South Africa, Australasia, the archaeology of European expansion in India stands on a distinct ground of its own. Here there is no abrupt break in the archaeological sequence—this is not a situation where new groups of people with a completely different range of technology and way of life appear all of a sudden in the landscape. Here the new groups of people are not really 'new', the landscape having seen a flow of traders from that general direction through the centuries, if not millennia. Secondly, the people who came lived here for about two centuries by being parts of the same time-honoured landscape. The 'cantonments' and 'civil lines' of the empire were still in the future.

Bibliography

Allchin, F.R. and J.P. Joshi. 1995. *Excavations at Malvan*. Delhi: Archaeological Survey of India.

Allchin, F.R. and Dilip K. Chakrabarti. eds. 1997. *A Sourcebook of Indian Archaeology*. Vol. 2. Delhi: Munshiram Manoharlal.

Badger, G.P. ed. 1863. *The Travels of Ludovico Di Varthema in Egypt, Syria, Arabia Deserta and Arabia Felix, in Persia, India and Ethiopia,* AD *1503 to 1508*. London: The Hakluyt Society.

Ball, V. ed. 1925. *Travels in India by Jean-Baptiste Tavernier*. Vol. 1. London: Oxford University Press.

Baram, U. and L. Carroll. eds. 2000. *A Historical Archaeology of the Ottoman Empire, Breaking New Ground*. New York: Plenum Publishers.

Beaudry, M.C. 2001. Flowerdew Hundred Plantation, Virginia. In T. Murray. ed. 2001, p. 520.

Begley, V. *et al*. 1996. *The Ancient Port of Arikamedu, New Excavations and Researches 1989-1992*. Pondicherry: Ecole Francaise D'Extreme-Orient.

Bellasis, A.F. (1861?) 1862. Old tombs in the cemeteries of Surat. *The Journal of the Bombay Branch of the Royal Asiatic Society*. 6: 146-156.

Bernier, F. 1968 (reprint). *Travels in the Mughal Empire,* AD *1656-1668*. Delhi: S. Chand.

Bhatia, Pratipal. 1997. Roman and Byzantine coin: Finds from India, Pakistan and Afghanistan. In Allchin and Chakrabarti. 1997, pp. 666-708.

Borsa, Giorgio. 1990. Recent trends in Indian Ocean historiography. In G. Borsa. ed. *Trade and Politics in the Indian Ocean: Historical and Contemporary Perspectives*. Delhi: Manohar, pp. 3-14.

Brown, M.R. III and P. Samford. 1994. Current archaeological perspectives on the growth and development of Williamsburg. In A. Shackel and B.J. Little. eds. *Historical Archaeology of the Chesapeake*. Washington: Smithsonian Institution Press, pp. 231-243.

Brink, Y. 2001. Africa, South, Historical. In T. Murray. ed. 2001, pp. 51-58.

Burnell, A.C. ed. 1885. *The Voyage of John Huyghen Van Linschoten to the East Indies from the Old English Translation of 1598*. Vol. 1. London: The Hakluyt Society.

Campbell, J.M. ed. 1877. *Gazetteer of the Bombay Presidency*. Vol. 2. *Surat and Broach*. Bombay: Government Central Press.

——. ed. 1879. *Gazetteer of the Bombay Presidency*. Vol. 4. *Ahmedabad*. Bombay: Government Central Press.

——. ed. 1880. *Gazetteer of the Bombay Presidency*. Vol. 5. *Cutch, Palanpur and Mahi Kantha*. Bombay: Government Central Press.

——. ed. 1880. *Gazetteer of the Bombay Presidency*. Vol. 6. *Rewa Kantha, Narukot, Cambay and Surat States*. Bombay: Government Central Press.

Casson, L. 1989. *The Periplus Maris Erythraei*. Princeton: University Press.

Chakrabarti, Dilip K. 1990. *The External Trade of the Indus Civilization*. Delhi: Munshiram Manoharlal.

——. 1997. *The Archaeology of Ancient Indian Cities*. Delhi: Oxford India Paperbacks.

——. 1998. The Indus civilization and the Arabian Gulf: An Indian point of view. In C.S. Phillips, D.T. Potts and S. Searight. eds. *Arabia and Its Neighbours: Essays on Prehistorical and Historical Developments Presented in Honour of Beatrice de Cardi*. Brepols: ABIEL II, pp. 303-314.

Chakravarti, Ranabir. 1986. Merchants of Konkan. *The Indian Economic and Social History Review* (hereafter *IESHR*) 23: 207-215.

——. 1990. Monarchs, merchants and a 'matha' in northern Konkan (*c.* AD 900-1053). *IESHR* 27: 189-208.

——. 1991. Horse trade and piracy at Tana (Thana, Maharashtra, India): Gleanings from Marco Polo. *Journal of the Economic and Social History of the Orient* (hereafter *JESHO*) 34: 159-182.

——. 1992/1996. The export of Sindan indigo from India to the 'West' in the 11th century. *Indian Historical Review* 18: 12-28.

——. 1998. Coastal trade and voyages in Konkan: The early mediaeval sources. *IESHR* 35: 97-123.

——. 2000. Nakhudas and Nauvittakas: Ship-owning merchants in the west coast of India (*c.* AD 1000-1500). *JESHO* 43: 34-64.

Chaube, J. 1975. *History of Gujarat Kingdom, 1458-1537*. Delhi: Munshiram Manoharlal.

Chaudhuri, K.N. 1985. *Trade and Civilization in Indian Ocean: An Economic History from the Rise of Islam to 1750*. Cambridge: University Press.

Churchill, Awnsham and George. 1704. *A Collection of Voyages and Travels*. Vol. 3. London: Black Swan.

Cimino, R.M. 1994. *Ancient Rome and India, Commercial and Cultural Contacts Between the Roman World and India*. Delhi: Italian Embassy Cultural Centre.

Cleuziou, S. and M. Tosi. 1994. Black boats of Magan: Some thoughts on Bronze Age water transport in Oman and beyond from the impressed bitumen slabs of Ra's al-Junayz. In A. Parpola and P. Koskikallo. eds. *South Asian Archaeology 1993*. Helsinki: Suomalainen Tiedeakatemia, pp. 745-761.

Cobean, R.H. and A.G.M. Flores. 2001. Mexico. In T. Murray. ed. 2001, pp. 878-896.

Commissariat, M.S. 1931. *Mandelslo's Travels in Western India (AD 1638-39)*. Bombay: Oxford University Press.

Commissariat, M.S. 1987. *Studies in the History of Gujarat*. Ahmedabad: Saraswati Pustak Bhandar (We owe this reference to Mr Y.M. Chitalwala).

Connah, G. 1996. The archaeology of European settlement in Australia. In B.M. Fagan. ed. *The Oxford Companion to Archaeology*. New York: Oxford University Press, pp. 75-76.

——. 1988. *"Of the Hut I Builded": The Archaeology of Australia's History*. Cambridge: Cambridge University Press.

——. 2001. The Lake Innis Estate: Privilege and servitude in 19th-century Australia. *World Archaeology*. 33(1): 137-154.

Cortesao, A. ed. 1944. *The Suma Oriental of Tome Pires: An Account of the East, from the Red Sea to Japan, Written in Malacca and India in 1512-1515*. Vol. 1. London: The Hakluyt Society.

Cox, G., J. Sealy, Schrire and A. Morris. 2001. Stable carbon and nitrogen isotopic analyses of the underclass at the colonial Cape of Good Hope in the 18th and 19th centuries. *World Archaeology* 33(1): 73-97.

Crawford, I.A. 1967. The divide between medieval and post-medieval in Scotland. *Post-mediaeval Archaeology* 1: 84-89.

Crooke, W. ed. 1909. *A New Account of East India and Persia. Being Nine Years' Travels, 1672-1681 by John Freyer*. Vol. 1. London: The Hakluyt Society.

——. ed. 1912. *A New Account of East India and Persia. Being Nine Years' Travels, 1672-1681*. Vol. 2. London: The Hakluyt Society.

Dames, M.L. 1918. *The Book of Duarte Barbosa: An Account of the Countries Bordering on the Indian Ocean and their Inhabitants, Written by Duarte Barbosa, and Completed About the Year* AD *1518*. Vol. 1. London: The Hakluyt Society.

Dasgupta, Ashin. 1982. Indian merchants and the trade in the Indian Ocean. In T. Raychaudhuri and I. Habib. *The Cambridge Economic History of India*. Vol. 1. Cambridge: University Press, pp. 407-433.

——. 1979. *Indian Merchants and the Decline of Surat c. 1700-1750*. Wiesbaden: Franz Steiner Verlag.

Deagan, K. 1988. The archaeology of the Spanish contact period in the Caribbean. *Journal of World Prehistory* 2(2): 187-233.

——. 2001. Florida and the Caribbean basin, historical archaeology. In T. Murray. ed. 2001, pp. 500-520.

Deetz, J. 1977. *In Small Things Forgotten: The Archaeology of Early American Life*. New York: Anchor Press.

——. 1993. *Flowerdew Hundred: The Archaeology of a Virginia Plantation, 1619-1684*. Charlottesville: The University Press of Virginia.

Desai, Ziyauddin A. 1994. Written Persian sources of the history of Gujarat. In P.C. Parikh, S. Bharati and T. Parmar. eds. *Dr H.G. Shastri Felicitation Volume*. Ahmedabad: Shastri Felicitation Committee, pp. 59-64 (We owe a copy of this paper to the kindness of Mr Y.M. Chitalwala).

Dillehay, T.D. and K. Deagan. 1992. The Spanish quest for empire. *Antiquity* 66: 115-119.

Donnelly, C.J. and Audrey J. Horning. 2002. Post-mediaeval and industrial archaeology in Ireland: An overview. *Antiquity* 76: 557-561.

Dowson, J. 1867. *The History of India, as Told by Its Own Historians: The Muhammedan Period. Edited from the Posthumous Papers of the Late Sir H.M.Elliot, K.C.B.* Vol. 1. London: Trubner & Co.

Dreyer, J. 1994. Cartridges and chronology: An exercise in relative dating. *Southern African Field Archaeology* 3 (1): 44-48.

Fairbanks, C. 1984. The plantation archaeology of the southeastern coast. *Historical Archaeology* 18 (1): 1-14.

Fawcett, C. ed. 1948. *The Travels of the Abbe Carre in India and the Near East 1672 to 1674.* Vol. 3. London: The Hakluyt Society.

Forbes, James. 1834. *Oriental Memoirs.* 2 vols. London: Richard Bentley.

Foster, W. ed. 1899. *The Embassy of Sir Thomas Roe to the Court of the Great Mogul 1615-1619, as Narrated in His Journal and Correspondence.* London: The Hakluyt Society.

——. ed. 1905. *The Journal of John Jourdain 1608-1617.* Cambridge: The Hakluyt Society.

——. ed. 1930. *A New Account of the East Indies by Alexander Hamilton.* Vol. 1. London: The Argonaut Press.

——. ed. 1934. *The Voyage of Thomas Best to the East Indies 1612-14.* London: The Hakluyt Society.

——. ed. 1939. *The Voyage of Nicholas Downton to the East Indies 1614-15.* London: The Hakluyt Society.

Funari, P.P.A. 2001. Brazil. In T. Murray. ed. 2001, pp. 180-193.

Fussman, G. 1997. The Periplus and the political history of India. In De F. Romanis and A. Tchernia. eds. Delhi: Manohar, pp. 66-71.

Ghosh, Amitav. 1992. *In an Antique Land.* Delhi: Ravi Dayal.

Gibb, H.A.R. 1994. *The Travels of Ibn Batuta,* AD *1325-1354.* Vol. 4. London: The Hakluyt Society.

Goitien, S.D. 1980. From Aden to India: Specimens of the correspondence of India traders of the 12th century. *JESHO* 23: 43-66.

——. 1987. Portrait of a mediaeval India trader: Three letters from the Cairo Geniza. *Bulletin of the School of Oriental and African Studies* 50: 449-464.

Gokhale, B.G. 1979. *Surat in the 17th Century: An Urban History.* London: Curzon Press.

Gray, A. ed. 1888. *The Voyage of Francois Pyrard of Laval to the East Indies, the Maldives, the Moluccas and Brazil. Translated into English from the Third French Edition of 1619.* Vol. 2. London: The Hakluyt Society.

Grey, E. ed. 1892. *The Travels of Pietro Della Valle.* London: The Hakluyt Society.

Goodwin, W. 1946. *Spanish and English Ruins in Jamaica.* Boston: Meador.

Greenlee, W.B. ed. 1938. *The Voyage of Pedro Alvares Cabral to Brazil and India.* London: The Hakluyt Society.

Guha, J.P. ed. 1979a and 1979b. *India in the 17th Century: Being an Account of the Two Voyages to India by Ovington and Thevenot: To Which is Added the Indian Travels of Careri.* 2 vols. Delhi: Associated Pub. House.

Gune, V.T. ed. 1979. *Gazetteer of the Union Territory. Goa, Daman and Diu: Part 2 and 3.* Panaji: Government of the Union Territory of Goa, Daman and Diu.

Gupta, Sunil. 1993. The location of Kammoni (*Periplus* 43). *Man and Environment* 18(2): 119-127.

Hall, M. *et al.* 1993. The archaeology of Paradise. *The South African Archaeological Society, Goodwin Series.* 7: 40-58.

Hall, M. and A. Markell. 1993. Introduction: Historical archaeology in the western Cape. *The South African Archaeological Society, Goodwin Series.* 7: 3-7.

Haudrere, P. 1990. The Compagnie des Indes Orientales. In V. Rose. ed. *The French in India.* Bombay: Popular Prakashan, pp. 22-37.

Head, L. and R. Fullager. 1997. Hunter-gatherer archaeology and pastoral contact perspectives from the northwest northern territory, Australia. *World Archaeology* 28(3): 418-428.

Herbert, T. 1638. *Some Years of Travels into Divers Parts of Asia and Afrique.* London: I. Blome and R. Bishop.

Howell, J. and A.K. Sinha. 1994. Preliminary report on the explorations around Sopara, Surat and Bharuch. *South Asian Studies* 10: 189-199.

Hoyland, J.S. and S.N. Banerjee. 1928. *The Empire of the Great Mogol.* Bombay: D.B. Taraporevala Sons & Co.

——. eds. 1932. *The Commentary of Father Monserrate, S.J. on His journey to the Court of Akbar.* London: Oxford University Press.

Huey, P. 1994. The Dutch at Fort Orange. In L. Falk. ed. *Historical Archaeology in Global Perspective.* Washington: Smithsonian Institution Press, pp. 21-67.

Hultzsch, E. 1882. A grant of Arjundadeva of Gujarat, dated AD 1264. *Indian Antiquary* 11: 241-245.

Hume, I.N. 1969. *Historical Archaeology.* New York: Alfred A. Knopf.

Irvine, W. ed. 1907. *Storia Do Mogor or Mogul India 1653-1708 by Niccolao Manucci Venetian.* Vol. 1. London: John Murray.

Jack, R.I. 1985. The archaeology of colonial Australia. In S.L. Dyson. ed. *Comparative Studies in the Archaeology of Colonialism.* Oxford: British Archaeological Reports, pp. 153-176.

Jain, V.K. 1990. *Trade and Traders in Western India.* Delhi: Munshiram Manoharlal.

Karttunen, K. 1997. *India and the Hellenistic World.* Helsinki: Studia Orientalia, Vol. 83.

Kelly, K.G. 1997. The archaeology of African—European interaction: Investigating the social roles of trade, traders, and the use of space in the 17th-and-18th century Hueda kingdom, Republic of Benin. *World Archaeology* 28 (3): 351-369.

Kervran, M. 1996. Indian ceramics in southern Iran and eastern Arabia, repertory, classification and chronology. In Ray and Salles. 1996, pp. 37-58.

Kohl, P.L. Diverse approaches to the Ottoman past: Toward a globally conceived, regionally specific historical archaeology. In U. Baram and L. Carroll. 2000, pp. 253-260.

Lange, Karen E. 2002. Unsettling discoveries at Jamestown, suffering and surviving in 17th-century Virginia. *National Geographic* 201 (6): 74-81.

Larsen, C.S. *et al.* 2001. Frontiers of contact: Bioarchaeology of Spanish Florida. *Journal of World Prehistory.* 15(1): 69-123.

Lawrence, S. 2001. Australia, Historical. In Murray ed. 2001, pp. 114-121.

Lokhandwala, M.F. 1965. *Mirat-i-Ahmadi: A Persian History of Gujarat*. Baroda: Oriental Institute.

Markell, A.B. 1993. Building on the past: The architecture and archaeology of Vergelegen. *The South African Archaeological Society, Goodwin Series* 7: 71-83.

Macmurdo, J. 1820. An account of the province of Cutch and of the countries lying between Guzerat and the river Indus: With cursory remarks on the inhabitants, their history, manners, and state of society. *Transactions of the Literary Society of Bombay* 2: 205-241.

Major, R.H. 1857. *India in the 15th Century: Being a Collection of Narratives of Voyages to India in the Century Preceding the Portuguese Discovery of the Cape of Good Hope*. London: The Hakluyt Society.

Majumdar, M.R. 1965. *Cultural History of Gujarat*. Bombay: Popular Prakashan.

Markham, C.R. ed. 1877. *The Voyages of Sir James Lancaster, K.T. to the East Indies*. London: The Hakluyt Society.

——. ed. 1878. *The Hawkins' Voyages During the Reigns of Henry VIII, Queen Elizabeth and James I*. London: The Hakluyt Society.

Mayne, A. and T. Murray. eds. 2002. *The Archaeology of Urban Landscapes*. Cambridge: University Press.

Mazzarino, S. 1997. On the name of the Hipalus (Hippalus) wind in Pliny. In Romanis and Tchernia. 1997, pp. 72-79.

Mazel, A.D. 1992. Changing fortunes: 150 years of San hunter-gatherer history in the Natal Drakensberg, South Africa. *Antiquity* 66: 758-767.

McCabe, Ina B. 1999. *The Shah's Silk for Europe's Silver, the Eurasian Trade of the Julfa Armenians in Safavid Iran and India (1530-1750)*. Atlanta: Scholars Press.

McEwan, B.G. 1996. Mission archaeology. In B.M. Fagan. ed. *The Oxford Companion to Archaeology*. Oxford: Oxford University Press, pp. 473-474.

Meghani. M.B. 1988. *Sodavi Sadinu Surat* (in Gujarati). Surat: Chunilal Gandhi Vidyabhavan.

Mehta, R.N. 1973-74. Urban Surat, an archaeological, topographical and toponymical perspective. *Journal of the MS University of Baroda*, 22-23: 81-92.

——. 1975. Khambat (Cambay): Topographical, archaeological and toponymical perspective. *Journal of the M.S. University of Baroda* 24: 18-29.

Milburn, W. 1813. *Oriental Commerce*. London: Black Parry & Co.

Miller, D. 1997. Archaeometallurgical studies in maritime archaeology at the Cape of Good Hope. *Southern African Field Archaeology* 6(1): 26-37.

Misra, S.C. 1963. *The Rise of Muslim Power in Gujarat: A History of Gujarat from 1298 to 1442*. London: Asia Publishing House.

——. 1964. *Muslim Communities in Gujarat*. London: Asia Publishing House.

Mitra, P.K. *Port Towns in Mediaeval India (AD 1605-AD 1707): A Case of Surat*. Calcutta: Punthi-Pustak.

Moir, R.W. and C.G. Sampson. 1993. European and oriental ceramics from rock shelters in the upper Seacow valley. *Southern African Field Archaeology* 2 (1): 35-43.

Mookerji, Radhakumud. 1912. *Indian Shipping: A History of the Sea-borne Trade and Maritime Activity of the Indians from the Earliest Times*. London: Longmans, Green & Co.

Moosvi, Shireen. 1992. The Gujarat ports and their hinterland: The economic relationship. In I. Banga. ed. *Ports and Their Hinterlands in India*. Delhi: Manohar, pp. 121-129.

Moraes, G.M. 1952. Surat in 1663 as described by Fr. Manuel Godinho. *Journal of the Bombay Branch of the Royal Asiatic Society* 27: 122-133.

Moreland, W.H. and P. Geyl. 1925. *Jahangir's India, the Remonstrantie of Francisco Pelsaert*. Cambridge: W. Heffer & Sons Ltd.

Moreland, W.H. 1937. Johan Van Twist's Description of India, *Journal of Indian History* 16: 63-77.

——. 1922-23. Dutch sources for Indian history. *Journal of Indian History*. 2: 222-232.

——. Pieter van den Broeke at Surat (1620-29). 1631. *Journal of Indian History*. 10: 235-250.

——. 1932. Pieter van den Broeke at Surat (1620-29). *Journal of Indian History* 11: 1-16.

——. 1939. The ships of the Arabian Sea about AD 1500. *The Journal of the Royal Asiatic Society*, (no volume number), pp. 63-74, 173-192.

Murray, T. 2001. Australia, Prehistory. In T. Murray. ed. 2001, pp. 121-126.

——. ed. 2001 *Encyclopaedia of Archaeology. History and Discoveries*. 3 vols. Santa Barbara: ABC-CLIO.

Nath, R. ed. 1990. *India as seen by William Finch (1608-11)*. Jaipur: The Historical Research Documentation Programme.

Nawartmal, H. 1999. Aksumite coins in India: Some new evidence. *The Numismatic Circular* 107(1): 3-4.

Nogwaza, T.G. 1992. Archaeo-historical investigations of the wagon-making site at the Lovedale Mission Station, eastern Cape Province. *Southern African Field Archaeology* 1(1): 40-45.

Orser, C.E., Jr. 1996. *A Historical Archaeology of the Modern World*. New York: Plenum Press.

——. 1999. The anthropology in American historical archaeology. *American Anthropologist*. 103(3): 621-632.

Orser, C.E. and P.P.A. Funari. 2001. Archaeology and slave resistance and rebellion. *World Archaeology* 33(1): 61-72.

Palande, M.R. ed. 1962. *Gujarat State Gazetteers. Surat District*. Ahmedabad: Gujarat State Government.

Parker, G. 2000. The artillery fortress as an engine of European overseas expansion, 1480-1750. In J.D. Tracy, ed. *City Walls, the Urban Enceinte in Global Perspective*. Cambridge: University Press, pp. 386-416.

Parsons, A. 1808. *The Travels in Asia and Africa*. London: Longman, Hurst, Rees and Orme.

Paterson, A. and A. Wilson. 2000. Australian historical archaeology: Retrospects and prospects. *Australian Archaeology* 50: 81-89.

Pearson, M.N. 1971. *Commerce and Compulsion: Gujarati Merchants and the Portuguese System in Western India, 1500-1600*. Ann Arbor: University Microfilms.

Pearson, M.P. 1997. Close encounters of the worst kind: Malagasy resistance and colonial disasters in southern Madagascar. *World Archaeology* 28(3): 393-417.

Pearson, R., Li Min and Li Guo. 2002. Quantzhou archaeology: A brief review. *International Journal of Historical Archaeology* 6(1): 23-59.

Prakash, Om. 1977. *Surat and Its Trade*. Delhi: Delhi University.

——. 1985. *The Dutch East India Company and the Economy of Bengal, 1630-1720*. Princeton: University Press.

——. 1998. *European Commercial Enterprise in Pre-Colonial India*. Cambridge: University Press.

Prasad, R.C. 1980 (rev. ed). *Early English Travellers in India: A Study in the Travel Literature of the Elizabethan and Jacobean Periods with Particular Reference to India*. Delhi: Motilal Banarsidass.

Purchas, Samuel. 1905. *Hakluytus Posthumus or Purchas His Pilgrimes*. Vols. 4, 9 and 10. Glasgow: James Maclehose & Sons.

Quin, H.O. 1896. *Gazetteer of the Bombay Presidency*. Vol. 1, Pt. 1. *History of Gujarat*. Bombay: Government Central Press.

Rao, S.R. 1963. A Persian Gulf seal from Lothal. *Antiquity* 37: 96-99.

——. 1987. *Progress and Prospects of Marine Archaeology in India*. Dona Pauila: National Institute of Oceanography.

Raschke, M.G. 1978. New studies in Roman commerce with the east. *Aufstieg und Niedergang der Romischen Welt II*. Berlin: Walter de Gruyter, pp. 604-1361.

Richmond, I.A. 1957. *The Archaeology of the Roman Empire: A Scheme of Study*. Oxford: Clarendon Press.

Ray, A. 1992. Cambay and its hinterland. In I. Banga. ed. *Ports and Their Hinterlands in India (1700-1950)*. Delhi: Manohar, pp. 131-152.

Ray, H.P. 1995. A resurvey of Roman contacts with the east. In M-F Boussac and J-F. Salles. eds. *Athens, Aden, Arikamedu, Essays on the Interrelations Between India, Arabia and the Eastern Mediterranean*. Delhi: Manohar, pp. 97-114.

Ray, H.P. and J-F. Salles. eds. 1996. *Tradition and Archaeology: Early Maritime Contacts in the Indian Ocean*. Delhi: Manohar.

Robin, C. 1997. The date of the *Periplus of the Erythraean Sea* in the light of south Arabian evidence. In Romanis and Techernia. 1994, pp. 41-65.

Romanis, F. De and A. Tchernia. eds. 1997. *Crossings, Early Mediterranean Contacts with India*, Delhi: Manohar.

Ross, Dennison. ed. 1931 *The Travels of Marco Polo*. London: George Routledge & Sons.

Rougeulle, A. 1996. Mediaeval trade networks in the western Indian Ocean (8th-14th centuries): Some reflections from the distribution pattern of Chinese imports in the Islamic world. In Ray and Salles. 1996, pp. 159-180.

Sachau, E.C. 1910. *Alberuni's India*. Vol. 2. London: Kegan Paul, Trench, Trubner & Co. Ltd.

Salomon, R. 1991. Epigraphic remains of Indian traders in Egypt. *Journal of the American Oriental Society* 111: 731-736.

Saitowitz, S., U. Seamann and M. Hall. 1993. The development of Cape Town's waterfront in the earlier 19th century: History and archaeology of the North Wharf. *The South African Archaeological Society, Goodwin Series*. 7: 98-103.

Sastri, S.M. 1927. *McCrindle's Ancient India as Described by Ptolemy*. Calcutta: Chuckervertty, Chatterjee & Co. Ltd.

Schadel, R.P. 1992. The archaeology of the Spanish colonial experience in South America. *Antiquity* 66: 217-242.

Schalkwyk, J.A.v., M. Naude and A.C.v. Vollenhaven. 1995. Archaeological investigation of a 19th century water furrow in Church Street, central Pretoria. *Southern African Field Archaeology* 4(2): 78-83.

Schavelzon, D. 2000. *The Historical Archaeology of Buenos Aires: A City at the End of the World*. New York: Plenum Publishers.

Schrire, C. 1991. The historical archaeology of the impact of colonialism in 17th century South Africa. In L. Falk. ed. *Historical Archaeology in Global Perspective*. Washington: Smithsonian Institution Press, pp. 69-96.

Scott, E.M. ed. *Those of Little Note: Gender, Race and Class in Historical Archaeology*. Tucson: The University of Arizona Press.

Schuyler, R.L. 2001. Historical archaeology. In T. Murray. ed. 2001, pp. 623-630.

Seamann, U.A. 1992. The Amsterdam Battery: A late 18th century Dutch military installation in Table Bay. *Southern African Field Archaeology* 1(2): 71-78.

Seiffert, D.J. 1994. Mrs Starr's profession. In E.M. Scott. ed. *Those of Little Note: Gender, Race and Class in Historical Archaeology*. Tucson: The University of Arizona Press, pp. 149-17.

Shackel, P.A. and B.J. Little. eds. *Historical Archaeology of the Chespeake*. Washington: Smithsonian Institution Press.

Shahani, L. 1997. Ethnoarchaeology of Harappan sea trade: A preliminary study. *Man and Environment* 22(1): 9-18.

Shinde, V. 1998. *Early Settlements in the Central Tapti Basin*. Delhi: Munshiram Manoharlal.

Sidebotham, S.E. and W.Z. Wendrich. eds. 1998. *Report of the 1996 Excavations at Berenike (Egyptian Red Sea Coast) and the Survey of the Eastern Desert*, Leiden: Research School CNWS.

Singh, Dilbagh and A.B. Rajshirke. 1992. The merchant communities in Surat: Trade, trade practices and institutions in the late 18th century. In I. Banga. ed. *Ports and their Hinterlands in India*. Delhi: Manohar, pp. 181-198.

Singh, M.P. 1985. *Town, Market, Mint and Port in the Mughal Empire 1556-1707*. Delhi: Adam Publishers & Distributors.

Singleton, T.A. 1985. *The Archaeology of Slavery and Plantation*. Orlando: Academic Press.

——. ed. 1999. *"I, too, am American". Archaeological Studies of African American Life*. Charlottesville: University of Virginia Press.

Singleton, T.A. 2001. Slavery and spatial dialectics on Cuban coffee plantations. *World Archaeology* 33 (1): 98-114.

Sinopoli, C. 1994. The archaeology of empires. *Annual Review of Anthropology* 23: 159-180.

Sircar, D.C. 1957-58. Rashtrakuta charters from Chinchani. *Epigraphia Indica* 32: 45-60.

——. 1961-62. Veraval inscription of Chalukya-Vaghela Arjuna AD 1264. *Epigraphia Indica* 34: 141-150.

Smith, I. 2001. In T. Murray. ed. 2001, pp. 934-937.

Sonawane, V.H. n.d. Nageswar: A Harappan shell-working site on the Gulf of Kutch, *Marg*.

Soundara Rajan, K.V. 1980. *Ahmedabad*. Delhi: Archaeological Survey of India.

South, S. 1977. *Method and Theory in Historical Archaeology*. New York: Academic Press.

——. 1999. *Historical Archaeology in Wachovia. Excavating 18th-Century Bethabara and Moravian Pottery*. New York: Plenum Publishers.

Stavorinus, J.S. 1798. *Voyages to the East-Indies*. Vols. 2 and 3. London: G.G. and J. Robinson.

Steensgaard, N. 1973. *The Asian Trade Revolution of the 17th Century: The East India Companies and the Decline of the Caravan Trade*. Chicago: University Press.

Subbarao, B. 1953. *Baroda Through the Ages*. Baroda: MS University.

Subbarayalu, Y. 1996. Chinese ceramics of Tamilnadu and Kerala coasts. In Ray and Salles. 1996, pp. 109-114.

Subramanian, L. 1996. *Imperial Capital and Imperial Expansion. Bombay, Surat and the West Coast*. Delhi: Oxford University Press.

Tchernia, A. 1997. Winds and coins: From the supposed discovery of the monsoon to the Denarii of Tiberius. In Romanis and Tchernia. 1997, pp. 250-276.

Temple, R.C. ed. 1914. *The Travels of Peter Mundy in Europe and Asia 1608-1667*. Vol. 2. 1628-1634. London: The Hakluyt Society.

——. ed. 1936. *The Travels of Peter Mundy in Europe and Asia 1608-1667*. Vol. 5. 1664-1667. London: The Hakluyt Society.

——. ed. 1923. *The Life of the Icelander Jon Olafsson, Traveller to India Written by Himself and Completed About AD 1661 with a Continuation by Another Hand, up to His Death in 1679*. Vol. 1. London: The Hakluyt Society.

——. (ed.?) *The Diaries of Streynsham Master 1675-1680*. Vol. 1. London: J. Murray.

Thomas, D.H. 1998. *Archaeology* (3rd edition). Fort Worth: Harcourt Brace College Publishers.

Trigger, B. 2001. Canada. In T. Murray. ed. 2001, pp. 249-259.

Varadarajan, L. 1984. *India in the 17th Century (Social, Political, Economical). Memoirs of Francois Martin (1670-1694)*. Vol. 2, Pt. 1, 1681-1688. Delhi: Manohar.

Voigt, E.A., I. Plug and C.G. Sampson. 1992. European livestock from rock shelters in the upper Seacow river valley. *Southern African Field Archaeology* 1 (1): 37-49.

Vollenhoven, A.C.v. 1994. An historical archaeological investigation of Fort Daspoort, Pretoria. *Southern African Field Archaeology* 3 (1): 49-54.

Watson, J.W. 1884. *Gazetteer of the Bombay Presidency.* Vol. 7. *Kathiawar.* Bombay: Government Central Press.

——. 1983 (reprint) *History of Gujarat.* New Delhi: Cosmo Publications.

Watters, T. 1905. *On Yuan Chwang's Travels in India.* Vol. 2. London: Royal Asiatic Society.

Webley, L. 1993. Archaeological investigations at the battlefield of Rorke's Drift. *Southern African Field Archaeology* 2 (1): 24-34.

Whitehouse, D. and A. Williamson. 1973. Sassanian maritime trade. *Iran* 11: 29-49.

Wild, Felicity C. and J.P. Wild. 2001. Sails from the Roman port at Berenike, Egypt. *The International Journal of Nautical Archaeology* 30(2): 211-220.

Wink, A. 1990. *Al-Hind, the Making of the Indo-Islamic World.* Vol. 1. Leiden: E.J. Brille.

Wright, A. 1918. *Annesley of Surat and His Times.* London: Andrew Melrose Ltd.

Yule, Henry. 1875. *The Book of Ser Marco Polo, the Venetian Concerning the Kingdoms and Marvels of the East.* Vol. 2. London: John Murray.

——. ed. 1888. *The Diary of William Hedges, Esq. ... (1681-1687).* Vol. 2. London: The Hakluyt Society.

Index